JUNE

JUNE

Roots of Steel

June Whitham Holroyd

iUniverse, Inc.
New York   Bloomington

JUNE
Roots of Steel

iUniverse books may be ordered through booksellers or by contacting:

iUniverse
1663 Liberty Drive
Bloomington, IN 47403
www.iuniverse.com
1-800-Authors (1-800-288-4677)

ISBN: 978-1-4401-5020-3 (sc)
ISBN: 978-1-4401-5022-7 (dj)
ISBN: 978-1-4401-5021-0 (ebk)

Printed in the United States of America

iUniverse rev. date: 07/29/2009

I hope my family and friends will enjoy my life's memories as much as I have. In recalling all my adventures, I think I have had a very active and interesting life, and I have loved all the ups and occasional downs.

I got into writing letters during my boarding school years, and later when we made our first visit to the United States. I wrote a weekly news letter to my parents. I have just wanted to record the calendar of events. Beneath the narrative is the undercurrent of the almost rivalling, yet ultimately fulfilling, relationship between America and England as it existed in the war years, the cold war, and up to the present.

This first book covers the period of my life from 1926 to 1945.

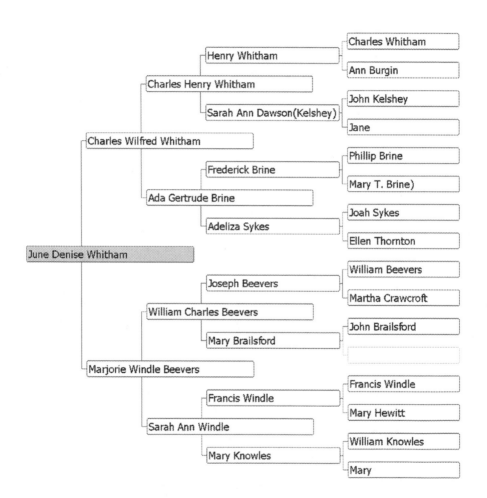

Family Tree of June Whitham Holroyd (née Whitham)

My Family and Early Childhood

I f we start at the beginning of my life, I was born eight years after the First World War. My father Charles Wilfred Whitham was the director of a steel business in Sheffield, England, Henry Whitham and Sons. He had inherited the file and steel works business when he was only thirteen, from his father, who died in his thirties from diabetes.

The Steelworks originally was started by my father's grandparents, Henry Whitham and Sarah Ann. (I have included a short pedigree chart, to help understand my family tree.)

Sarah Ann was the first child born to John Kelshey and his wife Jane in 1838, in Keadby, Lincolnshire, a rural farming community. She had four younger brothers. By the time of the 1851 Census, Sarah Ann age thirteen, had left home, presumably to be in service. We next find a record of her, the marriage to George Dawson from Ecclesfield, near Sheffield, on May 23rd, 1861. This took place in the church of Althorpe, county of Lincoln. (Althorpe is the village where Lady Diana Spencer, Princess of Wales was born, and is buried. I wonder if Sarah Ann had worked in the Spencer service?) In the 1871 census, we find George and Sarah Ann Dawson living at 44 Butterthwaite, Ecclesfield, and they had five children. Dawson had started a file cutting business. Recorded on this census, the family had a young apprentice living with them, his name was Henry Whitham, born in 1851, and learning the steel trade.

In this1871 census, Dawson was thirtyfive, his wife Sarah Ann was thirtytwo, and Henry Whitham the apprentice was nineteen. George Dawson died in his thirties of consumption, which is the same as tuberculosis today. It was a very common disease at that time. If you read any biographies from that period, most families lost someone to consumption. D H Lawrence is one person I think of, whole groups of his family died young from it, and he himself died of it too.

After George Dawson's death Henry Whitham felt it was 'his christian duty' (so my Mother said) to help Sarah Anne Dawson look after her five children, and help her run the steel works. In spite of the thirteen years age difference, they were married on the 10th July1876, and they had one child in 1878, Charles Henry Whitham, who was my father's father (see chart). By that time Henry and Sarah had moved to 118 & 120 Psalter Lane, in Sheffield, they had three Dawson children still living at home with them, Annie, Arthur, and Frances, and their own son Charles, plus Henry's brother, Arthur, who was living with them, and was also a file cutter. The Steel Works was then called Henry Whitham and Son. When Charles was old enough he also worked with his father, I have a good photograph of the two of them, father and son, standing at the door of their first workshop in Sheffield.

In 1913, after the death of Henry Whitham, his son Charles was in charge of the Steel Works. Charles met Ada Gertrude Brine, who had moved to Sheffield from Swindon, Wiltshire, where all her family lived, to work in Cole Brothers, a very elegant department store in Sheffield. All the girls who worked there lived in a large house in Broomhill, and on the early photos of my granny, Ada, she had exquisite clothes. I guess she was able to get them from Cole Brothers. Charles and Ada were married, and had a son on April 15th 1902, my father, Charles Wilfred Whitham.

Unfortunately, Charles had to travel to the United States of America. His agent and salesman for Henry Whitham & Sons, had been absconding with funds, so Charles went over to try to sort it out, and when he returned to England, with all the worry and strain, he had severe 'diabetes mellitus' for three and a half years, and was then in a coma for five days. He died on July 12th 1915. Ada Gertrude his wife, was expecting her third baby when he died. She was left with my father who was only thirteen, and his sister Dorothy, and another little girl, Joan, who was born after her husband's death.

Charles' death was registered by his brother in law, C.W.Street, who took over the management of the steelworks until my father was a little older. The Sheffield Telegraph of 12/07/1915 carried an obituary of Charles Henry Whitham – Wesleyan. A copy can be found in the Central Library, Sheffield.

Sarah Ann, Kelshey/ Dawson/Whitham, my Great Grandmother, was an outstanding woman. She had been a teacher and when she married Henry Whitham, who was twelve years younger, she taught him to read and write, as he had not had much schooling. Sarah Ann Whitham had lost all her menfolk. Her first husband George Dawson, in his thirties, then her second husband Henry Whitham died at the age of sixty two, in 1913. Her son, Daddy's Father, had died in his thirties, in 1915, so Daddy was the only man left. She apparently kept herself abreast with current events and mentally was very alert. Even at the age of eighty eight, she would invite a group of lively young people to her house, on Sunday evenings, and they had very interesting discussions. Daddy, her grandson used to go down and join her, and sometimes brought my Great Granny up to visit us in our house at 34, Barnet Avenue, in Bents Green, Sheffield.

Mummy told me that when Sarah Ann was young, she had to have her breasts removed, and apparently walked down to her doctors, no anesthetics then of course, had the surgery and walked back home, where she made a pot of tea and wrote a letter to her mother to tell her she was fine! What amazing strength some people had in those days, before any drugs and anesthetics! Not even any aspirin. She must be my most powerful relative.

Wesley Street ran the steelworks for a few years, until my father was about eighteen and was old enough to take over. Daddy had to leave school very young and had done a brief metallurgy course at the University of Sheffield at the age of 16-17. He inherited a lot of responsibilities for his Mother and 2 sisters, as well as the employees in the steel works, who had worked for his father and his grandfather before that.

Gradually they expanded and got larger premises and more workers and started to get their orders direct, not through an agent. By the time Daddy, a third generation took over, he moved to a larger factory on Countess Road in Sheffield, with perhaps 90 or 100 men. His family lived in the Totley Rise area of Sheffield, which is on the outskirts, and next to the Moors of Derbyshire. Although it must have been a very difficult time for him after his father's death, Daddy was able to have some wild boyish adventures with Wesley Street's sons.

They had an old motorbike and built some wings on to it and took it up on to the moors above their house, and got it to do some hedge-hopping, by driving it fast and pulling up on the handle bar! Daddy told me that one day they had seen a trickle of gasoline running down a hill, which they had set fire to, and it ran all the way up the hill to a car that it was dripping from, which apparently blew up!

When he was taken to tea parties, to an older relative, she had a new 'Flushing' toilet in the house, and the water cistern was up in the attic. My father used to play up there, and when he heard someone enter the bathroom, just as they sat down, he would press the ball valve and it would wet their clothes and underclothes! Maybe the seriousness of his life forced him to do these wild things, or perhaps it is what a lot of boys without a father would do; I don't know, but he was always pretty wild.

My mother's maiden name was Marjorie Windle Beevers, her father was William Charles Beevers, and he married Sarah Ann Windle born in 1870, the third child of ten. There is a photo of most of the Windle family gathered at her grandparents Mary Knowles and

Frances Windle's golden wedding celebration, which was held in Staveley Methodist Church on December 26th 1913. Sarah Ann and William Charles Beevers lived in Bolsover for a while, and later moved to "Ashbourne" in the Totley Rise area of Sheffield. My grandfather Beevers was a very relaxed and jolly person, and was my only Grandpa. My earliest memories of that household are that he was always around to play with me.

In the garden there was a spinney (a small clump of trees) and a greenhouse. Grandpa Beevers used to go in his greenhouse and call 'Freddy' and out would hop a little frog from behind his coke stove, that heated the greenhouse. Grandpa was always quite a dreamer, and very impractical.

My grandmother Sarah Ann Beevers was the opposite, and very strict. She had a number of young apprentices who she trained, and had working as milliners for her. She created the most elaborate hats, and even in the last years of her life she was constantly re-blocking her old hats for herself and re-decorating them with wonderful plumes and feathers. She was another diabetic, and was very thin and stood very erect.

Apparently my Grandpa Beevers needed a car for his drapery shops, but had such a dislike for driving and no understanding of cars. He would find his car would stop (maybe for lack of petrol- gasoline!) when he was a long way from home, so he would get out and kick it, but if it still refused to start he would take a train or bus back home, and then my grandmother would have great difficulty in tracking down exactly where he had left it, and getting it brought back home. They were amazing opposites in character.

My mother had a brother Clifford, and a sister May. Mummy was the baby. When she was quite young she showed a great interest and talent in playing the piano. After the school day finished in Bolsover, where they lived at the time, she took the train to Chesterfield for piano lessons. When she left school, she took more and more music lessons, with the idea that she should become a concert pianist. Her days were spent with 8 hours piano practice and lessons. Her family moved to Totley Rise, just outside Sheffield, and they attended Totley Rise Methodist Church. She was seldom out of the house, but on Sundays she was allowed to join the church choir.

Daddy's family attended the same Church at Totley Rise, and Daddy sang in the choir. In those days when there were no films, no radio, no T.V., no electricity and no telephones, it was popular to gather round a piano and sing. I remember my days of attending the Methodist Church, the singing was done with such gusto and when I stayed in North Wales with Daddy's Mother, the singing in a small welsh chapel, was even more amazing. People seemed to love to sing, especially the Welsh!

My mother had dark auburn hair, and sat in the front rows with all the girls, and my father was in the back of the choir, so my mother took a small mirror with her to choir practice, so she could watch my father while they sang. I don't know how they ever got past the mirror viewing days, but on September the second 1925, they were married at the same church in Totley Rise, and I was born on June 10th 1926. (My sister has just reminded me of something I had forgotten, Daddy did try to introduce himself to Mummy, but she told him they had not been properly introduced, and walked away. Luckily a friend did introduce them later, or I may not have been here at all!)

Mummy's older sister May, married Stanley Sawyer, and later they lived in Disley, near Stockport. They had 3 children, Desmond, a little older than me, and then Mary and the youngest Margaret. Both Desmond and Mary moved later to New Zealand, so now we have several relatives living down there. Mummy's brother Clifford was a mining engineer and lived in Doncaster. He had three different wives but no children, so we have no relatives from that line of the family.

Mummy and Daddy had such Victorian prudish parents, that they apparently had no idea that any birth control was necessary, so when they visited Dr. Jack, who became our family doctor, he laughed to find they had got into becoming parents without knowing anything about birth control! I was a honeymoon baby, and another financial responsibility for my poor young father.

Mummy and Daddy had built a house for themselves before they got married, at 34 Barnet Ave. Bents Green, Ecclesall, in Sheffield. In that house I was born, Mummy had an old nurse who came for the birth, and Dr. Jack was in charge. My father's middle sister Dorothy came over to help I think, I know she is on the early photos of my first walks out, up Ringinglow Road. We have some beautiful photos of my father on the front steps of our house showing me off to any neighbors he could. He always loved new babies and was always a tremendous support for me, we were very much alike and were great pals. We did disagree a lot when I was older, as we both had very strong opinions and personalities. But I am sure he played the strongest role in the making of my personality.

My memories of those early years are very scattered. My father's mother moved to Penrhyn Bay, a small seaside village next to Llandudno, in north Wales. Her youngest daughter Joan had a health problem, asthma, in Sheffield, probably due to all the steel works and pollution, and the doctor wanted her to be near the sea. Every holiday we could leave home we would visit them, my two Aunts, Joan and Dorothy, and my Granny. I remember we had a very tiny car an Austin seven and it took us a long time to drive from Sheffield to Penrhyn Bay, or so it seemed for a child. We always stopped in Chester for lunch, and Daddy bought me some wonderful sweets, they were like a tiny baby, all wrapped in swaddling clothes, all made of sugar. I loved them.

When I was two my mother was pregnant again. Granny Whitham her mother in law in Wales, got very sick with flu, so Mummy went over to help look after her and the 2 girls, and took me with her. I gather the work was so tiring that she had a miscarriage and was in bed. I had a fever and cold, but no one noticed until one day I just collapsed with pneumonia. No antibiotics in those days, of course, but one of the neighbors put hot suction cups on my back, and one of them was too hot, and gave me a very bad burn, I still have the scar. I was in an oxygen tent for several weeks, and was so long in bed that by the time I was allowed up, I was unable to walk. Photos of me when I recovered, are very sad, as I was so frail. In the spring Mummy and Daddy took me for a holiday to Cornwall to recuperate.

On the way south we called in Swindon, where my Daddy's Mother's family, the Brine's all lived. Her family were in Great Western Railway there, building trains. Their family portrait when she was in her teens, is a sad one as two of her brothers were killed a little later in the First World War. I remember great grandmother Brine in Swindon as she was so pleased to see us, and produced some horrible biscuits for me. They were black, charcoal biscuits. I think old people ate them if they had stomach problems. They tasted like briquettes of coal and set your teeth on edge to chew them! A strange thing to think a child would like them.

Daddy had a little open car and I bounced around in the back, waving to people we passed. When we returned from Cornwall, I was very brown and looked a lot better.

I was probably rather lonely for those early years; my mother said I would look out of the bay window in the living room and wave to an imaginary friend. When I was asked who was there, I always said it was 'my friend Rose'. One May morning when I was almost five, I had been out with my Daddy, and came home to find a nurse and a new baby brother, Charles David, there. The nurse asked me into Mummy's bedroom to see my new brother and just as I went in a big blackbird came down the chimney and was flying around the room, making soot stains on the walls. I remember I climbed in bed and under the sheets with Mummy and the new baby, until the nurse got the bird out of a window. I have always hated crows and blackbirds – it must have made a deep impression on me.

About that time I started attending a small school run by Miss Hambley; and Miss Givens. It was in an old stone cottage, and had just one large room inside. I remember it being terribly cold, there was no heating. We would wear our coats on the cold winter days, and we all wore mittens so we could hold our pencils. Between that one room and a small outside toilet they had a covered space where we put our coats on hooks as we went in. I had quite a group of friends there who all lived locally, so I began to have real friends to wave to.

The school was not too far from our house so after a while I was able to walk there. Every day I carried a small suitcase, which was empty apart from my 'Holy Bible.' Mummy used to ask me to leave my case at home, but there were a group of rough boys in the next road, who used to tease me as I walked home. We had to wear a school uniform and I had a very big panama hat, which drew attention to me. Anyway I used to swing my suitcase with my 'Holy Bible' in it for some weight, and keep the boys at a distance. It was strange that one of the boys called David Allford, was one of my first boyfriends at the University, when I was 18 years old. We both forgot the suitcase swinging days.

One day as I came out of my little primary school, my parents and my brother were there in the car to meet me. My favorite, Grandpa Beevers, with the little frog friend had just died. Granny Beevers had found him in his rocking chair when he got in from his work, I guess he had had a stroke. He was stout, but very jolly. He used to run cold water in the bowl each morning and put his face in, with eyes open, as he said it was so good for your eyes, and he never had to have spectacles. We were very good friends, he always played with me, and I was very fond of him.

My other memories of that school are very scattered. My Grandma Beevers, the one who made wonderful hats, sold her old Victorian rambling house "Ashbourne" when Grandpa died, and bought a new house, which I passed on my way to my little school, it was very much nearer to our house on Barnett Ave. Because she was so much nearer I got to know her better. When I was small she always seemed rather strict and her house had a real discipline about it - no space for young children to play. She had a maid living there called Madge, who was tall and thin, and I remember she used to collect a little soot from the back of the fireplace, and mix it with salt, and use it to clean her teeth. She did have lovely teeth, but I wonder if the coal soot was good for her. I think very few people cleaned their teeth in those days.

Dentistry was terribly primitive, my parents used to say the best thing they had done in their lives, was to have all their teeth out, and they were only in their early thirties. Mummy got pyorrhea after my brother David was born, and Daddy had the same trouble, I guess he probably never did a good job cleaning his teeth. He was always in a hurry.

The other thing I remember about Granny Beevers in those days, was that as she had diabetes, every morning she had a small methalated spirit lamp and a test tube to check her urine sample. I was always quite intrigued by this; I can still remember the smell of the methylated spirit lamp. She was the second branch of our family to have diabetes, Daddy's father died of it when he was in his 30's. They had no treatment for it then, I don't know when they started giving insulin injections.

Daddy had several friends from metallurgy school that went over to the Detroit area to the steel works there. Years later when my husband and I came over to Harvard in 1952 we visited one of them in Detroit, Wally Hakin and his wife Dolly. Wally and Dolly were from Chesterfield area, and came over every year to see Wally's father, who was a manager at Newton Chambers, and Wally's sister who lived at home and never married. They always came to visit us, and I remember Dolly had very fancy elaborate hats, and if Mummy admired any of them Dolly always gave them to her, but that is later, we are still in the early 1930's.

At some stage I was transferred to a secondary council school at Hunters Bar. It was another very grim building. Victorian- the stone was very ugly, all black from the soot. Most of Sheffield in those days was black. All the houses had coal fires, and all the steel works used coal or coke for the furnaces. Sheffield lies at the bottom of a hollow with hills on all sides, so the downtown used to have the thickest black fogs in winter. Often when Daddy was trying to drive us home, my mother would have to walk on the edge of the pavement, in front of the car, to guide Daddy, as it was impossible to see the edge of the road.

Every building in town had the same black staining, but I think our school was still one of the most ugly. The saying in Sheffield at the time, was "Where there's Muck there's Money!" We had a dreadful headmistress who seemed to really have it in for me. I think I probably was a little wild, and was always being sent to the head, she would give really severe canings. In those days most schools believed in corporal punishment, and it was legal. It was a rather rough school, in a poor part of town, and Mummy and Daddy decided to transfer me to a convent school, downtown. They had heard that the nuns made good manners a big part of teaching. They did not seem to have been worried about the Catholicism.

I had been christened in the Methodist Church at Bents Green, and we went to the Sunday service as a family, and then David and I had to go down to Sunday school on Sunday afternoons so Mummy and Daddy could take a nap, or so they told us. I think Sunday School must have been very boring, as I only remember one interesting thing. One warm Sunday afternoon the petrol station opposite the church caught fire, all the petrol in the tanks was blazing and set the trees on fire. We were just about to leave to go home so we were able to stand and watch. The other memorable thing from that church, was just before the long, boring sermon, they would hand out little tiny envelopes with small pastilles in, to all the children. When I got a little older and went to my Grandmother's Methodist chapel in Wales with her, the singing was the most exciting sound I had ever heard. Wonderful Welsh voices.

My parents were part of the swinging 30's at this time. They had a very wild life with parties most weekends. It was the days of the Charleston and lots of smoking and drinking. They had an old wind up gramophone and some wonderful records that I still remember:"Smoke gets in your eyes," " I Could be happy with you if you could be happy with me," "Tiptoe through the Tulips," "We'll have a Blue room, a Two Room," "What'll I do when you are far away," "If you were the only girl in the world and I was the only boy" All such wonderful sweet romance songs. Daddy also had some amusing records of "Two Black Crows," an American pair of comedians.

On Sunday mornings we were supposed to let them sleep later. We used to go downstairs and all the debris from the previous night's party would be around in the lounge. Half finished drinks, with cigarette ends floating in them. It was such a nauseating scene and smell, that I decided it was one thing I would never ever try, to smoke, and I never have.

I remember one Sunday it was getting quite late and as we always had our cooked dinner at lunchtime I thought I should start to cook a big leg of lamb that Mummy had in the pantry (no refrigerators in those days.) I carried it all down the road to some friends the Skipworths, to ask how I should cook it. When I got home my parents were awake so I did not have to cook my first roast!

We always had a live in maid, which left them free to go out any time. For years we had a maid called Francis. Mummy had got her from an orphanage. She was a very sad girl. She would stand and twizzle her hair round on one side with her finger and it would be a big tousled mess. On payday she went out and spent all of her pay on sweets, with the result that she had very bad teeth.

One night when Mummy and Daddy were out she woke David and me and told us it was the end of the world. She put our blankets around us and took us outside. The sky was wild with all different shades of colours, like a film was being projected in the heavens. David and I were sobbing, to find we were just with Francis for the end of the world. She said this was how her grandmother had told her the world would end. (Sheffield is far enough north to occasionally get a wonderful show of the aurora borealis, but poor Francis had never heard of it.)

She moved with us from Barnett Ave. to our new house in Dobcroft Rd. that Daddy had built, but she came to a very abrupt end, when Mummy found out that after they went out, Francis would have her boyfriend George around. He stuffed sausages for a job. He had to first take the bags from the intestines of animals and clean them, and then put in the sausage meat. I am not sure what they use for sausage skins nowadays, plastic probably.

Mummy and Daddy had absolutely opposite life styles. Mummy took an afternoon nap each day; she used to play the piano when we had any guests, and do embroidery and of course organised the food, but her life was very inactive, this seemed to be a remnant of the Victorian era, and their attitude to women. Poor Daddy would be working hard each day; he would always come home to lunch as that was when we had our main cooked meal, and then have to dash back to the works. In the evenings Mummy always had plans to go to a film or go dancing with some of their friends. They even went to a Ball in London, and returned home just as David and I were off to school the next morning. The drive from Sheffield to London in those days, with no good roads, took hours. Poor Daddy went straight down to the steel works when they got back, and I am sure Mummy retired to bed. They went with a group of their friends off on a cruise, and left David and me with Francis for a week or more.

Daddy had been brought up with the Victorian idea that the man made all the decisions, and earned all the money, while his wife stayed at home as a lady of leisure. Daddy led an incredibly active life. He used to go horse back riding most weeks, and would go cross-country jumping over stone walls on the moors. I remember one day we were waiting for him to come home in the afternoon, when an ambulance drew up in front of the house, apparently Daddy's horse had refused to jump a stone wall at the last minute, and thrown him. He had landed on his back on the top of the stone wall, luckily he had not broken it. He played a lot of golf, and tennis, and was always involved in active sports, which are a good way to relieve the tensions of a very tough job, which Daddy had.

He was away a lot on business, I think about six months of every year. He was the one in the firm who was always traveling to see that the customers were satisfied with their orders, and looking for new orders at the same time. He had a technique for visiting new factories which I remember, he would make an appointment with a new firm, and then to break the ice, he would introduce himself to the Managers, and offer them a cigarette from a beautiful silver case, which they always seemed to notice, it was a real talking piece, as long as they smoked. He had a huge repertoire of jokes, which he told very well and he felt it broke the ice with new people. I don't know how he remembered them all so well, when I am half way through a joke I often forget how it ends! The play 'Death of a Salesman' made me realise what a tough life it must have been for Daddy.

He had a number of firms he dealt with in Ireland, and he had some very good but wild friends over there. He would tell us of his adventures, kissing the 'blarney stone' while someone held onto his feet. He had one family, De Renzies he always saw, and she was a skater. She wanted to enter an endurance contest and Daddy said he would be her partner. I think they had survived for 18 hours; What a crazy guy.

Daddy was also a very fast car driver, right up to the end of his life, our children used to call him 'lead foot.' When he was young, he used to go in for some of the racing on the moors. The only driving accident I remember him having, was on his way down to the works, on Psalter Lane. A lorry went straight through a red light and hit Daddy's car on the side, knocking it across the road and into a stone wall. He was pinned in the car until an ambulance arrived and brought him home. I must have been very upset by his accidents as I remember them so well.

He had an amazing non-accident one day. He had dropped Mummy on the Moor, the big shopping street in Sheffield, to shop, as she was not able to drive, and he pulled out slowly looking behind to see if it was clear, he then proceeded down the Moor, but noticed people were waving to him and looking curiously at his car. He suddenly noticed the tip of a hat in front of his car, so he stopped and found a little old lady with a shopping basket was perched on his front bumper. As he pulled out he had scooped her up, luckily she wasn't hurt, and so Daddy took her home, I'm sure she was rather surprised by the wild ride!

I have always had the problem of driving too fast, and when we came to the USA the second time in 1967, and moved to California in 1968, I got 6 speeding tickets in a very short time, and had to go to see some State psychiatrists, as they think you have some stress problems when that happens. I explained that I had only just moved to California, and that my father and brother had always driven very fast. I feel that it keeps you very alert and attentive and is in fact safer. (I wish I had known then that the Germans and English who drive at very high speeds on their freeways have many less accidents per capita than here in the states) Anyway I was put on probation for 2 years, and as I was the only driver in the family, and you can't live in California without a car, I have had to learn to drive with my eye on the rear view mirror. I think my driving was copied or inherited from my father.

Another thing I remember, was his exuberance when we had any parties. When we had our Guy Fawkes celebrations, November 5th- we always had a huge bonfire with fireworks. We made a dummy of Guy Fawkes, he was the man who had been caught with dynamite in the basement of the House of Commons, planning to blow up the whole government, (Strange nobody has thought to do that in the US, under the Bush Presidency!!) and Guy Fawkes sat on the top of our bonfire, and he was the first thing to burn. Daddy used to pole jump right over the fire, through the flames! One time, the pole he had put in the fire for his leap, caught my leg, and burned it, so I remember that trick.

Bonfire Day in England was always such a treat, Mummy would bake potatoes and make batches of lovely gooey parkin, which we ate as we stood around the fire with all our friends, and watched the fireworks.

Back to my new school, David my brother and I were both sent to the convent of Notre Dame. He was only five and I was ten. It was rather a spooky place I remember. The corridors were very dark and had figures of saints in niches, with tiny red flickering nightlights in front of them. We were given rosaries and had to learn our 'Hail Mary's' along with all the Catholics. They had a big Nativity play at Christmas and David had a lead part in it with lots of talking, I was just an angel on the back row. The night of the performance I got flu and had to run out and throw up, so was then at home in bed, I remember David was very good in his part.

The best thing about that school was that it was just next to Glossop Road swimming baths. I went after school for lessons and loved that. From my early days I guess I was very much the same type of person as my Father, always active. Mummy never really understood me and towards the end of her life when she stayed with us in California, in the winters, she always nattered at me, telling me I should not work, I was too old, I didn't need the money etc. I used to say if I had no project to work on I would stay in bed and never get up again. Life to me has always been something I need to tackle with full energy, and be able to carry out anything I wanted to do. I believe you can do any task, if you really want.

I think the fact that Daddy worked so hard to get the Steel Works back on their feet after the depression, and earn sufficient money that we could always have a maid, and he could afford to send me to such an excellent school later after the convent days, put real pressure on him, the whole set up was entirely his to maintain. It was not a shared responsibility with anyone.

The Outbreak of the Second World War.

Germany had been left after losing the First World War, in a very desperate state, and the depression which was a world wide problem, had brought economies to rock bottom. In Germany, Adolph Hitler started the Nazi Party, and with lots of propaganda and parades, had given the Germans back some of their pride. His intentions were to take over all of Europe and to exterminate all the Jews, to create a perfect Aryan race. He first invaded Poland in September 1938, The Munich Agreement was signed in September 1938 and Neville Chamberlain who was the prime minister in England, returned home waving a piece of paper and saying "Peace in our Time."

Hitler invaded Czechoslovakia in March 1939 and we were all issued our gas masks. On Sunday September 3rd 1939 at 11am Neville Chamberlain broadcast on the 'please stop it' note that he had sent to Hitler--- "No reply has been received, and consequently I have to tell you that this country is now at war with Germany."

When war was declared, our family was in Bournemouth on the south coast, for a holiday. My father must have believed Neville Chamberlin, when he returned from his visits to Adolph Hitler in Germany and told the country he had an agreement with Hitler and there would be no war. We were far from home in Bournemouth, in the south of England when we heard Chamberlin's speech declaring war on Germany. We packed all our things into the car quickly, and set off for north Wales, to my father's mother's house in Penrhyn Bay. Everyone in England expected that as soon as war was declared we would have air raids on all our big cities, especially industrial towns like Sheffield, Birmingham and Coventry. Our News theatres had been showing the raids the German planes had been involved in, helping the Fascists in Spain. That looked terrifying. The air raid sirens did go off in London that very first Sunday. Anyway we were all in the mountain area of north Wales and far from any large cities.

My grandmother got a lot of rather coarse netting fabric, which we all worked hard at gluing it on the inside of all the glass in the windows. This was to avoid the glass shattering into the rooms in case of any bombing. We also had to put blackout material inside all Granny's curtains as we could not have a chink of light show after dark. All the headlights on cars had a metal cover put on them, it had small slits in, and an angled piece above each slit to direct the light to the road.

Daddy returned to Sheffield fairly quickly and I imagine had to carry out the same things there to our house. I do not know how long we stayed in Wales without him, but I know we went back home after a time of no air raids in Sheffield.

Notre Dame convent school we had been attending, was evacuated to Derwent Hall, which was a large country house just in Derbyshire, not far from Sheffield. Although we were still not far from home, it became a boarding school. My parents sent me there, as I was 13, but David was only 8, and so he was sent to King Edward's in Sheffield. It was not a boarding school.

Only two girls who went to Derwent were not catholic, and we both had a very hard time. We were put out of the service of mass and felt very ostracized and several of our friends tried to talk us into becoming catholics. I think the nuns had told them they would get special credit in heaven if they could convert us. I am sure in a catholic country like Italy, where they are in a majority, no one would have bothered us, but there were so few Catholics in England that it made them very aggressive. We were both told we would end up in purgatory, or hell, as no one other than Catholics could enter heaven.

On top of our religious problems it was not long before the Germans started very heavy air raids on Sheffield, as it was the centre of the steel industry. We could hear the German planes droning overhead with a slow throbbing, as they were so loaded with bombs. We were on their flypath, when they were heading for our families and all the steel works. We could hear the bomb blasts and see the red glow in the night sky from the fires. My parents came occasionally at weekends, but the petrol rationing meant you could not do much driving. All the petrol in England had to be shipped in, with convoys escorting the tankers.

We did have a few exciting adventures in our walks out from the school. The continuation of our valley had a huge stone dam wall across it, which was a Victorian structure. These dams were the ones where they filmed "The Dam Busters" in the war. There had been a plan before the war, to build a new dam wall a long way down the valley from the other dams, and to slowly flood the long distance of the valley between, which would drown several villages. Derwent, our village was on the way to being drowned, which made it very eerie to live in Derwent Hall. It was hopefully going to be sold and moved. (It was never moved to another location, but I think the dressed stone was probably moved by someone, and re-used).

The village church had a cemetery around it, and they had to dig up everyone who was buried there, I guess because the dam was to provide drinking water for Sheffield. They erected a sacking screen all around the churchyard, but we were all so curious, so would go and peep through holes in the sacking. The church itself they did not demolish and the church spire stuck out of the water for years. They finally had to demolish it, because when the water level in the dam went low in the summer, people would go out and climb the old spire, which by then, was unsafe.

I think on my parents visits, they realised I was very miserable, with all the taunting about not being a catholic, and the fear that they would all be killed, in the bombing, so they looked for another school where I would be happy.

End of my Convent Days, New School Hunmanby Hall in the Best Place of All, Bassenthwaite Lake, Cumberland, the Lake District.

They found the ideal place for me, a school called Hunmanby Hall, a Methodist Boarding School, which was normally in Hunmanby, near to Scarborough on the east coast. The army had taken over the school premises for the war period, as it was on the east coast, facing the Germans, who were by then occupying Holland and Norway. The junior school had been evacuated to the Lake District, to Armathwaite Hall Hydro, a large very luxurious hotel on the edge of Bassenthwaite Lake. It had boats on the lake, stables and horses and a huge acreage of beautifully landscaped grounds, it was the perfect place to have those early teen years, and I loved every second of it, from my first day on.

Most of the girls there, were really great and we quickly formed a very good gang, Judy England who we called BooBoo. I think it was because the day she arrived in school 2 chimpanzees were born in the Zoo, one was BooBoo and the other Jubilee. Judy's nose did stick up a lot at the end. Then there was Dotty, her real name was Dorothy Clough. The third member was Jean Hesketh, 'Hacket' and my name was ' Twit' as my proper name was June Whitham. We had a lot of other friends, Julie Flutter was one of them she lived fairly near the school in Cockermouth, but we 4 were pretty inseparable.

They had taken the bedrooms of the Hydro and put 4 or sometimes 6 beds in them. Usually there was one of the more senior girls in each. We had a pretty strict routine. At first bell we were supposed to get up and get dressed, and then 2nd bell we had to go down to breakfast. Our rooms were so cold so we would take our clothes into bed and try to get dressed under the blankets. We were often late down which gave you a disorder mark and at the end of each week, on Saturday mornings, you had to be given chores to work off the disorder marks.

Poor matron had such a job to find food for all of us. We were all at the big growth spurt of early teens, and rationing was so tight, I don't know how she was able to invent meals. We did have large vegetable gardens, and one of the punishments for disorder marks, was to have to work there, digging up potatoes etc. Another way to work off disorder marks was to be given mops and dusters and supposed to clean the dormitories on the weekends. I remember dusting some of the top corridors and shaking my duster over the roof, when it fell down, so I climbed out of a window, down the roof to get it. On my way back I saw a skylight and wondered what room that was, so peered in. The head mistress's maid was cleaning her bath. By the time I got back up the roof to the window she was there waiting for me. I remember another disaster I had, in our dormitory, there was a rail across the end of our beds, and I did a handstand on the rail, but went straight over, and the whole bed crashed to the floor! Miss Hargreaves, (we called her Harry) the headmistress, sent another letter to poor Daddy. I think he expected me to get expelled all the time!

Because food was so short, Matron had stocked up on sacks of porridge oats and some of them had gone mealy and had little grubs in. When we had our porridge we used to put the grubs on the edge of our bowls, but matron would not let us leave it, unless it made us sick. One morning I was sick trying to eat it, so then I was excused!

After breakfast we had classes from 9-12 then lunch, and we had 2 classes after lunch, but from 2-4 we had games and were outside which was lovely. It is such a beautiful area, we were near the slopes of Skiddaw, one of the high mountains, coming down to the lakes edge, and mountains all around us. We played netball, hockey and lacrosse and cricket and tennis in the summer. We could go riding, or swimming in the lake.

In the winters I was on the lacrosse team. It is a very rough game, as you cradle the ball in the lacrosse stick as you run, and you hold it up in front of your face, so anyone wanting to tackle you while you are running, has to hit your stick, to get the ball out, and very often you get hit in the face or on your head. I always seemed to have big bumps on my head or shoulders. I had my two bottom front teeth broken off, and had to go into Keswick, to a not very good dentist, who put two teeth on metal pegs down into the roots.

They were always coming out, and when our own dentist at home- Cliff Hardwick- finally looked at them, the gum had grown up through the drilled hole that was supposed to have the metal peg. I had to have the roots out and a little plate made, which over the years has wrecked the other teeth and gums. The whole dental world was very primitive.

I have one or two letters from my school days, that Mummy had saved.

February 16th

What a lovely week with two exciting parcels from home. Thursday was a topping day. A parcel from you and then in the afternoon played netball and then we had tea. Prep and a music practice and then after supper we had detention for Maths. Then Doreen Hearn who is a very boyish girl but great fun and her friend Beverley Monson, Jef and Dot and I all crept out after detention. We have done this a lot lately and gone down to the lake. When we got to the bridge over the main road we said we should turn back because of the time. Then Jeff and I saw a torch following us and then a whole gang of four more girls who had noticed us disappearing, got hold of us, and we were all good friends and they asked would we go to the lake again, so we went back. It's a long way, and then we went along the jetty right into the middle of the lake, (almost.) All this time it was black as pitch, and we just got in, in time for bed. It was scrummy. You mustn't think what a school because all that time we were breaking the rules but it's safe as houses as none of the staff ever go out at night.

Dorothy (Dot) has a lovely gramophone with all the latest songs "Whose little what's it are you" "The memory of a rose" "If I only had wings" etc so in changing time I change extra quick and go down to her room and dance.

At half-term I am in a cufufle what to do because Jef has invited me to her house in Cockermouth, and Dot to stay with her a day at the Pheasant Hotel and I have accepted both of these and then today to put the lid on it Dor Rob asked me to go with her for the whole time to Grange over Sands. But I had to say no thanks, because I had already promised Jef and Dot.

Last Sunday after letter writing in the afternoon I was walking near Harry's door when she said would I like to go to tea once again. So I wasn't chump enough to refuse, I went and poor Dot and Jef haven't been once, so I took them as well. We had chocolates and toast and ham sandwiches, lovely bread and butter and jam and scrummy cake and biscuits. After that, which was topping (I put a handful of biscuits in my pocket when she went out!) we were supposed to write more letters so I wrote to Aunty Dodi and Uncle Ted and then Dot and I went out. Jef didn't come because she was writing one of her long epistles to her father on the Gold Coast in Africa. It was marvellous and the sun was just falling into a lovely ruddy glow, that sounds funny but it is in a poem I have learned. We walked down to Wilson's Lodge and then through the woods and arrived at sunset at the lake. Such beautiful sunsets over the water.

The other afternoon Jeff and I were stroking a horse and she gave it a wine gum and the poor thing got its mouth stuck and it was still trying to undo it when we got to the top of the hill. You know how funny toffees stick, well like that only a good bit worse. I am glad the snow drops got their okay I was afraid they wouldn't because I gathered them and had to wait about five days before I could post them here, as we're not supposed to gather them. Soon you will be able to see them in the fields and round the Lodge near the main road. This place has three lodges.

You are lucky having "The Great Dictator" I could have told you it was coming if you wanted, because it was in our paper. I am very sorry you had such a bad night on Monday (air raids) *but I guessed you would because Tuesday was full moon. This week it shone in the lake marvelously and we had such great fun.*

Well here we are again Sunday rest. We had a dinner of meat, beetroot and potatoes cooked round the meat and apples for seconds. We went to the lake again last night and Dor and George who are great fun bounced out of the bushes to see if we were afraid but we weren't, and then on the way back we bounced out but they had gone so we followed behind and they were having a heated discussion on where Cylax (a star) was, George said to the right and Dor to the left of Mars.

Yesterday Jef's uncle and aunt came and took her around the places mentioned in Judith Paris and all the Herries books, and she had a tea of apple tarts and cream at a farm. Jef is really called Julie Elizabeth Flutter, she is rather plump, a round red face and dark hair. She is about two inches smaller than me and rather bonny she has white teeth and a good smile I think you will like her, at least I do. Next weekend it would be nice if you could come, would David be okay with Mary (the Maid) *although I would rather all come. But still I shan't see you much if it's not on the proper weekend. When you get to know, write and tell me straight away.*

The other night Dot, Jef and I went alone to the lake and when we got there someone was walking along the shore with a torch so we shot back like arrows.

We should have played a match (lacrosse) *at Rydall, yesterday but couldn't because of the weather. It was a pity, and it was a beautiful day, when it was too late to go. Are you sure my age isn't a year wrong because I seem much younger in looks and ways than the other girls except Dot, Jef, Dor and George.*

Yesterday I ate all my tuck except two biscuits in half an hour. Isn't that gluttonous. Then I stopped eating because it was dinner time and I had a large helping of macaroni cheese and two helpings of prunes after this and potatoes, cabbage, bread and lots of water I felt nicely satisfied. Now I feel empty like an abyss do you know what that is? A bottom less depth or well. Next weekend when I go to Jef's, if you don't come, we are going to the pictures in Cockermouth and we are going to have real fun. How is Granny getting on and is Mary (our maid) *back yet?*

Another letter sent later

"First of all I have something very important to ask you. This last week has been very full and I couldn't possibly fit one music practice in because they are supposed to be in free lessons so I went to Soapy with my timetable and showed her that I only have one free period and took eight subjects instead of 7. I take Maths, English, French, Latin, architecture, biology, history and geography. She asked me last terms Latin mark and she said it wasn't brilliant. All this boils down to please may I drop Latin? Harry is going to write you about it but she won't tell you how terrifically hard I had to work for the Latin test, all my free time, and I got 15/16 which tied with Porky was the top mark, but this doesn't matter. All I want to know is please may I drop it. Soapy says that with as much as I know I could take extra tuition after matriculation if it was needed but she doesn't think it will be. You see I must have more free time in which to practise and Dot has 14 free lessons and I have only 1. Please, please say I can drop it because it's terribly hard and we are doing Pliny's letters which are terrific.

Well now for news. Yesterday we went a very long walk, and when we got back Miss Hardy said we could have a dip, Dotty was at the dentist and Jeff was out with her father probably for the last time. We all complained of not having any swimming costumes but Ms Hardy said we could go in without. Not many liked the idea but four of us went in. I had the most super, super dip I have ever had. It was so free and I went miles out on the crawl and came back sidestroke. It was stunning, imagine if you can, anything like this at 'Ye Olde Convent!'

This last week, a bunch of sailors passed our window during the math lesson and we all sat up and took notice. Then Miss Creed came in and said that visitors were coming round. Naturally we thought of the sailors so we did our hair and sat pretty. After a few minutes in walked 2 old hags! Half the form burst out laughing. They will think we're an ill mannered lot. On Wednesday, Soapy who sleeps next door came in all flustered and said there was a mouse in her drawer. We all went in and she stood on a stool and conducted the traffic. She was a scream. Fancy Soapy scared of a mouse. We were going to feed it up and make it nice and large for her, but she caught it before we had time.

Mimi Fletcher a girl from Chesterfield has been very homesick and do you know what the daft chump did? She walked to the station and sent a telegram home. Isn't she crazy she's only new and says she made up her mind not to like it and therefore won't. She wants to come home at half-term and says she's going to stay there. How'd you like to have a mut like that for a daughter? Everyone is being frightfully kind to her and Harry (the headmistress) *was dancing with her last night to cheer her up. We go out with her and have ever such good times, but she still mopes with a long face, it's like 'Men of Boy's Town' trying to get that lad to smile!*

Would you please send me a face flannel because I forgot one and have to borrow Jeff's and Dot's and don't forget about the Latin.

P S. Oh horrors! Harry has just said I must keep on with Latin.

In my first riding lesson, when I went over to the stables I could see a lot of girls going on the leading rein, which looked very tame, so when I was asked if I had ridden before, I said 'yes'. I managed to get my foot up into the stirrup and swing up, but as soon as I was on, the horse just took off. I must have looked very amusing as I could not rein it in and we flew along. Luckily I wasn't thrown. When the others caught me up, the teacher said to me 'You never rode before did you?' It became one of my favorite pastimes and I can still remember the joy of galloping over those beautiful meadows and the wild rides we had when I got more proficient.

Another letter from me about riding and how I loved it.

"*This last week has been the most adorable ever. First of all I went riding, it was just stupendous, colossal and wonderful. I got on fine and Miss Barker* (The riding instructress) *is the sweetest girl I ever met. She is the sort of riding Mistress. I rode Jack who must lead the party, so Barker and I rode side by side and we chatted all afternoon. This was very good because the time before I'd had all on, to hold on. Jack is very big and does a bit what he likes, but coming up the drive I made him go at such a speed that we left the others miles behind and when Miss Denne shouted to me to stop, we stopped immediately. Jack's real racing name is 'Red Flash.' However when I had assured Miss Denne that he wasn't running away with me she let me canter to school and everyone stopped playing games to watch. You've no idea how super I felt.*

I am so sorry I did not write in the week to thank you for the riding britches they are lovely and only Miss Barker and I wear britches so I am very thrilled thank-you both a big lot. (Everyone else wore jodhpurs) *Yesterday was a lovely day, in the morning we had lessons and then we had tuck given out. After dinner we got letters and I had two. In the afternoon we played a few games of tennis but it was much too hot so we went down to the river and paddled all the afternoon until 4.15 when we came in and had to wash and brush up. I went to a birthday party yesterday and Friday. After tea we went to the lake and paddled and got brown. We stayed there until quarter to seven when we came back and then had supper and Scottie and Sod and I went down in the woods where it was cool and had Dot's gramophone on. After her music lesson she came too and we listened to all her super records.*

Next weekend Jeff is coming for me on the Sunday and after dinner we go to Allonby where the Flutters have a caravan and if we are lucky Jeff (Julie Flutter) *says we can go riding. Dot is going home on Friday and returning Monday.*

We have just had the Pilgrim Players giving 'Tobias and the Angel' it was super super and I enjoyed it a lot. Tobias was only about 19 and very funny, all the actors were extremely good and I did wish you could have seen it, you would have loved it. I have got all the actors autographs aren't I lucky?

We had grades this week and here's a list of what I got its better than last time

English A minus	*Geography B plus*
French B	*Latin B plus*
Arithmetic B plus	*Algebra A minus*
Geometry A	*Scripture B plus*
Science B plus	*Elocution B*
Piano B	*Aural Culture B*
Gym B	*Deportment B*
Games B	<u>*Total 28*</u>

Haven't I sent you a nice newsy letter? Sorry I can't think of any more and it is the end of letter writing now." (Every Sunday afternoon we had to write letters, first to our parents and if there was time to other relatives. I usually wrote also to one of my Grannies.)

After our 2 hours of sport we went in and changed and had milk and a huge hard biscuit, which was exactly like the dog biscuits we had for our big dog. I think matron was desperate to find enough food for us, the rationed food was so minimal. After that we had 2 hours of prep which was like homework, we had to work on our own. Then it was time for our dinner and after that we goofed around in the classrooms, we did handstands against the wall, and some games too, but we really didn't have much to do. Occasionally we would have a film or concert, usually on Saturday nights, and once or twice we had a theatre group came to perform a play. Usually bed was at 8.30 and lights out at 9. Looking at our routine I am surprised I loved school so much.!

One holiday I came home and Daddy noticed straight away that my right shoulder was much lower than the left. He took me to Dr. Mather, a chiropractor, who said I had been going around with a dislocated hip. It was probably from a riding accident, or from one of my many falls in lacrosse. I had several treatments during the vacation but I don't think it was ever properly corrected, as I had lots of troubles later.

I always looked forward to going back to school after the holidays. One of the reasons I think was when I was at home we had to go to our shelter almost every night. Daddy had first built an Anderson Shelter down the garden, but it was very miserable, very damp and cold and quite a long way from the house. They were half round corrugated metal, like a tunnel and you dug them into the ground and piled earth over the top. Later Daddy had the idea to line the walls of our cloakroom with heavy steel and it went across the ceiling and a plate over the window, and it was under the stairs structure so would have withstood the roof falling in on us, but not much withstood a direct hit, except perhaps being deep down in the London Underground, which is where crowds of Londoners spent the raids.

Our shelter was only a small space and we had some relatives billeted on us. They had been bombed out of their house. The old lady was very deaf, she had a large chair in the small space and whenever the house shook from the ack-ack guns or a bomb she would shout at her daughter (who must have been about 60 herself,) "Edie did I hear something?" I got to the stage that I preferred to stay up in my bed, as it was impossible to sleep in the shelter. Mummy would keep calling me to come down as she thought shrapnel would come through the roof if I stayed up there, but after lots of sleepless nights, I didn't care.

I remember the Christmas of 1941 when I was at home. We had some wonderful old elegant shops in town; one beautiful one, called Walshs, was owned by Harrods and had a large open atrium going up through the center of each floor, and they had a huge decorated tree in this atrium. They had such beautiful gifts and clothes in for the Christmas season, anyway in mid December we had a huge air raid on the center of town, not on the factories as usual, and they hit several big shops, and also the water mains so the fires from the burning buildings spread to the whole downtown area, and there were very few shops left standing. All those wonderful Christmas gifts gone!

As soon as the war started a group was formed called the Home Guard, and Daddy became a member. Later on in the war he was having a very hard time. His top man in the steel works, Ken Brown, had been called up and was in the air force, Daddy was very short of staff and had so many orders to complete so would come home absolutely exhausted. He would have tea and 3 or 4 nights a week, he still went on Home Guard duty. At first they had no guns but only wooden rifles to practice drilling, I think Daddy had made his. Everywhere in England they had H.G. units. I think they did a heroic job as they all had to work in the days, but each night after dark they were everywhere. They patrolled the streets to make sure no chink of light showed, and many of our big raids were on moonlight nights as the towns were totally blacked out. They had duties around all the main buildings to collect firebombs as they fell. St. Paul's in London had thousands of firebombs on its roof and a team of ARP and HG men on duty on the roofs would get them off. We had sand buckets everywhere to douse firebombs and large tongues to pick them up. Also the HG was trained and later armed as we all expected an invasion at any time. I think they were responsible also for getting Barrage Balloons up over the town and bringing them down when it got windy as they got tangled up in winds. Sheffield was ringed by huge barrage balloons. They had a lot of cables hanging from them so that low flying planes coming in on a bombing run, would risk catching one of the cables. All the names of towns were removed from stations, shops, everywhere, and if someone asked the name of a place we were not to give it. The German landing was imminent.

You can guess what a delight it was to take the train back to my beloved Lake Bassenthwaite, where the war seemed far away. Our train trips were fun too, as the trains were packed with troops, Canadian and English in the early part of the war. We had to change trains in Leeds, and sometimes would spend time there as they had a lot of restaurants with good tea dances, I think we were all getting interested in boys by then. We would put on parts of our uniform that looked like a WREN (women's naval corps) and hope we didn't look like schoolgirls. We usually had to take a later train back to Carlisle if we wanted to stop in Leeds. We were met there in Carlisle by buses to take us to school on Bassenthwaite Lake, in the heart of the Lake District.

Although food and sweet things were so short in the war, Mummy somehow managed to find things for my 'tuck box'. We took them back after each holiday and Mummy would sometimes send things to add to it during term.

We used to have great adventures after 'lights out' which made it very exciting. We had a wonderful cedar tree that we would climb. Dotty would bring her portable gramophone that you wound up. We each took a small bag with nibbles from our tuck box. Our tree had a series of level platforms of soft branches, and we would climb to one of the top ones, but you had to lie down on the branch for it to support you. We would lie and watch the moon and stars, with our music on very quietly, and chat, and eat our sweets. One night we were waiting for Dotty to come with the music and we heard her struggling up the tree, but suddenly we heard her crashing down through all the layers of soft branches. Apparently she had stood up on one of the branch platforms and the whole trick of our den, you always had to lie down. She was not really hurt and climbed up again. We were all quite hysterical after that. We had to be fairly quiet in case anyone was around.

When we were away in school we were always keen to get a tan before going home, the sun in the lake district never seemed to brown you, so one of our gang read in a magazine that some dark iron oxide crystals dyed you brown. We bought some and dissolved it in the bath, and then we all tried soaking in it. It was rather a failure though as I guess certain parts of our bodies were more greasy than others, the dry areas were quite dark so we ended up patchy and the bath took us ages to get clean, before matron saw it! We did a few of these crazy things at school.

Dottie saw in a magazine an advertisement for a cream to enlarge your breasts, and sent for a huge jar, as she was very flat chested. I used to rub it on my calves as my legs were very thin and shapeless. I don't think it worked for either of us!

Our other big adventure day was when we went bike rides with our Biology teacher. It was usually on Saturdays. We somehow would get as far as Keswick which was a nice little tourist town. It had good restaurants by the lake, and we would pop in and order tea with cakes. One time I remember when the bill arrived we didn't have enough money to pay it, so rather than make a great commotion, 2 of us rode back to school to borrow from anyone who had money. Another time the same thing happened and we asked the owner if we could help wash some dishes, as it was a very long ride back to school!

Sometimes at half term my parents would come up by train; almost no one had petrol enough for a long trip. They used to stay at a lovely hotel in Keswick or a very quiet one in Bassenthwaite Village. It was such a treat to go in and have some civilized meals, I sometimes stayed with them in the hotel. Because of my weekly letters to them, when they came to visit, they knew most of my news and all the scrapes I had been in!

I think we had some very good teachers, I liked Miss Drury our biology teacher, and we had a local man came in to teach us art, it was he who started my interest in architecture. We had a very strict Latin teacher, and a poor sad lady who taught us French who we all called Soapy. I don't know why, but we all teased her endlessly. When she came in the classroom we would all have the lids of our desks up, and she would try to get us to put them down. She usually had to go off to get Miss Hargreaves, the headmistress, for help. We had a very far out history teacher who looking back on it, must have been a communist. She changed a lot of our ideas, and as we were all from middle class backgrounds, her political ideas were quite a change.

Poor Daddy, when I went home I had all sorts of new ideas and he used to get so cross with me when I expressed them. Both of my parents used to say to me "What will people think" and I would get so mad and say I couldn't care less what anyone thinks. I remember I had a theory that we should have refused to fight in another war, and have worked on the idea of getting everyone to refuse to go, because England and Germany were destroying themselves once again. I thought we should put Churchill, Hitler and their ministers in a room until they could reach an agreement. As we had so recently destroyed lots of Europe and Europeans in the First World War, which had solved nothing, I did not see the sense of doing it all again. I think our history teacher started some of these ideas, but it made Daddy very cross.

The one sad thing about being in an all girls boarding school, and one so remote from people was that we never saw or met any boys. Sometimes we would have a delivery boy come to school and we were very pleased to talk to them, if we got chance. We had one young boiler stoker who everyone was in love with. Sometimes after dinner we would sneak down to the boiler house and chat to him. I am sure he was a very dull local boy, but we needed the change from such a female bunch. Another disadvantage of being away at school was when we went home for the holidays, our old friends at home had got new pals and we were left out. BooBoo lived in Tuxford, which was on the way to Lincoln. I used to cycle to stay with her, and she would return to stay with me. I still had one or two good friends at that time in Sheffield, Keith Harrison and Monica Walters. Keith's father was one of Daddy's traveling companions and they lived in a wonderful old house called Thrift House. I spent a lot of time with them, and Uncle Len, Keith's father, made beautiful models of old sailing galleons. He made an incredible galleon in the winter when I was there, which he gave to Daddy when it was complete. Nils now has it and I guess it will one day go to his son Dane, our 7th grandchild. I must remember to tell him about Uncle Len and all his hours of work.

Keith was called up into the Fleet Air Arm so then I seldom saw him. My other good friend from early school years was Monica Walters and I still saw her when I was home, and my cousin Desmond from

Disley was very keen on Monica, so would come over to us, or to stay with Granny Beevers to see her. There were so many great things though about being at Hunmanby. I had never lived in such beautiful surroundings. I also became a very independent person. If you are just in day school and return to your family every night, you always have the influence of their ideas. If you have any corners that need rounding your parents always seem to support you and do not find it necessary for you to try to change, and so you are torn between the people your age and the ideas of your parents. My father who was brought up by Victorians, was a very dictatorial person and tried to control me in the way he used to when I was young. In fact his ideas were far too narrow and we had some big arguments. It was a very freeing experience for me to be away from home and able to make my own decisions and opinions. I think Daddy had never thought what going away to a progressive school, and forming my own ideas about everything would mean to him. I was certainly a different girl. .

I think it had been a real struggle to pay my school fees and my brothers at the Leys School in Cambridge. Poor Daddy, I hope he appreciated me more when I became a woman, with a family and able to make decisions and support all 6 of us.

Whenever I went home it was so difficult to take the continual disturbed nights, with the raids. The house shook as we had some big guns on the hill near to us, so even if I stayed in my bed, I didn't get much sleep. It had a very depressing feeling in the town as so much was gone. We had to have our gas masks all the time and I couldn't stand the smell of mine, it was very claustrophobic. The eye piece was always steamed up, and the whole shelter thing was too small a space and often underground.

I probably had memories of being in an oxygen tent when I was 2 and unable to breathe, with pneumonia, but I think my brother David made it worse by trapping me in small spaces. Daddy used to go down to the steel works sometimes on Sundays and took us with him. While he was busy in his office, David and I would play in the works.

There was a small lift probably about 2ft x 2ft, that the files would be sent up from one floor to the next for packing. It had a metal square shoot fitting around it, and David and I would ride up and down. Sometimes when I was in it, David would stop it between floors and as the sides were so near my face, and it was all dark, I used to panic as I felt I couldn't breathe. For years I couldn't go in the caves in Castleton near to our town. I think I would still have a hard time with the "Little John" caves. Those are the ones you lie down in a boat and the man in charge walks on the ceiling as he lies on his back in the bottom of the boat. The roof of the cave is just down to the top of the boat, but then in the center there is a higher cave with a lovely purple crystal on the walls called 'Blue John'.

The visits to the steel works I enjoyed, were during the week when all the men and machinery were working, I loved visiting the steel works. Huge blast furnaces and giant metal hammers on machines that flattened and reshaped the red hot steel, it was very dramatic and exciting. The red hot blanks were immersed in large salty tanks, to harden the steel, it made clouds of hissing steam. Looked like Hades!

All the files they produced were hand cut, so that in the middle of the file, which got the most wear, the men cut the grooves deeper. They were huge files and rasps, and they also made ship's scrapers.

Our days in the Lake District were coming to an end, it was just for the junior years, and then we continued to our senior school which was evacuated to Ilkley, not too far from Leeds. There the school had taken over several large Victorian houses on the edge of Ilkley Moors. It was not the same as my beloved Bassenthwaite Lake, where we had so much freedom, because the Lake District was so beautiful, and the area around was wild, the staff did not know where we were most of the time.

We were part of a town in the senior school as we were near to lots of other houses. We had several strange events there. One day matron sent for some of the girls from our house, and asked us if we had lost anything. We had not noticed, but in fact all our underwear had disappeared. Each item of clothing had to have a name tape sewn in it, as they all went to the school laundry, and apparently the police had arrested a man and found all our underwear in his room. I think we had all noticed that we had no more clean things but just thought the laundry was late coming back.

The other weird thing I remember Dotty and I sneaked out of our house after lights out, like we did in Basenthwaite, as the apple trees in the garden had great fruit, and we had gone out to collect some for everybody. We were bending down to pick up fruit off the ground, when I saw the other side of the tree some very big boots, I couldn't see whose they were, maybe the 'Peeping Tom' who had stolen all our panties, but we just raced back to our dormitory and locked our door, which opened straight onto the garden. We had been used to such freedom in the Lake District with no one within miles of us.

The journey to school was much shorter, but we still went to our tea dances in Leeds. I think by then we had lots of American troops in England, so we enjoyed having more excitement in the stories they had to tell. BooBoo had a cousin Keith who was in the engineers, he was an officer and stationed near Tuxford, so when I stayed with her during the holidays, we used to go to dances at The Barley Mow, on Saturday nights. They were so exciting for us, and we would bath and try on all sorts of outfits to get the best effect, or so we thought. Keith had several friends stationed with him and we got to know a lot of them. Harry Sutcliffe was one of them, he had a wonderful old 1925 Bentley open car and BooBoo and I had some great outings in it, they came over to Sheffield to pick me up in it. It had a running board outside the chassis and was always open, I don't know if it even had a roof or top.

I am still in touch with BooBoo, who everyone now calls Judy. When I visited her once about 15 years ago in Retford, she told me she had an address for Harry and that he also was in California, where we have been living since 1968. I was pleased to find him again as I hate to lose touch with old friends. That seems to me to be the main reason to send Christmas cards each year to get any new addresses when people move. I have many old friends that I wanted to keep in touch with, as they are very hard to trace once you lose them. Recently there are various ways on the web to help find them but it is a matter of luck as most of the girls changed their names when they married. I was very pleased to find Harry again. When he came out of the engineers he went to University in Manchester and met an American girl who was over on a Fulbright I think, and they got married. When I discovered him they were living in Mill Valley just north of San Francisco. He was an engineer with Bechtel and I guess had become one of the top tunnel designers in the world. When we went up to see him he was working on the Channel Tunnel, from England to France. He had a fascinating film of the cutting of the tunnel with giant machines with rotating cutters on the front. It was a great engineering project, but I told him at the time that I will always fly across, or take the Hovercraft, if we have a car. The thought of the crazy French at one end blowing up the entrance, and the IRA at the other, you could be entombed forever in the chunnel, my old fears of not being able to breathe! The police in England recently discovered a store full of bombs near the tunnel entrance, so my fears are not unreasonable. Harry has worked on several big tunnels recently, the one in Denmark that was designed by a French engineer, that was getting sea water in. They called Harry in to solve their problem. He has worked on another one in Denmark, he has been over there to work, even though he is supposed to be retired.

He has apparently managed to trace his old Bentley. It was a 1925, 3 Litre Red Label short chassis, with Vanden Plas Body. When it was sold it went to Germany. During the sixties and seventies, Harry was a frequent visitor to Grasmere in the Lake District, where Chris Reekies was his favorite mohair shop. Little did he know that the Bentley was garaged a block from the shop!! In the late seventies a chap in the

British Officer's Club of New England looked it up in his handbook and told him it was in Chippenham, Wiltshire. Harry visited the old girl there. He said it looked good, but had been tarted up some, and its original 15 coats of lacquer had given way to modern car paint. Then he heard from a man with Xerox, a Brit, Ron Stokes, who has it in Upper New York State. Harry sent him a lot of stuff on it, he says it is now worth a million bucks!! He thinks Judy (Boo Boo), he and I should find a pub in New England and have a photo taken to bring our old one up to date. On our original photo we had John Collinge with us, but he killed himself by attaching his exhaust to the interior of his car, so perhaps the new owner Ron could take his place. You can tell from all this research Harry has done that he is a 'super sleuth.' He has also been able to trace his family back to the times when records were first started. I don't know how he has done it, as I have tried and it is very hard work. I did meet him in Salt Lake City, where he did his research in the big Mormon Library, and he got me started on my families genealogy.

Keith, Boo Boo's cousin moved to Toronto after the war and Judy (Boo Boo) has just been to try to see him, but he has Alzheimer's and his wife said he becomes very agitated if anyone goes to see him, so she never met him.

That is such a tragic disease- Keith used to be such a vital, handsome fellow when we were all friends. (I have just received his obituary from Judy, he had been the director of a very successful development company in Toronto, and they were the developers of the Canary Wharf scheme, on the Isle of Dogs in London)

Dotty Clough, who was one of our gang at school, I have lost. For a while we were in touch. After school, she became a journalist and worked on the Sheffield Telegraph so I saw her at that time, as I was at the University there, and then she visited me in London in 1949. I heard she was going to Australia to marry someone there, but she met someone on the boat going out and decided to marry him instead! Don't think I ever heard of her again.

Judy has traced Jean Hesketh (Hackett) recently, and I telephoned her in Australia, and had a long chat, but she had had a stroke, and was not too well.

As I didn't live in England, I never went to the old girls re-unions, and the school has now been closed. I think because it was an all girls school, most of the 'public schools' that have survived became co-ed. Funnily enough since I wrote that, I just had an invitation to a re-union at Armathwaite Hall, for all the girls that were evacuated there. It was very short notice and a long way to go from California, so I think I will miss that. (I just heard from Judy that our friend June Mc Adam went and Judy said not many of our contemporaries were there, so I am pleased I didn't go over specially)

My days at Hunmanby were almost finished too, I took the School Certificate exams and passed, so I guess I had been learning something during all our crazy adventures. I remember going home on the train on the last day, and throwing our uniform straw hats out of the window and into a river as we went over a bridge. We wartime students never went to the real school, the buildings that were built for it specially, and taken over by the army, so that was sad, but I don't think we would have had the joy and freedom of our surroundings in the Lake District.

My brother David was at the Leys, and their base was in Cambridge, but all his schooling was in Blair Atholl, in Scotland. I am not sure he ever went to the Cambridge school. I think the big Hydros and Hotels that were so far away from the big towns, were pleased to lease their buildings, as nobody had enough petrol to drive, to stay there during the war.

Several of my friends had their brothers killed in the war, one boy I really liked was Pam Hicks brother, he was in the air force and had been trained in Canada. Not long after he came back from his training he was killed in a dogfight over England. I heard a lot of the boys trained over there, were killed quickly after they returned. Perhaps it was not a realistic place to train, so many miles from the real fighting.

When I was about to leave school, I heard they were training 'ferry pilots' to fly planes over from the USA and Canada so I wrote off to volunteer. I had always dreamed of being a flyer and this seemed a great chance to get my pilots licence. Daddy had heard how many of these ferry pilots got shot down, as they had no gunner on board, and as I was under 18 he was able to say 'NO' to that idea. I had to start to think of something to do that he would agree to.

The New Life --Starting at University.

I had been enjoying our art teachers ideas of studying Architecture, and when it came to having to make a decision about what to study at University, Daddy and I had different goals. He felt I needed a career that would enable me to support a family if it was necessary, and he did not think there was any money to be made in architecture, and as I had very good grades in Biology he wanted me to enter medical school as a dental student. He and I went to see the head of the dental department, and I needed to bring up my grades in Latin. I guess that was one of the required subjects in those days.

I had a Latin tutor for the following year, Johnny Rushton. I had always found it a very dry dull subject, and wading through Virgil's Aenid and Homer's Gallic Wars was all very boring stuff to an eighteen year old, who had just been released onto the world from my all girls boarding school.

There were suddenly so many wonderful men around. A very distant cousin from Daddy's side of the family, John Knowles was in the RAF and used to come and stay with us, he was really a sweet guy. I still visited BooBoo in Tuxford, and saw the gang there. One of Mummy and Daddy's girl friends had a friend in the Engineers, he was a major, John Steele, and his family lived near Harrogate. Whenever he was on leave he would come over to see me, he was a lot older than me, I guess he was 32 when I was only 18. He was very impressive for me as he had a great tailored uniform, as he was a Major. The non-commissioned men had terrible uniforms in the English forces. They were very scratchy material and had silly little triangular hats that were hard to keep on. John was a man of the world with a more mature manner about him. He took me to wonderful expensive places for trips and out to good restaurants.

One weekend he had come over to Sheffield and we were having lunch in the Grand Hotel, which I thought was very posh. I suddenly had the most excruciating pain and rushed to the ladies room where I was sick. I think John phoned my parents but the next thing I knew, was I came around in a bed in a nursing home, Claremont, run by nuns, which was like a nightmare, after my days in the convent. My appendix had burst during lunch and so they had decided to operate immediately on me. I think the surgeon was called Dr <u>Little</u>, anyway I thought very <u>little</u> of him. He had cut me from the edge of my pubic hairs to 2 inches higher than my navel, and I had a series of big metal clips all the way along the cut, that caught on the gauze bandage on my tummy, very painful.

I asked him later how he could have made such a huge cut, as my brother had his appendix out, and had a very small incision on his right side, I think he said something about if I needed a caesarean in the next few years. It may have been that as it had burst he needed a large opening to clean up. I was completely shattered, at that age to have a massive scar on my tummy, and then to be in another creepy place with rosaries clinking around all the night, like the Notre Dame days.

I think I went home after a couple of weeks, back to my Latin cramming. I found after a while that I was not very hungry and feeling rather miserable all the time. Mummy took me to the family doctor, Dr Jack. He thought the best thing I could do was to go to work for some really unfortunate people, as he wanted me to see how lucky I really was, so they got me a job serving lunches at the British Restaurant at the Scala Cinema. These were started during the war as very cheap or even free places to eat, and all sorts of homeless folk went there, people who were bombed and in shelters. The food was awful, huge pans of mushy peas and weird smelling main course dishes. I guess we got used to eating anything during the war. Something helped me to slowly get over my depression, from the shock of the surgery, but I don't know what it was.

On June 6th that year, 1944 the armed forces landed on D day in France. I know John Steele was over there as he sent me a box of grapes from France or Belgium. We couldn't get grapes in the war, in fact we had very little fruit.

In the summer we had english apples, cox's orange pippins, and we had so many, so we dried them. We cut them into thin slices and took out the core and threaded the rings on poles near the ceilings to dry out. They were good for apple pies or applesauce during the winters. We also put a lot of whole apples up into our attic space on newspapers and we had to remember to turn them fairly often. My mother also used to get a lot of eggs in the summer when chickens were laying, she had some huge earthenware pots in the pantry, and she would carefully pack the eggs in, and then she would make up a mixture of 'eisenglass' whatever that was, and pour it into the pots completely covering the eggs. We did get powdered eggs, which you could use for baking, but they were not good for anything like an omelette.

Our food was terrible all during the war, so much had to be shipped in, and it was so difficult to get convoys through. We had 2 ounces of meat and cheese each week, we had pasta a lot with very little on it. English people had not been very adventurous in their taste for food before the war. They did a funny programme later on T.V. showing farmers harvesting spaghetti off branches of trees! I don't know how many people realised it was done for a joke.

Daddy had a cousin with a farm in Friskney, Lincolnshire. He would send us a package of sausages, bacon, and other pork cuts when he could spare them and he had killed one of his pigs. We also received food parcels from America. We loved the Spam meat but they also included several cans of peanut butter, which we had never heard of. They should have given us some instructions on what we could do with it. Mummy thought it must be the same as butter and so would try to fry our food in it. Don't think we ever realised you could eat it on bread!

It is hard to think of my memories of the war, I remember we had a lot of news theatres, and as we did not have any television, that was the one way to see all the fighting and results of the bombing raids. We had a very good BBC news at 9pm every night on the radio, and I think almost everyone in England listened to that. Churchill gave the most rousing speeches when we were at our lowest point and expecting Germans to land at any minute. We all followed the sea battles very carefully, as our battleships were always chasing the German boats that were blockading us from our supply lines. We had some terribly exciting ones- when the Scharnhorst was chased around the north of England, and finally sunk up there. Then in May 1941 we had the great search to find the 'Bismarck' it had been up in the North Sea off Norway, and was heading down into the Atlantic to join in the battles with the convoys bringing many of the supplies to England from the States. There were three possible routes, one to sail the northern route and come down the Canadian coast, and HMS Hood was sent to defend that route, and sure enough that was the route the Bismarck took, and the Germans attacked and sank the Hood, and 1,415 men were lost, there were only 3 survivors. The last survivor Ted Briggs just died in England, in 2008, at the age of 85. After H.M.S. Hood was sunk in the battle of Denmark Strait, the Royal Navy in retaliation chased the German "Bismarck" in one of the biggest battles of the war and three days later, the Bismarck was sunk. I remember the cheers in all the pubs as we all rejoiced. The war pulled us all together like nothing else has ever done.

It brings tears to my eyes now, to remember that tough spirit everyone had in the darkest days of the war. We were fighting ALL

ALONE, the huge German army, that Hitler had amassed for years. Luckily we had a GREAT leader, Winston Churchill. He was on the radio almost every day, spurring us on, in the darkest days of the war, when an invasion was expected at any minute. When our troops, who had gone over to help the French, in their battle against Hitler's invading forces, were trapped, because the French never warned us they were about to capitulate. Our troops were caught deep in France, we suffered huge casualties, in their retreat, and it took every single small boat in England to go across the channel, to Dunkirk, to ferry the soldiers that were still alive, back to England.

The French are a very arrogant race, they never credit us with sending so many of our soldiers to die, to help save them, in TWO wars. De Gaulle came to England for the rest of the war, when France was occupied, and gathered some French army, called the Free French. After the war when he became President, and they were discussing the formation of the EU, De Gaulle was emphatic that England must not be allowed to join!! What a great way to repay our help and Hospitality he had enjoyed during the rest of the war.

The whole country mourned the loss of the Ark Royal and for several days spirits were very low. Our whole lifeline depended on goods and troops being brought in by sea. We were on a roller coaster ride emotionally, nothing was secure, and people in the forces were living each day as if it might be their last. Lots of romances because you didn't know if anyone would survive, and in case they didn't, people were grabbing at any pleasure they could find.

The Convent School had been asked to knit scarves, mittens and balaclava helmets for the sailors on HMS Sheffield. I had never learned to knit, but got some big needles and khaki wool and knitted a very long scarf -must have been about 8ft by the time I had it finished. I was sad to hear that HMS Sheffield was finally sunk in the 1990 Falkland war. Wonder if my scarf went down with the boat?

After the 2 old ladies who were billeted on us had moved, we had some WAAF's (Women's branch of the RAF) from a nearby air base, stationed with us. I remember a very pretty one Barbara Bullock, she was so sweet. She was very fond of poor Daddy, who was really beginning to show the strain of work, and loss of sleep from home guard duty every other night, so Barbara would sit and rub bay-rum and cantherides into his scalp to help him relax. I think it was also to stimulate hair growth.

Daddy was beginning to get very bad pains across his shoulders, and was having a difficult time sleeping. Dr. Jack decided to give him a course of quinine injections in the winter of 1944-45. They were given with a very long needle into the buttock. It was to be a series of 5, and Dr. Jack would come on Sunday mornings to the house, and Daddy stayed in bed until after he had had the shot, and then he and the doctor would have a glass of sherry together. On the Sunday that he had the 5th one, Dr. Jack had just come down to the hall and was about to leave, when Daddy called out in terrible pain, his right side was completely paralyzed. The needle had hit the sciatic nerve.

There was nothing to be done. In the next few months we had all kinds of therapists came to give him treatments, but for a year he just lay in bed. He had always been so active, never still for a minute. He had played golf a lot, gone riding, and dancing and of course during the war had been seriously overworked and stressed.

On April 25th 1945 when Daddy was in bed paralised, Mummy had a baby girl, they called her Elisabeth. She really saved my Father's sanity. He adored babies and young children, and I remember Mummy would put Elisabeth down on his bed and he sat and watched her for hours. Mummy would sit and read to Daddy, as he had never sat still long enough to read. After his incredibly active life, I do not know how he was able to stay sane, when he could not move at all.

When Mummy had found out she was pregnant we were having our tea in the lounge and as we were pushing out the tea wagon, Mummy was telling me about it, and laughing so much that she fell over the edge of the carpet and rolled over. It did seem hilarious, I was 19 and my brother David was 14. I guess the contraception they had used, had depended on the same quinine, and during the war they had to use a substitute as it came from abroad. It obviously didn't work, but it turned out to be the best thing for both of them, to have a new baby. I was very seldom at home, I was in my first year at University. My brother David was in Pitlochry in Scotland. His boarding school, The Leys, in Cambridge, was evacuated there.

After about a year of electric therapy on his leg, Daddy had an iron made for his right leg, it was attached to his shoe and strapped to his leg, with a spring to keep his foot up, so he was able to walk with a stick. He was very unsteady but was able to be up from his bed. Over the years he did get a bit of use back in his right arm but he never got his right hand back properly, and over several years got to the stage of a wheelchair for every day. He was barely 40 when it happened, but Mummy rationalised it, that Daddy would not have lived long at the wild pace he had been going, and he did live until the fall of 1984 when he was 82.

I don't remember how it happened or when, but Daddy allowed me to switch from dentistry to Architecture. The thought of poking around English sets of teeth seemed very depressing, but Daddy was right about the pay being better.

To go back to 1944 and my first days at the University. The Architecture Dept. was in a tower of one of the buildings, that was where we had our studio. Everyone had a large desk and we had to buy a series of drawing boards, Imperial size and Double Elephant. Our lectures were given in different parts of the University, our surveying classes and engineering were given down the hill in the Engineering School. We were on the whole fairly fresh out of school. One of the boys David Allford, was in my first year. He was one of the gang I met when I walked back and forth to my first little school, run by Miss Hambley and Miss Givens, and I always carried my holy bible in my suitcase to tackle him. He was my first serious boyfriend, and remained one of my best friends until he died in 1997, he was a little younger than me.

There was a real mix of boys in my year, Peter Hickson who was from Doncaster the son of rather a great old guy, who was an architect. I was very good friends with Pete and often went over to stay with him at his parents home, and he came with us to stay at my grandmothers (Daddy's mother) in North Wales in the summer of 1945. Pete died very young of cancer. Morton Taylor who was also from Doncaster, was a good friend for a while, but he was very quiet and not a lot of fun.

There was one older guy who had been in the merchant navy, Pete Pickerell, he was a very wild fellow, I don't know if any of us really understood him. He had some incredible stories of adventures he had had in the merchant navy, I remember one of them. They discovered on the merchant ship, that there was no cutlery to eat their food. Apparently the guy who was in the kitchen, whose job it was to wash cutlery, had had some sort of problem, and tipped all the cutlery overboard!

We used to have a sketch design day every week, we would have a simple building to design and to draw it up and have it submitted by the following morning. We worked sometimes through the night, but after we went out to eat dinner in the student union, Pete would say 'lets go out for some air on the moors'. Sheffield is on the Pennines, a chain of mountains down the middle of England, and it has wonderful rock outcroppings, they are the ones that Kathy and Heathcliff used to climb on in Bronte's 'Wuthering Heights.' I still go back to them each time I am in England.

My brother David and his wife bought a wonderful old stone farm that we used to look down on from Stannage Edge, and they made it a very comfortable place to live in, without spoiling the beauty of the old group of farm buildings. When Pete and I went up it was usually howling wind and we would race through the heather and climb the highest peaks, it really blew the cobwebs away. I think Pete was married and lived in Chesterfield, I heard that he got some terrible illness and also died young, he was a very wild man of the moors. Gerry Sheard, and Ray Moss were 2 friends, in my year. Ray lived with his parents in a huge hospital, The Royal Infirmary, his mother was matron and his father was superintendent. Ray was a good friend of David Allford's, he played in a band, he was always drumming with 2 pencils in the studio and had sharkskin trousers that he had got from the States! He imitated Glenn Miller, had the same glasses and looked very American. The Moss family had lots of parties in their flat in the hospital, they always seemed to have very good food, I guess because it was such a big hospital with large food allocations.

I used to go to the Saturday dances in the Union, and then we would go on to someone's party afterwards. Dave Allford had lots of friends, and we would go to dances and pubs with them, and to films, there was quite a gang. Always someone coming home on leave, so we had to celebrate that.

There was only one other strange little girl, Miss Cooper, studying architecture, in my year, she seemed to have some sort of social problem. Whenever anyone spoke to her she would go very red, and sometimes cry, but never answer. I was virtually on my own with a class of about 25 men. After my years away at an all girls school I really wanted to find out what variations of men there were, so I would do some things with one friend and dance or swim with another.

At one of the parties I met an engineering student Doug Atack, and I started to see a lot of him, he was called up into the engineers. After his training in England he was to be sent out to Singapore and he asked me if we could get engaged before he left. He was abroad for ages, and when he came back I broke off our engagement and returned his ring. He was not right for me at all. I think I had agreed to become engaged because he was just off to a war that you never knew who would return, and he wanted to keep our attachment alive.

While we were all in our first year of studies, the film 'For whom the Bell Tolls' came out and Ingrid Bergman was in it, she was called

Maria. She had her hair about 1 inch long, all over her head. A lot of hair salons were advertising the 'Maria' cut, and as I was always busy and would swim and be out in the wind a lot, I thought it would be a good style for me. I remember the day I got it done, I went back to the studio and no one liked it, Pete Pickerell, the wild one, jumped into a huge trash bin we had for all the scrap drawings, and screamed. Luckily it did not take too long to grow. I learned then that most men liked women with long hair.

One of the really hard things for me was to find some clothes for my new life. I had only worn school uniforms for the past five years. Our clothing ration was so low it only entitled you to one outfit per year, so we took some of Daddy's plus- four suits, from his old golfing days, which he realised he would never wear again, and found that with the wide trousers we had enough fabric for a skirt, and we had Daddy's tailor make me some skirts and jackets, so I was free to get some sweaters and shirts with my coupons to wear with those. I remember we could get some very pretty shoes, but there was no such thing as nylons, and silk stockings were impossible to get hold of, unless you knew one of the US troops. You could buy a bottle of liquid tan for your legs which made them look like you had very fine silk stockings, and if I was going out to a dance or somewhere special, I would ask my brother to draw the seam line up the back of my legs, because all silk stockings had that seam. The liquid stockings made your legs very dry, which was annoying.

The first summer of our Architecture Course we went on a measuring trip to Ludlow in Shropshire. It was and still is a beautiful town, many half- timbered buildings, and some first class Georgian houses. We camped down near the castle and each day we crawled all over one of the classical houses and had to take our own dimensions, and later draw it up. In our second year our measuring trip was to Edinburgh in Scotland, where we tackled an even bigger building.

Stephen Welsh, the head of the school, was an old Rome Scholar and he basically thought women were not good for architecture, or for anything much. After the first few terms he would start off his criticism with my work, and say this is no good, occasionally pulling my drawing off the wall. I started not putting my name on my work, and asked several of the boys I knew to do the same. He was absolutely furious. I went to see one of the deans to put in a complaint about him as he was unfit to give criticisms to us. He was the only one I had any trouble with in school, he was old and victorian in his ideas and still thought women should stay at home.

Gradually many of the boys who started in my first year had to go off to the forces. David Allford went into the air force, and very quickly was sent out to India, which he hated. Even when Indian food became so popular in England after the war, he would never have any, as it had been so bad when he was out there. About the same time Doug Atack went off too, Gerry Sheard went into the army, I am not sure how the ones who stayed got out of it, perhaps they had some physical problem.

The war in Europe finished in 1945, it was my second year at the University. We had tremendous celebrations after 6 years of war, the whole town went crazy, and although we were bombed to pieces, and our rationing was worse than ever, it was wonderful to know that no more 'doodle-bugs' would be over. They were the most sinister of weapons, they came over without any pilot, and had their own engine, which had a different sound from the planes, but suddenly the engine stopped and then you held your breath, waiting for the crash and explosion as they fell.

It is very nostalgic to think of all our emotions during the war. I had a very good radio given me for my 21st birthday and I remember listening to a programme called 'Munchen House coffee time', every night about 12 o'clock midnight, it was broadcast from Munich. It had all the great American Bands on it Glenn Miller, and Tommy Dorsey, it was to entertain the US troops in Germany and in Europe. Our soldiers had Vera Lynn singing 'There'll be Bluebirds Over the White Cliffs of Dover' and the German song 'Lillie Marlene' which we all sang.

I think at the end of our 2nd year the young group we started with were called up, as we still had troops all around the globe, and all the de-mobbed men came to join us in third year. We moved from our tower in Brocco Bank into an old chapel on Sherwood Rd., it had one very large central space, with good top light, and smaller rooms all around. Our year suddenly swelled to about 60 and I was now the only girl.

Whilst Daddy could not drive at all, he let one of his friends teach me to drive. We would take Daddy's car out to the moors, where there was little traffic, and poor Harry Rastall, Daddy's friend, who had volunteered to teach me, would come back every time absolutely shattered, as I guess I drove too fast for him. Daddy had always been a very fast driver and I guess that had made me think about the quickest way to get somewhere.

Once I had learned to drive and had my driver's licence, Daddy let me take the car to the University, as he could not use it. One day we had our engineering class down at St. George's, engineering school. It was a good walk up the hill, so I offered some friends a ride. There was one stop light as we went up the hill, and it was green in my direction, so I didn't slow down, and suddenly there was a truck flying through his red light, and it hit me on my side, at full speed. I phoned poor Daddy who was still in bed at that stage, he was pleased that none of us was hurt, but he must have been pretty upset about his car. The driver of the truck had to go to court, and I went as a witness. He lost his licence, as he had done the same thing before. I remember when I got home I was pretty shaken up and was saying to Daddy that I had the green light to go, but he said what is the point of saying you had the green light, if you were dead! (I now remember he had had a similar accident when I was young, and he got hit by a lorry running a red light)

In the summer holidays I went over to north Wales to my Granny's and I got a job for the summer in Colwyn Bay. I loved that area, they had some lovely little trams, single story ones that we called toast racks.

They were single deckers, open on top and on the sides. The ride into Llandudno was through wild fields, it was a very beautiful area.

Auntie Joan (Daddy's youngest sister) and I used to go early in the morning onto the Little Orme, and collect fresh mushrooms, and we took them back for breakfast. On the other side of Llandudno was the Great Orme, and there was a road that went right around the Great Orme past the Happy Valley gardens and the Grand Hotel at the end of the pier. At the other end of the Orme was another big hotel and it was around there that Alice in Wonderland had been written by Lewis Carroll, about a little girl called Alice Liddell who lived there. I loved the statue of the white rabbit on that beach, when I was young.

Daddy's youngest sister was always a good friend to me, she was probably only 14 years older than me, she had married late, during the war. She married someone in the RAF and he went to India very quickly after they were married, and there he developed a brain tumor and died out there. She had always lived with her mother, Granny Whitham, and she was the child born after her father had died of diabetes. I think she worked in various stores after she left school, she was plump and very jolly. It was a very relaxed household as Granny Whitham always seemed to have no worries and was a very happy, easy person to be around and I enjoyed staying there very much. (Looking back on her relaxed personality, I realise that all her life Daddy supported her and her 2 daughters, amazing!) Joan liked the same films as I did, and she loved swimming at the Rhos pool.

She was a member of the IFL, the International Fellowship League, and they were always having social events and asking lots of foreigners, which made it seem lively. We went to the Isle of Anglesey with them and also to Caernarvon Castle, and Portmeiron, it is a beautiful area that part of north Wales. All the resorts on that west coast were very lively, I guess there were no holidays abroad, so many of Mummy and Daddy's friends had houses and boats in places like Anglesey. The Trickett family were on Anglesey, in the summers, they had a very nice sailboat there, so we would drive over to spend the day with them.

My other Aunt, Daddy's other sister Dorothy had married several years before, in fact I was a bridesmaid at her wedding when I was 6 or 7, and Daddy had given her away. She was living in Chertsey near Hampton Court in London and had a boy Stephen and a daughter Christine. Granny Whitham, had had an amazing life, moving from Swindon up to Sheffield all on her own, she was beautiful when she was young and wore very beautiful clothes, as you can see on her early photos. When her husband died and left her with 3 children, she knew someone called Vernon, who she believed had a lot of money. He owned Vernon's football pool, which was a betting pool on soccer teams. He was apparently bankrupt at the time and Granny thought he was wealthy, and she did not tell him what a bad state the steel works was in from the Depression after Grandpa Whitham died. They were married, but it turned out after he moved into Granny's house, that not only was he broke, he was also an alcoholic. He had 2 boys of his own and had plans to send Daddy away to a boarding school. I think the marriage lasted about a month. I don't know if Granny was ever divorced as when I used to stay there she still got letters for a Mrs. Vernon. Vernon's pools did very well later, I think they were millionaires and his 2 sons (Daddy's half brothers) were big fat fellows who drove Rolls Royce's around Sheffield.

As well as my holidays in Wales I went to France with about 20 architecture students and 2 faculty members. It was not long after the war, so France like England was starting to rebuild. We first went to Paris staying in the Ecole des Mines, and then had a coach take us down the Loire Valley, we stayed in Orleans, and Blois, and Tours, and took trips out to various chateaux. I remember that the ones in Blois, Chenonceaux, and Chambord were all wonderful, and some of the small ones, Azay le Rideau, and Ambles had a great charm. We went to lots of the caves in the banks of the Loire, as they had wine stored in the cool cellars, and the day we went to Vouvray, the wines were so delicious that several people got quite drunk. The worst case was our stupid Welsh instructor who got very ill on the bus and then passed out, we could not revive him, so he went into hospital in Blois, and when we returned home, we left him there.

In Blois we stayed in some religious places, the 19 boys were all in a monastery but I was in a very poor convent, on my own, as I was the only girl. Those poor nuns lived in such terrible conditions, the toilets were indescribably dirty, and every meal while I was there was just boiled potatoes.

One night all our gang went to the cathedral in Blois and the organist who was blind gave us an amazing organ recital. The whole structure vibrated with it, we were all quite stunned. I think he played all Bach. Our French guide was young and very attractive, so I went out dancing with him several nights. I found French men and Italians very different from English and for several years I seemed to be very impressed by them. Probably totally unreliable though, but I needed to get over that phase of finding them so attractive.

When David my brother was quite small, perhaps 14 or 15, he went over to France one summer to stay with the Gilmaires, Daddy knew them through business, and they had a son Patrice who was David's age, and a daughter Sylvie, who was a little younger than me. They lived in Paris but spent the summers in a large family house in Brittany owned by the grandparents. David went to stay with them in Brittany. Guess they ate very different food from ours, which had been so plain all during the war, and maybe the water was not drinkable, anyway poor David got sick and could not find anything to eat, and when we went to meet him at the station, I remember him looking terrible, very thin and like he was about to die. Guess that had been his worry while he lay in bed. Funny that he now lives most of the time in his house in Pezenas in south west France, it obviously did not put him off completely.

When we got back to Paris after our stay in the Loire Valley, I wrote to my parents from there so I will include that letter.

We are staying in a very nice student house on Rue Tournefourt. My room is huge and the windows are very different from at home. My window goes from floor to ceiling, about twelve foot high and opens inwards, with shutters outside for evenings. Each window has a little wrought iron balcony. The buildings are all without exception, very beautiful. The eaves are wide and even the poorest slum houses have the most amazing details on-say a chimney or a doorway. It is definitely a far better land for breeding artists than England. The people are quite dramatic and very excitable, when they talk, they get very keen on whatever they are saying and don't half-heartedly enter a conversation unless it is an English one!

In Tours, Blois and Orleans, we didn't meet anyone who spoke English our guide of course did, but no one else, 'so avec ma Dictionnaire' I was able to carry on long conversations. The driver of our bus couldn't speak a word of English and I used to talk to him going round all the chateaux and my French improved no end. Sylvie and I are going to speak all French when she comes (the Gilmaires had asked if Sylvie could come and stay with us in England for 3 months to learn english) *she says my French is good but I must speak a lot more of it. Her English is quite good too. She has been practising what to say to you Mummy, when she comes.*

I went to see them on Friday morning. On Thursday evening when we got into Paris we had a meal and went to the Casino de Paris. It was terrific, the stage went up and down round and round and it was really spectacular. I got a bus round to the Gilmaires this morning and Patrice came to the door, his mother says he looks better but he's very pale. Patrice and I went to Bon Marche, shopping in the morning we also had two glace framboise, which are strawberry ices and I had four cream cakes. They are wonderful here, when we were in the Loire they were very cheap. Madam Gilmaire asked me back to lunch there as they were going to Brittany in the evening and then after lunch Sylvie and I went to the Louvre. All our crowd were visiting it. They are all a very nice family Mr. Gilmaire is particularly nice, but doesn't speak English at all so I had to use my French again. I went back there with Sylvie and had a cup of tea and then came back here and washed and changed and in the evening we went to the Paris Opera House *to the ballet. We could only get In the fifty five franc seats so we didn't have very good ones but the place is absolutely <u>marvellous.</u> In the interval, which is very long over here with huge lounges, they are bigger than the theatre in most places, as everyone goes out and it's a sort of fashion parade. We walked all around the place and it was terrific. Afterwards we went to a little cafe near the Opera and then back here on the Metro, which is the underground. These shows are very late they start about 8.15 or 8.30 and finish about 11.45 so we have all been a bit dozy as we've walked around all day and been up to leave at 9 most mornings. The first evening here we met a solitary Swede at the casino. He is a student and quite nice, he speaks a little French and a little English, so we can make ourselves understood in a fashion. He's been with us every night. Last night he got three seats for Phil Liversidge and me for the Folies Bergere. It was very good too. Today we are going to Versailles, lunch is at 11.30 and then we are off. We have another guide here in Paris, he's a real Bohemian and has been a student at the Ecole de Beaux Arts as our other one had. The Swede is coming too to Versailles, as he has a bit of a job finding his way round on his own.*

Our day's are all planned in Paris and very well too. Yesterday we went to the Rodin Museum it's over near Les Invalides, I really love his sculptures, they are very sensual and powerful. We went to the Eiffel Tower but didn't go up as it was not clear and costs one hundred and fifty francs. We then walked to the Luxembourg from there, in fact we walk all day and every day. This morning is the first we have not left at 9, so you can guess we're having very full days. Yesterday morning we went to the Palais de Justice, It's on the island you know. We sat on the tip of the island for quite a while, the guide was telling us about the crowds when Princess Elizabeth and Philip were here, they went to where we were. At 10.30 we set off for the Ecole de Beaux Arts and went around there. There are some real lads in that place, well there are all over France. We went and had some wine with them after our trip and one gave me a book about the school so you will see it.

Some people are going home on Tuesday, but we are going to stay until Thursday or Friday. This place is only 250 francs (2 shillings and 6 pence) so our money will last out fine. We shall arrive in London in the evening whichever day it is, so if you could ring or drop a card to Auntie Dot (my fathers sister who lived near Hampton Court) *and tell her I will make my way out to her place if it's OK. I will ring her when I get into town at any rate.*

Paris is not really so lovely as the Loire Valley, that was marvelous, *but it's very big and very beautiful buildings and very well laid out, elegantly proportioned streets. There are too many tourists! Not being one myself!*

The whole holiday had been wonderful, and so exciting. It was a real treat to be able to get out of England because for 6 years we could not go abroad at all.

I think it was at that time I drove Daddy to visit all his old customers in the Birmingham- Wolverhampton area, we stayed at all his old hotels which he had not been in since before the war, and everyone was very pleased to see him. By then he was able to walk with a stick and he had recovered his sense of humour, so was fun to travel with, but I did find the driving in the areas I did not know was pretty tiring. Anyway I got back for the new year at University, after the people my age had gone off to the forces, we had all older men return after they were de-mobbed. Some of them had not studied architecture before, and they all entered our third year, so some of them had a very difficult time, to get back to any studies, most of them had spent 7 years out of school, from 1939 to 1946 and several of them had a family already so had to be sure they could support them after their studies.

There were a number of very interesting men in my year though, I worked next to Alan Mather one year, he was the adopted son of Dr Mather the osteopath, who worked on my dislocated hip. Dr Mather and his wife were very correct and staid, and after they had adopted Alan, they had a son of their own who became a medical doctor and was a very serious person. Alan had been a physical training instructor in the Fleet Air Arm, I thought he was very handsome, he had a very tough physique with a broad face, and a cleft chin like Kirk Douglas.

He played Rugby for one of the Sheffield clubs. He was a first class swimmer, and in the warm summer days he would say lets take off and go to Matlock Bath, where there was a lovely hotel and huge pool. He had an open car and it was too hard to resist on a sunny day. Alan was married to a sweet girl, Barbara, from London, she had been in the Fleet Air Arm or Navy when they met, and they had a little boy, David. I think she had accepted she was married to a real rogue. Every lunch time Alan would go down the road from our department, to the pub. I think he drank pink gins. His parents must have spoiled him, as he seemed to do just as he pleased all the time. A friend of Mummy's knew Barbara well, and when I was qualified and living in London, I heard from her that Alan had been racing in his car, over to see some new girlfriend in Barnsley, and was apparently drunk and killed someone on their bicycle. He did not live a lot longer and I never heard how he died.

There was one little group Ted Harrison whose father had a steeple jack firm in Sheffield, and he had a good pal Crosby, who had a little M.G. car and if I didn't have Daddy's car he would drop me off sometimes on his way home. Crosby was married, and was a very steady type, I think he and his wife ran a little country pub. I asked Ted and Bing, as we used to call him to my 21st party which we had at the Maynard Arms in Grindleford. Judy (BooBoo from Hunmanby) came. After we left school she went to Leeds University, but I guess she was also having a wild time like me, and she got mono or pleurisy, so had to go back home. She was engaged to someone in the south of England, but when she met Ted Harrison, at my 21st birthday party, she was so bowled over by him, she broke off her engagement and married Ted fairly soon afterwards.

My future husband was also in our year, Geoffrey Holroyd. He had just come out of the royal engineers, was a very serious and very good student, and he was very involved in theater. He did the sets for plays in the Army, after they got through to Germany. He had landed on D-day in France, and they worked their way over through France and

Belgium to Germany. In Hamburg they set up a theater pool where they put together plays, which toured all around for the troops. Geoff had done the sets, and had met some really great friends. Felix Barker who was in the Balmorals, and was an actor, and John Brinkworth who was a painter who worked on sets, and after the war became a portrait painter in London, we always saw a lot of them. One quarter, my desk was next to Geoff, I think he was probably surprised by my wild behavior. I remember I got behind on one of my schemes, probably from taking time out to have some fun, and I asked him for some help, I think he did not take me too seriously!

At the beginning of my fifth year Sylvie Gilmaire from Paris came over for 3 months to stay with us, she wanted to improve her English, and I think her parents wanted her to take a break before her marriage to Yves, he was quite a lot older than her, and she had been very protected from meeting many people her own age. She really went wild once she was away from her parents, we would go to the dances at the Student Union and she met someone in my year called Roy, and when we got home she was awake all night so excited, talking to me about him. After her return to Paris she was quickly married to Yves, and had 2 or 3 children. On some of my later visits to Paris I saw her with her children and I remember going once when she had a very tiny new baby, and she was changing his cloth diaper and his bottom was red raw, the top surface of skin seemed to be gone, and she was cleaning him up with a bottle of alcohol and the poor little thing was screaming. My baby sister Elisabeth had never been sore like that. Poor Sylvie died of cancer a few years later, a very sad little life.

After a few weeks her parents asked if her cousin Pierre de la Landes could come over, he was an advocat (lawyer) in Paris, and needed to learn good english for his job. We did not have room for him in our house with Sylvie and Elisabeth and my brother, who was in the air force by then, needed a room when he came on leave. Mrs. Atack had an empty house as Doug, who I was still engaged to, was abroad, and Mr. Atack had died, so she said she would be pleased to have Pierre stay there. He spent most of his time at our house, and had all of his meals with us. He was an amazing looking guy, very tall, and dark haired and I thought very aristocratic. After a short time he cornered me in the cloakroom and said how much he loved me, and I was very fond of him too.

It was my last year of studies and I had so much work to do. I was doing my thesis on Maternity Hospitals, and had all my other subjects to swat for. That winter we had a lot of snow, so after we had both studied hard each day, Pierre and I would take our big Norwegian sledge up to the hills behind Thrift House, and go down the hills, it was a very good winter for our snow.

Pierre was very interested in my models I made for my thesis, and helped me with the photography of them. I think he returned to Paris just before my final exams. They were pretty tough and I needed to give them my full attention. I remember the morning we all had to go to be interviewed by the external examiners, the older fellows were all so nervous as they had families and commitments to cover, and had got themselves into a very tense state, I felt very sorry for them.

Hooray! Graduation, The End of My Student Life

As soon as the whole thing was over I sailed off to France to join Pierre in Paris, I think at that stage we were planning to get married. I still had my passion for French men and Italians. By the time I got to Paris I felt a total wreck from all the work and exams, didn't feel hungry or anything. I think the excitement of being back with Pierre had suddenly got to me too. Anyway Pierre took me to a wonderful restaurant and after a very good aperatif we had a superb dinner and I was back on my feet again.

My diary letter to my parents covers all this in great detail. I think I will include it here.

I took the train from Sheffield to London, and after an overnight hotel, took the boat train to Dover, and from there the ferry to France. Pierre was there to meet me. He had invited me to meet his rather formidable family. We had one night in Paris, and then took a train to Poitiers. The train was electric, beautifully clean and very fast, better in every way than any English train I have ever seen, so I'll never believe any more tales about French *Railways*. All the towns on that line Orleans, Tours and Poitiers were bombed by us, as the Germans had taken them over.

In Poitiers we collected the De la Landes car, an old but very big and powerful Hotchkiss, with a lovely wind horn! We came on to Boisguerin in the evening. I had never realised how wealthy Pierre's family was, they were big landowners in the Landes area near Bordeaux. They have a large townhouse in Bordeaux, Boisguerin a beautiful limestone house where we stayed, and then they have a big estate in Brittany where the women and all the children go for the summers. The men stay in Paris and join the family for brief visits. It is beautiful country all-round, like an ideal in England with no dreadful red roofs to ruin everything. This house is really very elegant, beautiful lime stone as in all the buildings and pan tiles. The hall and dining room are panelled with a lovely staircase and wrought iron balustrade, the lounge is papered with brocade fabric, furniture, typically French. My bedroom is one of 18, and is large, with a bathroom with bath and lavatory basin and all the water laid on, and a dressing room on the other side! Pierre's family are very nice though his father is still in Bordeaux so I've not yet seen him. Everyone is very kind to me and Pierre's mother talks quite a lot of English.

Pierre wanted to take me over to the west coast, so after a short stay in Boisguerin, we took the Hotchkiss to La Roche sur Yon, we had our lunch in La Roche and had langoustines, which are a big fish in its shell, like a small lobster. We had Dubonnet to start the meal and white wine with it and after lunch we bought some sun tan oil, as it's very hot here, and then we pushed on to the coast. We went first to La Bernerie, which is quite a good beach, miles of sand, but Pierre had hopes of something better, so later on, after a drink in La Bernerie- we went on to Pornic. This as you will see from my photos is a wonderful little fishing harbour, we got in at a Hotel de France, without any booking and our rooms looked out over the harbour and beautiful blue sea. It was more like a tropical sea, and everywhere so beautiful and hot and the buildings are all white. We had dinner in the hotel about nine, it was very good, and the meat is so delicious, as it was last year. England was still rationed for food.. After dinner we went along the coast and looked at various little coves ready for the next day, it's a lovely coastline, rocky headlands with sandy beaches. The water near Pornic was crystal clear. There was a lovely breeze the whole time from the sea so that kept us a little cooler as the weather was very hot.

It was such a fantastic change from all the studying and exams I had just left in England. I was really ready for the break. We visited so many lovely beaches, Tharon was about four miles away, it has has all sand with no rock, but it was very hot as it's more of a bay with the island of St. Nazaire sticking out in the sea. We were just below the mouth of the Loire and not far from Nantes. It is not a busy tourist place, so the beaches were uncrowded. We were in and out of the water all afternoon and about seven we went back to Pornic, and had dinner at a posh looking hotel right, on the front, we were staying more on the hill above the harbour. The dinner though wasn't really as nice as at our own place, though it was very formal, finger bowls with lemon in etc. After dinner we went and sat on some rocks with the sea all around them, and watched the sun set over the land and the moon streaming down over the sea, and then we went back to our hotel.

The days seemed to fly, and already it was time to return to Boisguerin as Pierre's father wanted Pierre to drive him to a farm, one of their farms which is on the other side of Niort. I was pleased to meet Pierre's father, when we got back. He was very much like Pierre.

Our next project was to drive Mme De La Landes, Pierre's mother to Vichy, which was in the other direction, south east France. It is a Spa town, and she was going down to take the waters there. On these trips Pierre looked up a number of interesting roman churches that he knew I would love to visit. On our return journey to Boisguerin we went to Aubusson which is very famous for the tapestries made there. Aubusson was really the first tapestry manufacturing town in France. The Spaniards who brought the technique, found the wool dyed well in Aubusson because of the water in the river, so they settled there and made the first tapestries. Pierre was determined we should see some, so we went to the works of one of the manufacturers, and he showed us around. It was most interesting and the modern ones were absolutely splendid, lovely colours, a square yard is about 40 pounds. I think the chap thought we were going to buy one but he was very good and didn't seem to mind. Pierre explained to him I was an English architect and was very interested.

We went and had an ice in the town afterwards and the man who owned the shop said he knew some tapestries we must see, so took us around to the house of an old pal of his, about 75 years old. This old fellow had spent all his life making tapestries and was so proud of them they were done in very fine silks, much finer than the others we saw and must have taken much longer, but the colours weren't really astounding, too many pinks. Pierre was so sorry for the chap, he said how awful it would be to spend 60 years or so and never produce a masterpiece! We left Aubusson and went to a beach by a river and had a lovely swim, then we set off again for home, Boisguerin. We had dinner in La Dora, and saw the Church then we drove on to home and arrived about 2 am. We came back a different way from going, so really I saw an awful lot and in the eight days we did about eight hundred miles so were tired.

Thursday 14th July Bastille Day!. Pierre and I were going back to Paris, so we packed our things and left about 4pm, and had dinner in Poitiers. We went in the hall where Joan of Arc was put on trial, before being burned as a witch. Our train for Paris left at 6pm, and we got to Paris at 11.30pm.

When we arrived there were crowds all wanting taxis to go round and see all the lights in Paris, so Pierre left me with the cases and went to find a taxi. After he had been gone a few minutes two men came and stood near me and one said did I want a taxi, I said I had a friend who had gone to look for a taxi. He said get in my taxi and we will go and find your husband. I said would he put the cases in the taxi, then we could look for Pierre, but he said his friend would stay with the cases. They got me in the taxi and it suddenly dawned on me it may all be a scam, so I leapt out of the taxi and the guy leapt out shouting "Quel

Idiot!" to everyone. It was a scream you would have howled if you had been there. Eventually they persuaded me to go down the station approach and leave the bags so I opened the window and shouted all the way "Pierre, Pierre" The chap drove along as if he'd got a lunatic in the back, of course Pierre was nowhere to be seen so we went back and much to my relief the bags were still there. Pierre was about 2 cars behind us!

We had the taxi all around Paris to see the Louvre, Notre Dame, Arc de Triomphe, Tuileries Gardens, Place de la Concorde, and Admiralty, they were all floodlit and a huge V of light from the triumphal arch in the Tuileries. I remember Bastille Day, everything was wild, floodlit and looking so beautiful. It was an amazing day to arrive in Paris.

Pierre and his cousin have their flat straight up the Champs Elysee and up the avenue de la Grande Armee to Neuilly. We went up there and had a cup of tea and went to bed. It's a lovely flat two bedrooms and living room, kitchen, bathroom and a store room. Pierre and his cousin go halves and do all their own cooking and have a woman to clean every morning.

Joan (my fathers youngest sister) and I had planned a holiday together, first in Paris and then on to Italy. I went to meet her at Gare St. Lazarre, and then we went to the Albert Hotel in Paris. We made a trip to to show her the Tuileries Gardens, Champs Elysee, and the Place de L'Etoile and we went to an exhibition of French furniture and interiors, it was a superb one too. The most beautifully made furniture I have ever seen. Then we went up to Pierre's flat for lunch and had a splendid meal with ice-cream cake to finish, which was delicious. Later we went up the Tour Eiffel. We had dinner at Pierre's flat and went to see some of the beauties on the boulevards after, very smart usually too.

We had a few more days looking around, we went to see the Invalides inside, then we got the train to Versailles and went first to see the petite Trianon and then to the Grande Trianon and around all the gardens and then a little of the main building, we were very tired after all this. We got a bus from Versailles to Pont de Sevres, and from there a Metro to Michel Ange to these friends of Joan's for dinner. We had a very good evening with them.

The next day Joan and I took a bus for a trip to Fontainbleu. We had a lovely drive there through 42,000 acres of parkland. It's a colossal place and is the chateau where Napoleon signed his abdication, we saw his rooms and some superb ceilings in carved wood, painted. The furniture and floors everywhere are in excellent condition. The whole place is really lovely.

We had lunch in Fontainbleu village, and then went to see the artists village of Barbazon where Robert Louis Stevenson wrote "Travels in Idleness" or some such book. Corot, Maillot, Luini, Rousseau all lived and worked there. These artists had lived in a small Inn, which we visited and they had painted on the doors, cupboards and everywhere. It was a very interesting spot.

Pierre came to pick us up at 7.30 and we went to his place for dinner. We went down to Place de L'Etoile and had coffee and cognac.

We had a last day looking around, lunch with Pierre and in the afternoon I went to the Trocadero, where I met a boy from Colwyn Bay! (where my grandmother lived in north Wales) dinner with Pierre, and then we went to the metro station near Pierre's, it's a direct line to Gare de Lyon, 16 stops on the line but no changes. Pierre saw us off safely, and was going to see his father as he was in Paris on business.

We had a carriage to ourselves so each had a seat to lie on, and were able to sleep. We woke about 5a.m. in Valorbes with Customs, we had breakfast and back in the train to Domodossola. The Swiss scenery was really splendid with the early sun over the snow on the high mountains and all the quaint little places on the hillsides. The boundary between Switzerland and Italy is in the middle of the Simplon tunnel, which we were going through for about 20 minutes. We passed Lake Maggiore, and went through Stresa where Mussolini and all the aristocrats had had their villas. Huge houses too.

The houses on the Swiss side of the tunnel looked all spotlessly clean with Freshly painted wood and the gardens so neat and prosperous looking. Then to the Italian side, it looked so dilapidated and uncared for. Very quaint little houses with all the tiles slipping down the roofs. We arrived in Milan at 12.30 pm after 15 ½ hours of travel, got a taxi from the Stazione to the hotel, and found it a very good place indeed. Just at the back of the Duomo, and very central. We went to a little place opposite the hotel for dinner and had spaghetti. The italians were very amused about the way we tackled it and we had several lessons from chaps nearby, but still made a hopeless mess of it all. We got long ends hanging down that we finally had to pull off!

The next day we walked to the Castello Sforza, which is the Palace of the former Dukes of Milan. It's a most unusual building and as you will see from my photos, if they come out, it is quite impressive. One of the first Dukes to live there was an old chap of 39, married to a girl called Beatrice D'Este who was only 15, he became engaged to her when she was six. The Castello in those days must have been beautiful as Beatrice being so young, was always trying to outdo the French court. Leonardo Da Vinci painted one of the ceilings there, but it has been restored in rather a poor way. We went to the park beyond the Castello and sat there and had an ice-cream and watched all the peculiar chaps going past. I don't think I've ever met such a crowd. They all have a crack at talking to you and they stare all the time and grin, they really are wild. There are very few fair complexion ones, they are dark like gypsies, with skins nearly as dark as their hair and very cheeky faces. About 2.30 we went back to look around the galleries in the Castello and saw some very good pieces of early Italian furniture and early chairs and paintings as well as some old pottery. The paintings were by Bramante- the architect and one very good one of the supper at Emaus by Caravaggio I've got a photo of it. The other good ones were by Luini, Foppa, De Predis, Bellini and Corregio. When we left there we walked to Santa Maria della Grazie to see Leonardo da Vinci's last supper, which someone has cut to put the top of a door through. After that we went into the Duomo and had just sat down inside to have a breather, when a chap came up and said in English "I am Official Guide" so he took us all round the cathedral and along the roofs. You get on to the roofs in a lift so it is quite easy. When we got down and had seen all round he said that he would like to show us Milan in the evening, not as a guide but as a friend, so he called for us at 8.30 and took us on the tram to a park outside Milan, where we had drinks and ices in a cafe with a band, and he refused to let us pay as he said he was very pleased to be able to use his english with someone. We came back here about 11. He was quite an interesting fellow telling us all about Milan and showing us where Mussolini and his mistress were hung by the people. When you see them in groups in the streets and the Piazza Duomo it is quite easy to understand why they would do such a thing, without a moments thought. They stand and shout and appear to argue at all hours of the day and night in the Piazza, there are literally hundreds of men just arguing and waving their arms about. What a crew! In the cafes from early morning to late at night they sit and talk in groups of about a dozen. This guide, Angelo, was saying that he has seen families sitting about in the Piazza, having come to find work here, and not succeeding and having no money, no food, nothing, and yet they sit all day and laugh with other folk. This seems quite a good picture to have of them. There are very many wealthy families in Milan because of the huge millinery trade, which took its name from the place, and yet at the same time there are 26 thousand or so unemployed, so quite a lot of poverty.

Angelo had some amusing stories about country people coming to Milan, thinking they can make some money. One story was that some poor person had been told by a tram conductor, that you could buy a tram, they were all privately owned. So the fellow paid him, and sat on the tram until the end of the line, to collect all the fares, but was then told the truth, and told to get off! Another thing he warned us about, a lot of people in the Piazza are selling cloth. Because of our clothing shortage, people were buying fabric, but when they opened up the roll, it was just a few feet of cloth, the rest was paper.

It is a strange place, the streets are narrow, very narrow after Paris, with funny clanging trams. Joan and I got on a tram the first day and we got on at the wrong doorway where you should get off, so all the tram was in turmoil inside, then we stood instead of going down to pay so the driver stopped the tram to tell us to go to get our tickets! The ticket collector sits by the back door at a little desk.

It is a dreadfully hot place, all these trips we have done have been in stifling heat, the shutters are always to the windows and water is running all the time down the hotel roof like the hotel in Vichy. You can't imagine how hot you can get, and every time you sit you get up feeling as though you have wet your pants, it's so boiling. When we walk along a street, we creep against the wall like Miss Cooper, (the poor girl studying architecture when I was there) to enjoy a bit of shade.

<u>Friday 22nd July</u> We went out early to book our hotel for Rome, we went to Stazione Nord and got a train at 10.15 for Como a one hour trip on the train when we arrived we got the boat up the lake to Cernobbio, where the Villa d'Este is. We went to a very nice hotel for lunch which we found had quite a few English, Swiss and French there, so catering for tourists, they charged a lot. After lunch looking out on to the lake we walked to the Villa d'Este and then got a boat back to Como. The boat was only 40 lire each way and was a large steamer and so was very cheap. These lakes are not anything like the Scottish ones you know. They are so long that when you are on them, they are more like the sea. On arriving in Como we went to a lido and changed to swimming suits and bathed. It was lovely there and the first breeze we have felt. We went in and out of the water until about seven o'clock. A crowd of Italian boys were talking to us, they could speak a little French so we talked in French and I translated to Joan in English. After we had changed and when we came out, two chaps had waited for us. We were quite pleased as we wanted someone to ask how we

could get a cheap meal and they walked into Como with us and took us to a place looking over the bay. We were nearly finishing our meal when they arrived back having eaten and washed and changed. They ordered a bottle of Muscato, which was delicious and they wouldn't let me pay for it at all. Then we walked over to the station to find we had 50 minutes to the next train so we went to a cafe opposite and had ices. They are so delicious here, mostly home made, and the most refreshing are the sorbets. Joan and I did laugh as she was trying to talk to the chap on her right, but he could speak only Italian so Joan told me in English and I told the chap next to me in French and he told the other one in Italian, then the answer all came back again! They came and shook hands most politely when we left and our opinion of the Italians went up a little on meeting them, especially after the wine and ices.

Here in Milan they're like a lot of old Shylocks and as soon as you leave the hotel they are around you like flies taking your photos and thrusting cards and books at you. They do all to rob you, except snatch your purse. When we got back we were both tired out and my throat was aching on the right side, so bed immediately.

<u>Saturday 23rd July</u> I woke up with a terrible sore throat so got up briefly to go round to the chemist to get some medicine for it, and then back to bed. We had booked to go to Rome today but my throat is very raw so we're going to cancel it. I had breakfast and lunch in bed. Joan went to see San Ambrosio this morning and is now asleep. We are having a terrific storm at the moment, which is super as at last it is possible to breathe. We are planning to go to Lago Maggiore tomorrow as Milan is not the place to recover and Rome they say is dreadful at the moment. My throat is a nuisance, but a few of the waiters who have been up to our room, said in Italian that they get bad throats with this heat.

We went to Ghiffa, a small place on Lago Maggiore. It had a beautiful hotel where we stayed, and it was a very lively area. In the evenings a group of boys from Pallanza would come up to our hotel. It had a lovely bar and restaurant. The Bar had a wonderful collection of drinks that we had never heard of, so while we were there we tried most of them. This gang from Pallanza all came up on their little Vespas. It was the time when the buzz of their engines was in every spot in Italy. Pippo Vitalli and his friend took Joan and I all around the area on the back of their Vespas, we went round the lake to bars on terraces where they had dances, some of them were on wooden decks just over the water. Most of the boys were working at Coates Cotton in Pallanza, and some of them were just off to Argentina as Coates had their big factory there. In the daytime Joan and I went swimming in the lake, and we took a bus up to Ascona and Locarno in Switzerland. I bought a beautiful dress in Locarno, it had some very elegant shops.

Our hotel in Ghiffa, when we first arrived was very full, as it was a weekend and a lot of people had come up from Milan, to escape the heat. The restaurant had splendid food with lots of choice, but on the Monday they asked us what we would like for dinner, and we told them and we said we would like the same cake for dessert as the one on the weekend. We saw two boys take off on their moped in the morning and return late afternoon with a big box from Milan, which was our cake! It really was a very good one, but we had to eat it every night on our own as the restaurant was almost empty each night during the week, and we felt we should eat it up, when they had gone all the way to Milan to buy it. We had a very relaxing holiday there on the lake, with day trips out to Isola Bella, and sailing on Maggiore.

By the time we had to return to Milan I was completely recovered but we had missed going to Florence and Rome. I was able to go later but poor Joan never got there. Our train back from Milan to Paris was so full, people were cramming themselves in, and then when it was full to capacity they were hanging onto the outside. Luckily the majority were just going short distances, we stopped at several small places near to Milan and they got off, we were still very full, so I decided to climb up on the luggage rack and lie down to sleep. I was sound asleep when suddenly the train came to a screeching halt, the brakes of our carriage had caught fire. Everyone had to get out, and they disconnected our carriage from the train and we had to pile into another one. (My son Nils just read this and said he wondered if I had kicked the brake handle while I was asleep on the luggage rack!)

When we were back in Paris, Joan took a boat train for England, and I went out to stay with Pierre in Neuilly. By then he was back at work, so I had lots of time to really get to know my way all around. It is such a beautiful city, I don't think it had been damaged in the war as they just gave up once the Germans crossed the Maginot line. The French had put out such publicity before the war on this infallible defense they had constructed on their eastern borders, I remember news films showing the French army on small open trains going underground all along the Maginot Line, but when the Germans got to it they went straight over it, and the French capitulated straight away, leaving the British Army stranded. The retreat to Dunkirk was chaotic, the German army was in full pursuit, and every small and large boat from the south coast of England that could be sailed, set out across the Channel to pick up as many men as they could save. I think a total of about 320,000 men were brought back, but many soldiers died.

I asked Pierre how they could have given up so quickly, without warning England to pull out its army, and he was weeping about it. He cried very easily, and I had never seen a man cry, most men in England would have been ashamed to show their feelings like that. This was the second time English troops had gone over to help the French fight off their neighbors. (I have just read an article about Scandinavia, and they always call them the arrogant French, which I think is true.)

Pierre came home for lunch most days, or I met him somewhere. We went to some very good art galleries, I remember going to Gallerie Maeght to see a new artist who had just come to Paris, it was Chagall, and his first show there. We went to the opera and some concerts. I bought some amazing shoes to go with my dress I had bought in Ascona. After a couple of months I had to return to England. I had a job fixed up in London in the architectural office of Hillier Parker May and Rowden, Estate Agents. They were on Grosvenor Street just near Grosvenor Square.

My Aunt Joan had a friend who lived in a mews just behind Kensington Church Street, so I first went to stay with them. It was a real heat wave when I was there, very airless, and all the underground trains on that Kensington line rattled the house. It was hard to sleep, and I had to be up early to get to work, so I decided to look for a better place in Kensington, and found a small hotel that was full of long-term guests. My room was very nice, cooler and a good size, but there was nowhere to cook, and the bathroom was down the corridor. Every time I wanted to take a bath I had a big box of 'vim' and had to scrub the bath first.

I enjoyed working in that office, they were very friendly people, and were very sympathetic when I was often late for work. I used to sleep through my alarm, as I was always doing something after work, and I didn't get to bed early enough. I was working on the United Press offices on Farringdon St., the architect who was the head of the office was Mr. Davie, he was a nice gentle person, and as we were under the very successful estate agents Hillier Parker May and Rowden it was unlike most architect's offices where the pressure of business plays a large part. There were some very nice young people in the estate office side, and one boy who lived in the outskirts of London used to ask me to his home on weekends. His parents and younger brother were very kind to me.

Pierre used to fly over from Paris every other weekend, so we were able to explore London, the same as we had done in Paris. I had begun to doubt whether I could happily marry Pierre. His grandmother who owned all their houses was in fact very rude to me when I stayed in Boisguerin. I had only my English summer dresses with me and they all had short sleeves, and as it was very hot, they were as much as I could have worn. Anyway when I went into the huge dining room, the miserable grandmother sat at the head of a very long table. Pierre's uncles and aunts, all sorts of cousins, and Pierre's sisters were all living at the house, the table must have had 25 or more people at it, and the grandmother used to say to Pierre that I should have my meal in my room as she did not want to see my arms! I said to Pierre that he should tell her I was a guest and that it was very rude to treat someone like that. He didn't dare to say anything to her, as he said all the family wealth was in her hands, so she was able to behave like a tyrant.

When I was living in Paris with him, I began to see what my life would be like with Pierre. He was a lawyer with the family firm who did business with French Indo China. He said we would live in Paris, but every summer I would go to the house in Brittany with all the other women and our children and the grandmother who owned everything. I could imagine what my summers would be like with the tyrant and all the other feeble women who got shipped there, and I wondered what the husbands got up to in Paris on their own. I had found that the French men I'd met were very attractive, but I don't think I would trust them out of my sight. They were also very annoying; always talking about "La Belle France" they did not seem to be very fond of other nationalities. It is a beautiful country, but I think many countries are also, and it is tiresome to have them always praising themselves.

I had joined the linguist club in London, at Hyde Park Corner, I went to French conversation classes because I wanted to get more proficient in chatting with French friends. I met some French boys in that club, they were all working in restaurants and learning English. Two of them had a wonderful flat in Chester Square, in the heart of Belgravia and after knowing them for a while I heard they were going to go back to Paris. Bernard the nicer of the two, asked me to move into their spare bedroom, I was still in my rather awful room in Kensington. It was difficult to find places to live as not much rebuilding had been done since the wartime bombing. I decided to move into 12 Chester Square with them. It was very amusing as I think Bernard had told his friends I was moving in with him, but I put my things in the spare room, and although I was still very friendly with them I locked my door at night. Bernard made a great commotion each night about it, shouting to his pal what a bitch I was, but I only had a short time of it, as they soon went back to Paris, and then the flat was all mine.

The couple who owned the house were very interesting, an old professor from Vienna and his wife, Professor and Mrs. Weidenfeld. They lived on the ground and first floor and the second floor had a separate flat, and I was on the top, above the cornice. It was so beautiful up there as you just looked onto the tops of the trees in Chester Square, and did not see any of the cars crossing the square, or hear them too much either. There are a series of squares all with very elegant houses, Belgrave Square was the first, next to Hyde Park Corner, then a long square Eaton Square, and then Chester Square, backing onto Eaton. It was a very grand address Terence Rattigan the playwright lived a couple of doors away. George Weidenfeld, Professor and Mrs Weidenfeld's only son, of Weidenfeld and Nicholson, the publishers, lived next door to us, and I think he had bought our house for his parents.

Mrs. Weidenfeld would start cooking their dinner as I was leaving for work in the morning she did very elaborate meals, and George who lived next door would often eat with them. She was always asking me to go in her kitchen and see her amazing creations. She used to cook a full pig's head and would stuff an orange in its mouth. She made very extraordinary cookies with lots of poppy seeds on, some she called 'gugelhupf,' or some word just like that. She and Max her husband, were very sweet to me.

When I was suddenly on my own in the flat I realised I needed someone to share it with. By that time I had started seeing Geoffrey Holroyd quite a lot, he had graduated the same year as I had, and we were the only 2 architects from our year, who had gone to London to work. Geoffrey was working for a well known architect, Maxwell Fry and Jane Drew. He telephoned me one day suggesting we went to a theatre. He had been very involved with theatre, in the army after the fighting had stopped, and also he had put on plays at the student dramatic society at the University. We had such great evenings together, he was so entertaining. He was living with John Brinkworth and his wife Joy, who he had got to know in the army, they had both been part of the theatre pool in Germany which Geoff had been in, once the fighting was over.

Mummy and Daddy did not think it would be a good idea for Geoff to move into the flat with me, but Geoff had a friend from the University, Tom Margerison, he was a scientist, and he had just moved to London and was working for Jackson's Cookers, near Sloane Square. We had both known him in Sheffield. He moved in, into the second bedroom. It worked out very well, Tom did all the cooking, he was a great cook and we had very good healthy dinners together, and I did all the house cleaning as my share. Geoffrey would often come round for the evening, and John and Joy often asked me over there.

I continued to work in Hillier Parker May and Rowden, but Geoff got a very interesting new job with James Gardner, designing the 1951 Festival of Britain. They were working on the Festival Gardens, and it was the sort of work that Geoff was so good at. It was a little like the theatre days, very imaginative designs, but not real buildings - very playful architecture. Gardner was an exhibition designer and was very well known, so Geoff was very pleased.

Daddy had to go over to Basle in Switzerland, on business, and as he could not drive because of his paralysis, I went up to Sheffield to pick him and Mummy up in the car. I remember 2 nights before we were due to leave, David had borrowed the car to go into Derbyshire to some pubs with a friend, and on the way back over the moors they had hit a sheep. These animals are so stupid, they are all free and roaming in the heather, and sometimes when you are quite near they suddenly jump up and dash across the road. Luckily the front axle was only slightly bent and the garage was able to repair it so we left on time. I think David was home on leave, as he was then in the Air Force.

We took the ferry over to France, and then I drove down to Paris, where Pierre had reserved us an hotel, we did some sight seeing and went to some strange shows, but then had to start out for Basle, where

Daddy's agents gave us a wonderful time. I remember the wife had cooked the most delicious dinner. We were still severely rationed in England, but the Swiss had not suffered anything during the war, no shortages, no bombing, and they like Sweden had continued to build during the war period. (It now has been discovered in 1998 that both countries were in collaboration with the nazis.) They had some very interesting new hospitals and apartments in Basle, I had done my thesis on a maternity hospital so it was great to see the very modern ones there, so I got a lot of photos and toured around them. They also had a very lively graphics scene, the posters and advertising were really good. We then drove on to Lugano and stayed in a luxurious hotel on the edge of the lake, I think that was just a holiday break before we drove down to Italy to Milan. Daddy's agent there was a Mr. Seeber, he had visited us in England, and he took us all around in Milan. I had met a very sweet Italian doctor in London at the linguist club, he was from Milan, Dr. Angelo Baron. He took us to several great restaurants and the first time he came to meet us he brought Mummy a huge bouquet of roses. After our stay in Milan, I then had to drive the whole way back, I think I survived it O.K. but was pretty tired when I got back.

Unluckily when we got home, my little sister who was then about 5, had caught measles, and I was so sorry for her and used to read to her and look after her. Mummy seemed to think I had had measles, but either I hadn't or I got it twice. I suddenly developed it, and I was really sick, and it took about a year before I really got my full energy back.

Poor Pierre who still came over from Paris could see I was very involved with Geoff, and he used to write a lot to Mummy, who he called 'Ma'. I think Mummy had been very impressed by his very polite manners, and thought he was wonderful. He wrote to her that he was so desperately unhappy to lose me, so he had decided to go to the family business in Saigon and worked there in the import/export business. I was sorry for him but I was sure it would not have been a happy marriage. I think I came to the conclusion, about this time that it would be good to have a husband from the same background as me. I sort of knew what to expect and we shared the same interests and attitudes.

Another New Phase – Married Life.

Geoffrey and I decided to get married. Mummy and Daddy wanted me to be up in Sheffield, partly to plan our wedding, but mainly because of 'What will people say?' if I had stayed down in London with Geoff when we were not married. They had such weird ideas, but anyway I went up for quite a few weeks before the wedding. Geoff used to come up on weekends and when I used to drive down to meet him at the station in Daddy's car, I would feel quite sick with excitement!

As our clothes were still rationed I decided not to have a white wedding dress, but got a very smart tweed dress instead. I can't remember if I wore it much after, but that was the idea. We were married at the Methodist Church on Psalter Lane on September 2nd 1950, my little sister Elisabeth who was 5 by then, was my bridesmaid. Mummy and Daddy had planned a big reception, which we had at the Victoria Hotel.

It was wonderful to get on the train for London, afterwards, just the two of us. We were going to spend the night in my flat in Chester Square. Tom was moving out to the flat onto the floor below, but he had taken his Austin 7 to pieces and had cans of oil with car engine parts in soaking, all around his bedroom in my flat. Whilst we were on our honeymoon I had told my Auntie Joan from Wales that she should come down for a holiday in my flat, and when she arrived the bath was full of water with dozens of shirts soaking, she thought poor June has not had the time to get the laundry done, so she proceeded to wash and iron them all. She was very surprised when Tom came up and said they were all his, and that he had just put them in my bath, to soak! He was a very strange guy. Anyway we spent the first night in my room, we went to the Polonia restaurant in Victoria for dinner and then back to the flat. Our boat train to the south of France was leaving from Victoria fairly early the next day, and we woke up rather late and had a real panic to get round to the station. I remember closing Geoff in the clothes closet in my haste, but we did just make the train.

It was a great trip down to Avignon, we had a sleeper and during the night as we stopped at little stations we looked round the corner of our blinds and saw all the activity. We stayed in Avignon for a few days. It was a beautiful old town, the papal palace had been moved there at one time from Rome, so it had all those buildings, and then all the little squares with very good restaurants. Unfortunately Geoff got a very bad cold, so I was trailing round trying to find a good cold cure in France. The weather was very hot, as it was early September, which is a bad time to have a cold. The Pont D'Avignon and down by the river was lovely and very quiet compared with the crowded streets and busy tourists.

After a week we went south to Marseilles, which was a big seaport and seemed to us to be rather violent. We were looking for a post office, walking across a big waste open area, when a fellow went running past us wielding a gun, and a whole group of 'gendarmes' were chasing him and firing their guns. We were total strangers to guns and police chases, as England in those days, was very law abiding, and nobody including the police and the criminals had any guns. We also had a hard time finding a hotel, as they were so sleazy inside. We were only staying there for one night, as we wanted to visit Le Corbusier's new Unite D'Abitation, which had just been completed.

It was a very exciting project, it had a children's nursery on the roof, and several sports and family activities up there. The apartments were mostly on 2 or 3 levels, which meant you had access corridor /streets every 3rd floor, and these were open and wide. We were all thinking of the problem of housing many homeless families as after the bombing we had huge numbers of people needing a new place to live. A group of architects were all thinking that with the increase of population and rising cost of land, we could no longer afford the luxury of single storey houses, each with their own garden but it turned out later that people did not like to be up in the air like that, as they couldn't see their children as they played, and they had no space for a bit of garden. In later years these huge apartment complexes seemed to produce a lot of violent people, and crime. Many of the housing projects from that period in England have recently been demolished.

At that time though Le Corbusier was a big hero. We had a handful of architects that most students admired. Gropius and Mies van der Rohe, Schindler, Neutra, Breuer, all Germans, Maxwell Fry and his wife Jane Drew in England were a few. I feel sorry for the students nowadays as there are no heroes, or at least I don't think there are any. There are a lot of 'Stunt' architects who make buildings that look like freaks, widening at the top, like they are standing on their heads, or clad in crazy materials. What happened to the qualities we always have admired, proportion, scale and timeless elegance?

After the visit to Corb's building we went to a small restaurant in Marseilles. It smelled very fishy, but Geoff decided he wanted to have bouillabaisse. I decided to eat something else, which was lucky. We took a bus after lunch to go on to Cassis where we had booked to stay for a while, Geoff began to feel sick from his fish stew lunch. When we got to our hotel he decided to go to bed, but when it got near to dinner time I thought I would go to eat on my own, as I was hungry by then. The hotel had a lovely big terrace towards the sea, and all the tables for dinner were set out there. The waiter showed me to a table, which was on the side next to a group of bushes. I think it was a set dinner, and as they always did at that time in France, each vegetable, or meat course came on its own. They brought me something that I had never seen before. The tables were all lit by small candles, and I could not see any other tables very clearly, but I could see people had taken off all the leaves of the thing I had been given. I first tried to eat a leaf, but they were awful and had a spike on the end. I decided there must be some tasty part in the center, so I pulled off all the leaves and tried the centre part, which was just like a thistle. I gave up on the whole thing. I often laugh at the thought of the waiters taking my plate out to the kitchen and realising the silly English did not know how to tackle an artichoke! We had never had them in my family, as I guess during the war they were unobtainable.

It was the same way with bananas, quite a time after the war we suddenly could buy bananas, and a lot of people had never seen them and did not know you had to take off the skin, so there were stories of people in the student union telling other folk that you just sliced them with the peel on, and ate the whole thing.

After my tussle with the artichoke I noticed a little pair of eyes in the hedge by my table, just catching the candlelight, and it was a tiny mouse. He was probably waiting to get the breadcrumbs from my table. I don't think he would have enjoyed artichokes either. Geoffrey was amused by the whole thing.

It was a wonderful unsoiled area round Cassis, and we spent our days strolling on the beaches, and swimming out to different rocks. I have never been back there but I am sure it would be unrecognisable now, as that whole coast has been so over-developed and spoiled. We both of us were looking very healthy and brown by the time we left, and ready to go back to our hard work in London. More recently Geoffrey and I have returned to Cassis. We were in Europe for 3 months in the year 2000, to celebrate our 50th wedding anniversary, and we went to see several friends and my brother David in the south of France. We also made a trip to Cassis and it was still wonderful, not overdeveloped like so much of that coast.

I had a new office to go back to as I had given up my first job because Mummy and Daddy had wanted me to have time to take them around the continent and afterwards to stay in Sheffield to plan the wedding, and it was too long to be on holiday from Hillier Parker. My new job was in Russell Square with a firm who had an office in Cyprus as well, so they had a lot of work abroad. The partners were Harrison, Barnes and Hubbard. They were doing work on the New University of The Gold Coast in Accra. I worked on the Science and Physics buildings and really enjoyed all the new ideas of designing buildings with a special structure to keep out the sun with brise-soleil because it was a very hot climate. There was no air conditioning available. I worked with a Professor at London University who had studied the angles and altitudes of the sun at all times of the year in Africa, and I designed the overhangs of my sun protection Brise Soleil screens using his information.

The buildings were very formally laid out and symmetrical around courts, I think Mr. Hubbard had been classically trained and was an old Rome scholar. The type of building structure was very unlike anything in England. We had pitched roofs on all buildings, but the roof space was all open, with louvres at each end and we faced these end walls to the direction of the breezes. It was to try to stop a heat buildup in our roof spaces. Maxwell Fry's office was also designing in the Accra area, but their buildings were all modern with flat roofs, and Hubbard was delighted when they got the rainy season, to hear that water had poured in from a butterfly roof, into their building. So Hubbard was convinced that our style was the best and no changes could be discussed.

I designed all the laboratories with their demonstration benches, we had visits from some of the staff when they were over in London, and one Professor was about 6ft 3ins, so he wanted his demonstration benches to be designed for his height. I heard that by the time the building was complete, he had already left and the next Science teacher was a very short little man, who had to stand on a box. So much for designing for a particular client! The other building on the campus

I worked on was the hospital for students, which looked the same externally but inside was 4 and 6 bed wards.

Our office did all the working drawings but we had an architect and a site office in Ghana, and Mr. Hubbard went out to the job pretty frequently. Most of the work in Africa was designed in England or France at that time. We had a big hotel to do on the Zambesi river, by Victoria Falls. I worked on that for a while too, when I had finished the University buildings. We got a big Hospital in Kuwait, Persia which Mr. Hubbard gave me to work on.

This was another unusual scheme, as we talked to the nurses who were to run it and they wanted to have a 3 legged star on plan, with a central staff facility in the middle of the star, so only one night sister could see and check all 3 corridors on her own. I designed some 4 bed and some 6 bed room wards, but was told rather quickly that those would never work, as all the relatives of each patient came in as well; they did not trust their relatives in a hospital on their own, and they brought all their cooking pots to set them up on the floor to prepare their own food. It was impossible to think of keeping any standard of hygiene as they all slept on the floor around the patient. Our client for the job was one of the vastly wealthy oil princes and he wanted to spend some money on the people as they had absolutely nothing, and I think he was worried they might realise he had more than a fair share of the oil revenue.

In London I worked on Dulwich College Science Building, which we designed to fit into the style of the other buildings, I had to detail all the benches with glass demonstration tanks, and I used the standard height requirements for my details this time.

My cousin Desmond Sawyer, (he was Mummy's sister May's, oldest child), had studied pure mathematics at St. John's Cambridge and then he had been in the army, his first job teaching when he left the army, was at the University of Otago in New Zealand, that was in 1948, and in 1952 he went to Accra to the New University of the Gold Coast, our new buildings were not completed so he was never able to use the new premises, and he left in 1954 to go back to University of Otago, in New Zealand. He had married a girl called Pam Clayton from Disley, which is where his parents lived, and they had one little girl called Carol. I remember he said that if he stayed in Cambridge to teach, he would be waiting to step into dead men's shoes, and be quite old before he got anywhere.

It was rather a popular idea among a number of intellectuals in England, to move out to New Zealand as they felt it was safe, and the place of the future. There was fear of atomic warfare, and Europe had twice proved it could not live at peace. A group of architects we knew bought an island off the coast of New Zealand, and they formed a group of teachers, potters, agriculturists, they tried to get every trade they would need to live on their island, I don't know what happened to them all. Anyway Desmond took his little family down to Dunedin which is on the south end of the south island and it did not take him long to become the head of the math dept. When I visited him in 1983 he seemed a little disappointed I thought, that New Zealand had never risen to its full potential. Everyone we met there told us that it was a lovely quiet place to bring up children. I did not think there would be enough stimulation for a lively person. It seems a very beautiful and unspoiled place and I enjoyed our visit there, but it is pretty remote from the rest of the world.

Desmond's sister Mary had married his best friend from Cambridge, Arthur Aiken, he was another pure math guy, and they were living near Manchester. Mary had a son Jonathan, and then became pregnant again, but Arthur, her husband got polio in a big epidemic we had, and died very quickly, and Mary's sister Margaret, who had been a physical education teacher, was said to have got polio in the same epidemic. She was expecting a baby at the time and Margaret recovered, but her baby girl was born with some sort of problem. Mary had a very hard 2nd pregnancy, after Arthur died, and she had to spend all the time in bed so she would not lose her baby. After her baby girl (Elisabeth) was born, Desmond asked her to go and stay in New Zealand for a while, so she took the boat out via India with Jont, her little boy and her new baby, Elizabeth. While she was there she met a doctor in Dunedin, Peter Jerram. His wife had died and he had four children, but they were older than Mary's two. Mary and Peter got married and he got a practice in Wanaka. Mummy's sister Auntie May, had 2 of her children in New Zealand, so she and Uncle Stan used to sail out to visit them. Mary had 2 daughters with Peter, Sophie and Lucy, and I think between them Mary and Peter had a total of eight children. When we stayed with them Peter was retired, and was drinking rather heavily, and died not too long afterwards. Mary is still living in Nelson on the northern edge of the south island, a very beautiful area. We seem to see her here in California quite often. She likes to make a stop here on her long flight to Europe.

To get back to our life in London, I was very busy during office hours, but Geoffrey was even more hectic, designing the Festival of Britain, and they had to camp out on the site a lot to oversee all the building work and had to work every night. I decided to start doing pottery in the evenings at a school in Notting Hill Gate. I found it really very pleasing as I loved to create something, with my own hands, instead of making architectural drawings for someone else to create.

Finally all the festival buildings were complete. On the South Bank of the Thames they had the permanent buildings, and then in Festival Gardens they had the more playful and entertaining part. There was a tree walk, which went through the branches of trees, very high up, and there were little villages of small people among the branches. There were all kinds of rides, roundabouts etc., it was all planned to be exactly 100 years after the Crystal Palace Exhibition of 1851 which Prince Albert had planned. All during the war and for a few years after, we had not done any building in England, so everyone wanted to do something exciting, to raise the spirits in England again after such a grueling war.

Our flat in Chester Square was so central so we had people staying with us the whole summer of 1951. We had several people from France and Italy that we knew, and seemed to have sleeping bags on the living room floor all the time. We had a very sweet girl Rosa Lucini from Bergamo Alto, in the lake area of Italy, to visit us. I knew her through my Aunt Joan and the I.F.L.(International Fellowship League) She had a friend, a doctor in Bergamo, who was in London too, and we got to know him at the same time. In the September we went over to Italy, on vacation, and Rosa asked us to visit her family. We took a crazy train up from Milan, with people fighting to hang on to the outside of the train, as the inside could not take one more person. It reminded me of my stay there with Joan in 1949, when I climbed onto the luggage rack to sleep.

Rosa's family had a lovely old house in Bergamo Alto, which was the old hill town and very picturesque. She had 3 brothers. I remember the oldest one had just qualified as a doctor. He had just had a tragic accident; he had been sleeping in the family house and there had been a very violent thunderstorm which woke him in a real panic, and he had rushed for the door and crashed through the large glass panel in the upper part of the door and cut his main artery in his neck and was left paralyzed. The glass in the doors and windows in France and Italy was always so thin and was not safety glass. He was a terribly handsome boy, but was in a wheelchair and I thought it seemed so tragic, especially after he had just graduated and become a doctor.

On the Sunday morning we were there, the other 2 brothers and a servant put some little blind birds out into the garden in cages, they had taken out their eyes, so that they would sing in captivity, and attract other birds. They spent a long time catching small birds when they came to join the captive ones, and then they were all cooked and we ate them with polenta. This is the delicacy of Bergamo, "ucello and polenta." The poor birds were so small and had their heads wired to look up, which made you feel awful for them. The polenta tasted smoky, it was not a very memorable meal for me, I do not think I ate much at all.

The other strange thing I remember of the town was that a lot of people had goiters on their necks, and in the sweet shops they were selling small goiter shaped candies as a memento of the area!

I think English people can be a bit silly about animals but the Italians and Greeks are very cruel with their total disregard for animal life. Once when Geoff and I were in the countryside in Greece, I found a little bunch of new kittens trying to shelter from the sun behind a rock, I picked some of them up and went to a nearby cottage and tried to tell the woman about them, but she just shrugged and waved me away. I am sure they were from one of her cats as there was no house in the area, within miles. When we were in Athens the railway lines underground had a triangular opening up to the street, and there were so many dead cats down on the electric lines. I imagine they were unwanted and had been thrown down there.

Rosa's friend who was a doctor in Bergamo asked us to go for lunch one day, unfortunately he had an emergency in the hospital at the last minute, but when we arrived at his house, his old servant had cooked a huge meal for us. It was a chicken and it still had its head and feet on, we were surprised as we never serve them like that. We had a very good lunch and a bottle of great wine, and after we had eaten, the servant was ushering us into a bedroom, I think she wanted us to have a siesta! We did not want to be in Roberto's bed when he returned, like goldilocks and the three bears so we thanked her and left.

Whilst we were in Italy that visit, Geoffrey had an appointment to see the editors of 'Edilizia Moderna' an architecture magazine, in Italy, based in Milan. Geoffrey was writing a series of architectural articles for their magazine. Geoffrey had his meeting with them and they took us out for a wonderful meal. It was the first pizza we had ever had and it was a beautiful restaurant with great pizza ovens all around. I wonder if that was the time when they first started to make them? We had never heard of them before.

From Milan we went down to the coast, east of Genoa, to what was then a very small and pretty resort spot called Nervi. It was lovely, hotels and restaurants right on the rocky coast. It was the first year that the Germans were allowed out of their country since the war ended, and a lot of them were staying in our hotel. Because there was no sandy beach the hotel provided nice thick padded cushions to lie on the rocks, but by the time we had eaten our breakfast, all the cushions had been taken by the Germans. Some of them had 3 or 4 rolled up and under each leg etc. I asked one woman if I could have one and she just shrugged, pretending not to understand. I gave her a great shove and pulled 2 of her cushions away. I thought they would have come out of Germany for the first time, feeling rather sheepish, and subdued, but they were just the opposite of course!

When we were back in London and all the Festival of Britain excitement was over, and not much building was happening there, we had a plan to go to Brazil, as Geoff was going to work with Oscar Niemeyer. He was a very well known architect, who had worked in Rio de Janeiro with Le Corbusier. He had just been given the new Capital to design- Bello Horizonte. Brazil was really booming then. There was not a lot of building going on in England, too many architects fighting for too few jobs, so the chance to go to Brazil was very exciting, and the Italian firm of Olivetti had asked Geoff to do an exhibit in Rio de Janeiro, which was where we were planning to live.

After a number of letters back and forth with Niemeyer, and Geoff was already working on his Portuguese, we were never able to find out if we would be expected to pay him to work there, or if he was going to pay us the sum he kept mentioning.

We got Stefan Zweig's book, 'A Land of the Future' he quoted Amerigo Vespucci

"If Paradise exists anywhere in the World, it cannot be far from here" He had moved to Brazil, to escape the Jewish persecution in Europe, and we got a lot of information from that, but then we found out the poor man and his wife had committed suicide there, so we did not think it had turned out to be a good place for them. We had heard how incredibly expensive Brazil was, so we decided it was not a good time for us to go there either. We felt rather sad because Brazil was thought to have tremendous potential and was doing some exciting buildings and landscape designs. Matarazza was in charge and it was perhaps the best time to be there, because it has never lived up to everyone's hopes. (except maybe now in 2008, it seems to be more prosperous.)

In the meantime Geoffrey had been awarded a postgraduate scholarship to go to the United States, to Harvard University in Cambridge. It was a scholarship for his Phd. tuition only, so after we used our money for our transport to the US, it was dependent on me supporting us with my job. We both went to the US Embassy in Grosvenor Square, and applied to get a green card, as that was the only way we would both be able to work. We had to have chest X rays, and blood tests, and also had to be inoculated for smallpox. Daddy had never allowed us to have any vaccinations or shots, he felt it was a dangerous procedure. It is strange that he should have been the one to be paralyzed by his shots from Dr. Jack. Anyway I had a very bad reaction to mine, I had very high fever for about a week, and my arm was like a football.

We did not have long to wait for our visas, the quota was so high at that time, and was never filled. We were sad to close down our lovely flat in Chester Square, it had been a beautiful area to be in, in London.

Whilst we were there in 1952, George Weidenfeld had had a very elaborate marriage to Jane Sieff, who was the daughter of Edward Sieff. His sister was the wife of Sir Simon Marks who was the owner of 'Marks and Spencer' a large chain of stores in England. We had become quite friendly with George, and gone through the drama of Jane being sent away for 6 months to South America, to see if the romance would survive the separation. George was quite a lot older than she was, and she was still in her late teens. When she returned she was still in love with George. He was a very interesting man, with amazing friends and connections. He started a publishing company Weidenfeld and Nicholson. Nigel Nicholson was the son of Harold Nicholson and Sackville West, so a very academic and well- known family. George had also had a very good education, he was the only child of Professor and Mrs. Weidenfeld, and before the war when they still lived in Vienna, his mother had taken him all around the world. She had really spoiled him I think, and really thought he was perfect. He had bought the house next door to ours in Chester Square, and I think he had bought our house for his parents.

Before his wedding he had his house beautifully re-done. He bought some old tapestries for the walls of the living room, and the whole house was done with beautiful taste. Their families were both Jewish so the wedding ceremony was planned in a big synagogue in St.Petersburgh Place, Bayswater. "It was a clash of two worlds: Jewish patricians, manufacturing tycoons and courtiers, facing a group of Bohemians, radicals, friends from the BBC, Austrian refugees, debutantes and dandies" (This is George Weidenfeld's description) Geoffrey and I were invited, and we were very interested in the whole proceedings.

As we went into the synagogue all the men went into a small room and appeared in hats, Geoffrey was followed into the room by Ben Nicholson, the painter, and he had chosen his own special hat which was a very big and elaborate one, everyone else had small skull caps. As he walked down the aisle someone came and grabbed his grand hat, as it was the one for the Rabbi!! Everyone laughed.

It was a traditional ceremony; they all stood in a sort of fourposter bed, with the crushing of glass underfoot. After the wedding, the reception was at the Dorchester Hotel on Park Lane, and was a fantastic colorful affair.

Later George and his wife had a terribly pretty little girl, Laura, and Mrs. Weidenfeld was very pleased about that, but not long after that I remember when we came home one day the household was very upset, as Mrs. Weidenfeld had popped around next door, and found George's wife in the bath with Cyril Connely. He was a terrible rogue, in all sorts of marital troubles. I think George's wife eventually went off with her ski instructor. In George's recent book he has a photo of his baby Laura, and a recent one of her with her husband and their four children. Anyway we were sad to leave such an eventful house, and the life we had had there.

Mrs. Weidenfeld had a sister Mrs. Bauer who lived in Boston, Mass. When they had all fled Vienna, her sister and family all went to the States, and Mr. Bauer had developed a very good chain of wine stores. Unluckily for him just before we went there, he had to have very expensive heart surgery, and as there was no medical insurance in America then, he had spent his life savings on hospital bills. He was very near retirement age and he had been saving for that, so the shock of losing all his savings was a terrible blow for him. He sat most of the time looking completely wrecked by it, whilst we were there with them. It made me appreciate the very good health scheme we have in England.

Mrs. Weidenfeld suggested we go and stay with the Bauers in Brookline when we first arrived, so we were pleased to know we had somewhere to go, whilst we looked for an apartment.

In our last weeks we went up to see all the family. We stayed in Penrhyn Bay, North Wales, to see Granny and Joan, and then to Sheffield to see Geoff's family and mine. I remember my little sister Elisabeth was very sad to see us off. We did have a nice holiday before starting out on our big adventure. We were I think the first batch of students to go to the States since the war, and had no idea what to expect of that huge country.

Sarah Ann Kelsey/Whitham in 1900. Born 1838 in Keadby, Lincolnshire.

Henry Whitham, born 1851 in Wortley, Derbyshire. He married Sarah after her husband's death, and was able to take over the steel works. He named it Henry Whitham and Son.

Henry Whitham with his son Charles Henry, at the doorway of their first steel works.

Ada Gertrude Brine, center, the wife of Charles Henry Whitham, with her family in Swindon. Her mother Adeliza Sykes on her left, and her father, Frederick Brine on her far right.

Four generations, R to L, Ada Gertrude Whitham (née Brine), my father Charles Wilfred Whitham, Joah Sykes, and his daughter Adeliza Sykes.

Charles Henry Whitham, Daddy's father, with his son, Charles Wilfred Whitham in the latest in perambulators.

L to R. My father Charles Wilfred Whitham, his father Charles Henry Whitham, Dorothy the new baby and Ada Gertrude Whitham (née Brine).

Daddy's father on the left, just before his death from diabetes, my father, Dorothy and Ada Gertrude (née Brine).

Dorothy Whitham and her brother Charles Wilfred Whitham, my father.

My mother's family, William Charles Beevers, standing, Sarah Ann (Windle) Beevers, holding Marjorie Windle Beevers my mother, May Beevers and Clifford, Mummy's brother.

My mother in her fancy perambulator, with sister May and brother Clifford.

Sitting: Grandpa Beevers, Mummy, and Granny Beevers, May and Clifford standing.

Francis and Mary Windle's Golden Wedding Party on Boxing Day 1913 at Staveley Methodist Church. Charles Beevers, second from right on back row, Clifford Beevers fifth from right on back row, May Beevers second from right on second row from back, Marjorie Beevers, my mother in front of May, Sarah Ann Beevers (née Windle) my granny end of second row from the front, on right.

Sarah Ann Beevers (née Windle) and William Charles Beevers my grandparents, first passport photos to visit the English soldiers' graves in France, 1919.

Daddy at the age of twenty-one.

Daddy on the farm in Friskney.

September 2, 1925, my parents wedding. Daddy's mother, front row, second from left. Mummy's mother and father, front row, second and first from right.

June 1926. Proud father! Daddy showing me off to the neighbors in Barnett Avenue.

My parents with someone looking eager for life!

Great Granny Whitham visiting us at Barnett Avenue in 1928, I was two and she was ninety-two.

After my long bout with pneumonia, I was taken to Cornwall to recover.

Me dressed up for May Day, in the garden at Barnett Avenue, Sheffield.

Daddy and me at sea in Bournmouth.

The Sheffield school was evacuated to Derwent Hall, in Derbyshire, to move us out of the bombing.

Daddy visiting me in Derwent Hall.

Derwent church with sacking around the graveyard, while they exhumed the bodies.

Derwent village as the waters encroach. Derwent Hall is in the background in ruins, the chapel windows remain on the right.

The church tower remained as a memorial to the village.

Later it had to be demolished, as people were climbing it during a drought period.

My move to Hunmanby Hall School, evacuated to Armathwaite Hall Hydro on Bassenthwaite Lake, the Lake District.

My view from the dormitory of the lake.

My favorite horse in the riding school.

Our gang of four, L to R, Jean Hesketh, Dorothy Clough, Me, Judy England.

Me in a Summer Masque, fourth from the right.

Judy and I on Harry's Bentley.

University days.

My twenty-first party at the Maynard Arms Hotel.

At university, me sitting fourth from right, front row, with the staff.

Rag Day in the university, begging to raise funds for the poor.

THIS IS TO CERTIFY THAT

JUNE DENISE WHITHAM, DIP. ARCH.

261, DOBCROFT ROAD, SHEFFIELD, 11,

Having passed the Qualifying Examination established in 1882,

was elected on the twenty-ninth day of November, 1949,

ASSOCIATE

OF THE ROYAL INSTITUTE OF BRITISH ARCHITECTS,

Founded in the year of Our Lord, One thousand eight hundred and thirty-four, and afterwards constituted, under Royal Charters granted by King William the Fourth, Queen Victoria, King Edward the Seventh, and King George the Fifth, a Body Politic and Corporate for the general advancement of Architecture, and for promoting and facilitating the acquirement of the knowledge of the various arts and sciences connected therewith.

IN WITNESS whereof, the Common Seal has been hereunto affixed, at a Meeting of the Council, held at No. 66, Portland Place, London, this third day of January, 1950.

Chairman of the Meeting.

Member of Council.

Member of Council.

Honorary Secretary.

The Secretary of the Royal Institute.

Registered Serial No. 11,192

This Diploma is held subject to annual notification of its renewal, and under the conditions of bye-law 25.

Free at last, graduation! My R.I.B.A. certificate in 1949.

Pierre de la Lande.

BOISGUÉRIN-SOUVIGNÉ (Deux-Sèvres)   *Collection Max Ménard - Niort*

Pierre's family residence, Boisguerin, France.

My Swiss dress from Ascona, Switzerland.

Living in London, me at the Serpentine.

Geoffrey Hulette Holroyd during the war in army uniform.

September 2, 1950, the big day, our wedding day.

Vacation in Wales before we left England.

Geoff on the deck of the Liberté.

Our first glimpse of America, sailing into Manhattan.

New Life in the New World.

As soon as we arrived we mailed our first letter from New York. After the compulsory letter writing from my school days, I just continued it again, and wrote regularly, like a long diary. Mummy luckily had kept ALL my letters. And they have been very useful in writing this.

TheLiberte. (The old German Europa)   *Thursday24thJuly 1952*

My dear All,

What a wonderful send off you gave us! It was so lovely to see everyone there, waving, and then when we woke up yesterday morning, so good again to get all the telegrams. We had 4, from Ted and Dodi, Gran and Joan, Elizabeth in London and one from you Mummy and Daddy.

The journey to London went much quicker than I thought it would, and we got all our cases over to Waterloo by about 10 past 6, we bought our tickets and then rang Felix and Anthea. We met a friend in Waterloo, just by chance, so had a chat and said we were just going off to the US, he was surprised! We met Felix and Anthea at Hennekeys Wine Lodge, on the Strand for a drink, then they came over to the station with us, to see us off on the boat train. They had had a super holiday in Italy, and were very brown.

The boat train left at 8 and got to Southampton about 9.30. It was the most beautiful evening, and all the countryside looked lovely, it was really looking its best in the evening sun. When we drew into Southampton the Queen Mary was there, very large with 3 floodlit funnels, then we went on further and there was the Liberte, one mass of lights with 'LIBERTE' on the top in fairy lights. It looked almost as big as the Queen Mary but has only 2 funnels. We got through the customs quite easily, our trunks were there at the customs bay, then we trotted up the gangway onto the boat. It doesn't seem too much like a boat, downstairs, the shops and corridors, but our cabin is very much like a boat. It's really very tiny, hardly room for two of us to be standing out of bed at the same time.

Anyway we went up to the lounge and had some sandwiches and a drink there and then at 11.30 pm. we watched all the excitement of leaving. The tugs pulling us away and hooters blowing, and the pilot ship taking us out of the estuary and round the Isle of Wight. We could see plenty of lights on both sides, one side would be Cowes and the other Christchurch, Bournemouth and places, I guess.

The boat is really very good except that our end has a terrible bumping, it feels as though we have a square wheel that we are going along on, anyway it doesn't sway too much and we have both slept like logs. I never hear the steward come in our cabin and call us, and this morning we missed our breakfast, so had to have it brought to the cabin about 9.30! Breakfast is 7-9 and consists of a huge menu, first all fruit juices, then grapefruits, then all kind of cereals, then soup! (We have not tried this yet as it seems to be too french for us) then eggs 2 or 3 then toast and marmalade, or comfiture, and coffee. People seem to eat it all too.

The lunch and dinner are 2 huge meals, dinner last night for example, I'm copying the menu, as I pinched it to send to you.

> Watercress soup.
> Fried Whiting and lemon.
> Artichoke

Poached chicken and rice.

Mixed salad and eggs

Emmenthal and Roquefort cheeses

French ices.

Fruit, grapes, pears, or apples.

As much wine as one wants. (free)

Coffee, tea (china, ceylon, linden, camomile, mint, vervain.

What about that! I eat everything too which is more surprising.

(This may sound foolish now, but Food rationing was still so miserable in England.)

We have a ships newspaper every day in french and english giving us the latest news, and all details of the ships programme. We have films, a different one each day, we saw "The River", and then we have dances, and yesterday they had horse races or something, but we didn't go. The weather has been too nice to be inside much, but today (Friday) is grey and rougher than we have had it so far.

They are all french or American on the boat, we have only met 2 english people. We feel we are almost in America already as the boat is full of them. They seem rather funny! We met a crowd of chaps from Oxford, they have been over for 2 years on a scholarship studying law, and are all from American universities, one is going to Harvard again, he's been already and is returning to do research. They are so different from English people that we have not got used to them at all yet. They say some of the most odd sort of things and aren't a bit embarrassed. One of these law chaps was talking about himself, (they all like to do this very much) he said he was wondering how he would feel back in America, for in these 2 years he felt he had changed. They were the critical years of his life and he felt he had matured in them! It was the way he said it, and to us, strangers as well, it did seem funny. They talk a lot of politics and all the American journals around are full of the election. We keep hearing groups discussing all the different European peoples and they say such funny things, and in such loud voices. The dining room is bedlam with French and Americans all bawling at one another. Anyway it is breaking us in for America, they will soon seem more normal I guess.

The first afternoon on board we had our fire drill, it was funny we all had to go to our cabins, put on our Mae Wests, check our lifeboat numbers and then all walk up to the first class where the lifeboats were. We used it as a good chance to see over the whole boat. The first class is <u>amazing</u>. They have tremendous rooms, about 40 ft high, all incredibly furnished, with very few people in them, they have huge decks with an odd one or two people on, a giant swimming pool, a gym with all sorts of fat reducing things for the ladies, lots of deck amusements, and very ornate stairs with wrought iron handrails etc. It seems very ridiculous that so few people have three-quarters of the boat, plus all these extra things. They have a beautiful nursery which when we went in had one little boy plus 2 nannies, and that was all. They only pay double our fare but each person must have 300% or 500% more space plus all the extra facilities. The cabin class has a better average space not ridiculously lavish but well designed and without the square wheel effect that we have, as they are further forward. They have a nursery, packed, but with one nurse. Our part is just the back end, with a small deck only, very small cabins, and this tremendous bumping which seems to be only in our part and nowhere else. We have decided that the ship is very badly designed of course, after all our research! There is plenty of space for everyone to be fairly well placed, and the decks are quite big enough if properly divided, and the height of the rooms in 1st class could be reduced by half and still be spacious. They could achieve the lavish effect in decoration, not by putting 3 or 4 people in the same space as 50 or 60 of us share at the back. If you could see their decks! Anyway our tourist class is supposed to be as good as accommodation in other boats, and better than some, and the french food is of course wonderful, so we don't wish we'd booked any other boat. I think if you came on this boat but cabin class you would be fine, I'm not sure how much more cabin class is or what they charge for children.

It's funny you don't realise, until you are on these liners the class distinctions, or money distinctions there are. It is the place where it is most apparent I think. Up at the front you would never know you were on a boat, not a sound, no smoke from the funnels, no vibrations or people. At the back, bags of smoke, vibrations and many people.

We were going to phone you from the boat but it is very expensive and we are pretty low on money as we only had 6 pounds for drinks etc., and then found that to get a chair on deck cost us 3 pounds 15 shillings for the 2, so we were down pretty low straight away. I think it is much too dear as you have to have a chair, otherwise there is nowhere to sit except in the cabins or to see a film. Anyway it will mean our tips are low!

We keep hearing stories of the heat in New York at the moment, so if it is still on when we arrive we won't stay long at all. I think we dock next Monday morning, so that means only 2 complete days left. The Queen Mary will pass us, en route, as she was due to leave soon after we left. Since we saw the last tip of Ireland with its lighthouse we've only seen an odd little boat bobbing around, and yesterday and today we've not seen anything. We seem to go so fast all the time, maybe that's why we bump so, I think they want a new propeller or some oil on this one!

Yesterday we had one very exciting thing happen, suddenly the ship turned about very abruptly at a tremendous angle, with water out of one side of port holes and nothing but sky on the other. Everyone ran on deck and there were tales of children having fallen overboard, and as you can imagine on a French boat, quite a panic. We turned a complete tight circle and then we were able to see life belts and a head bobbing in the water. They quickly lowered a lifeboat and set off to this bobbing head. We all cheered when they hauled this person on board and then as the lifeboat was pulled up we all went to have a look who he was. Apparently he was a stowaway who had been in a cell for a day or so and they were taking him for an exercise walk when he leapt overboard. Poor chap he must have been desperate, to leap over as we were a full day from land, he could only have drowned if we had left him.

On Saturday night we had a beautiful dinner and at 10pm we had a party, paper hats, streamers, rattles etc., during the evening Geoff and I walked right to the bow of the ship, to the front of the first class. (The recent film of The Titanic reminded me of it, when they stood on the bow of the boat together*) It was absolutely quiet, the sky was full of stars, and it was so silent it was like going into another world, as you couldn't see a thing but slight waves on the water as the boat sliced its way along. It's been boiling hot the whole way and we've been in bathing costumes while we were out. Some of the time we sat in cabin class in the reading or writing room, and sometimes in first class. It was such a luxury after ours.*

This morning we got up at 6am and saw the first signs of land, lighthouses and small fishing boats in the mist, then we saw Long Island vaguely but not too clear, it seemed to be packed with racing cars all glinting in the sun. We had breakfast about 7 and tipped everyone and then came up

Monday 28th.

We have just docked and have sent off a wire to let you know we have arrived O.K. We docked at 9 and now at 12 are still waiting on the dock, for the customs! It's boiling and we are sitting on a pile of suitcases, waiting until the queue moves slightly before we join it.

The Americans are still quite surprising to us, anyway you'll see when you come. Whereas in England visitors are treated first and called visitors, we are treated last and called aliens! Very rude I think. We have just had a cup of coffee sitting on our suitcases. The cup of coffee was fifteen cents, the piece of cake fifteen cents and the cheese sandwich thirty cents. (14 cents = 1 shilling) so our snack, which was only small cost us four shillings and twenty eight pence!

Geoff adds a note.

3pm. Just arrived at Hotel Windsor and resting in our very nice room on 7th floor. New York so far has reminded us very much of Milan, so we don't feel strange. We are seeing our friend John Glenn tonight at 7pm, so are looking forward to seeing the sights and the lights. We must go now to get our first big meal today, after our terrible morning with the customs- I have never known anything so bad in Europe. June and I both feel a little dizzy as if the room is moving just like the boat did! I suppose we have got so accustomed to the movement. It was very nice to be greeted at the hotel desk by two letters from home, thank you very much everybody.

Thank you also for our very pleasant holiday at home- it was just what we felt like!

This is the end of our first letter, so lots of love from both of us. JandG

Our second letter mailed from Boston.

> *C/o Mr. and Mrs. Bauer,*
> *25 Beals St.,*
> *Brookline 46 Boston*

My dear All,

Well as you can see we have arrived in Boston. We had Monday and Tuesday nights in New York, but it was exhausting with the heat and the high prices, so we came on to Boston on Wednesday. Arriving about six in the evening.

After we had sat so long waiting at the docks, we took our cases with us in a taxi to our hotel and arranged for the French Line agent to take our trunks to Grand Central to wait there for us. It cost us six dollars which is over two pounds to have the trunks just delivered, anyway things just don't compare with english prices, so we've given up converting money into sterling equivalent, as it's so worrying.

New York seemed amazing to get out into, the streets were just packed to overflowing with huge honking cars, and the people looked so different too. We certainly felt we were abroad. The town is such a mad collection of very high buildings with these slices out for streets that the breeze from the Atlantic never gets into town, and all the buildings hold the heat all night so that it is always the same, tremendously hot.

Anyway our hotel room was very big, with a lovely bathroom with shower, but it wasn't air-conditioned which was a great pity. We sat on our beds and had showers for the afternoon when we arrived, then we rang up John Glenn and arranged to meet him at our hotel in the evening at seven o'clock

We had heard of a good French restaurant from a very nice French chap on the boat, so we trotted round there for a meal, and found it was closed on Mondays, but next to it was a place which looked quite good and was air-conditioned so we went in and ordered ham salad which on the menu was seventy five cents. It was a huge plateful and when we had struggled half way through it the waiter came and said he was sorry but we had seen the lunch menu by mistake, and in the evening the price was one dollar twenty five cents each! We have heard since from various folk that it's really impossible to eat out for less than one dollar even here in Boston. We had a real day that first day, but apparently everyone does. The taxi from the docks to our hotel charged us double too, so we certainly decided to put a stop to that.

This French chap from the boat by the way, decided he couldn't stand in this long queue at the docks, the same as we did (some folk queued from eight thirty am. when we docked until two thirty pm, to get an inspector to show their cases to) so he, his girl in New York and Geoff and I all had a coffee, which his girl brought from outside, then he saw some girls he had got to know on the boat, at the front of the queue at about two thirty so we went up and gave them his slip and ours for the trunks, that is how we managed to get away when we did, we left a very long queue of people, the poor things. He was very good to us this chap all the time giving us addresses and tips about NY, and he gave us his office and flat address so that next time we are up in NY we can get in touch with him. After we had had our meal we went to meet John and went with him to the hotel opposite ours, which was air conditioned and there we sat and chatted and had a drink. Then we walked over to the East River to see the UN Buildings, which are one of the conversation topics of architects, world wide. They are very impressive compared with the ornate and Gothicky skyline of the old skyscrapers, so we sat for a while by the river where there was air, and watched lights, neon signs and boats.

We then went with John along by bus to Times Square, which was brilliant and dazzling. I have never seen such ingenious lights and trick advertising. One building has a waterfall pouring off its roof, and another had smoke and moving figures and the brilliance is tremendous, but our opinion on the whole is that it is rather vulgar. Quite a lot of things though are rather vulgar, the whole picture of towns as one walks about is certainly astounding at first, they have got gadgets and modern ideas off to a high degree.

We walked from Times Square to 6th Ave., and when we were waiting for the bus, (with John luckily) a gang of chaps came and asked us for some money. We hurried off very quickly into a busier area so we were all right. We had been warned not to take much money out as there are lots of hold-ups every day in New York. Our first evening there a policeman was shot in Central Park by one of these gangs, and there are daily shootings. We were amazed as we thought all those days were over, anyway they aren't.

We were glad to get to bed though, and both of us felt very dizzy as though the whole room was rocking! We weren't ill on the boat but the effect was worse when we got on dry land, as when we lay down we could feel the same motion as the boat!

It was so hot that we didn't seem to sleep so well, so the next morning we stayed in bed until late. We phoned Wally and Dolly (the Hakins who were friends of Daddy's from metallurgy school and from Sheffield, and lived in Detroit) and each had a long chat with them both. It was very nice to hear them and they said if we got in any trouble in NY to be sure to phone them. Wally is coming to Boston in a few weeks so will see us. They sent their love Mummy and Daddy and sounded very pleased we had arrived O.K.

Tuesday morning we woke late and went to a place called Horn and Hardart, an automat for breakfast. You put a nickel or 2 nickels in various machines and get your whole breakfast. It sounds very queer but it is wonderful. You go around with a tray to all the different glass boxes of food and collect what you want, open up the little glass doors. The whole place was air conditioned and we had frozen fruit juice and toast and marmalade and coffee. We decided that as the heat was so impossible we'd spend all the day in air conditioned buildings as they are just wonderful, like stepping into a refrigerator. You can't imagine what this heat is, it's worse than Milan and just makes you feel dead. It is very humid with the heat too, which makes it much worse. It's been much cooler in Boston since we arrived, but even here it is pretty killing, yesterday afternoon was 85 degrees, and still very humid.

After our breakfast we went to Radio City, a tremendous entertainment centre in the Rockefeller Building. It's air-conditioned and has the largest theatre in the world, 6,600 seats and its usually about full. We first saw a film, "Where's Charley" which was quite amusing, then a news and a Disney cartoon, and then from below ground a huge orchestra came up and played an interlude, then the curtains went up on a tremendous stage. They had all the theatre effects we should use in England but don't, a cyclorama with clouds and sea in full speed at the back of the stage, lots of things like a pageant going across the stage with horses (real ones) and a lovely train puffing across with people in it. Finally a firework display over some buildings, with ballet dancers whirling and all the fireworks done with lights, bursting rockets and everything, it was a very amazing thing and all so big again, but they don't seem to use these things in the proper way, it was all a bit of a poor taste show.

Afterwards we looked all around the foyers and halls, they are on a colossal scale, then we went out to another automat for lunch. We decided until we got the hang of the money they were the safest places to eat. After lunch we went along 6th Ave. to 53rd St. and went to have a look at the Museum of Modern Art. It is one of the wonders of the world really, they have such a tremendous collection of modern paintings, a lot of modern architecture with a modern house built from time to time by different architects. They have a huge film library, and really go in for all modern art. It must be one of the best museums in the world for modern art.

(Geoff adds the next section)

Then we thought that a good way to get to know American living would be to see the big shops, so we went to 5th Ave. and into a dress shop ' De Pinna' and June looked at a whole range of beautiful, gay coloured clothes- very modern and well designed, especially summer evening dresses and beach dresses. I looked at shirts, but they didn't have any with collars as small as I want, which seemed rather funny.

JUNE: Roots of Steel

We were going to Saks but they were closed by the time we got there. The window displays are marvelous, and the shops so new and modern that we were amazed. We went into a church, which is always photographed- among the skyscrapers, but it was so hot (not air-conditioned!) that we had to come straight out. It is a funny sensation to come out onto the hot streets from cool buildings, and seems to be the wrong way round. We were so tired by now that June said she must sit down, and we went into Central Park by a fountain and with old fashioned horse carriages with tasseled awnings and drivers in top hats, very like the south of France, standing along the boulevard.

Back in the hotel we rang the friend of Auntie Dot (June's father's older sister) June and I arranged to have breakfast with her the next day. Also we phoned an American, Jim Sherlock who we met on the boat who was a reporter, but he wasn't in. We went out again with John for a drink in Greenwich Village, which is supposed to be the Chelsea of NY. We met him in a square called Washington Square, with an arch like the Arc de Triomphe, in it, and trees. It was just going dark (very early between eight and eight thirty) and the square was packed with people of all ages, sitting about to keep cool. Little groups sat around portable radios and ice cream tricycles with bells and lights went around everywhere. We walked through it all into side streets full of shops selling paintings and antiques, and funnily enough leather sandals and bags and belts -all designed and cut out by long haired chaps while you watched. June went into one to ask the price of some sandals (of course we couldn't have bought them) and a girl was standing on a big piece of leather on a stool having the soles of a pair of sandals cut around the shape of her feet. We found a good Italian place to eat and drink. The best drink to cool you is a Tom Collins, which varies wherever you are, but is mainly gin and fruit juice and soda with fresh fruit in.

Then we said goodbye to John - he had asked us to see his flat in Brooklyn but we were too tired and his wife Natalie was ill and had gone home to Philadelphia, so we said we would like to see it when she was there. Back in the Hotel we packed our things ready for Boston, because we decided it was too exhausting (and expensive!) in New York.

(June resumes)

About ten fifteen the next day Jean Beckwith came around to take us out for breakfast. We gave her the gifts from Auntie Dot, and then went off in a taxi with her to a place called 'Hamburger Heaven' where all the hamburgers in the window have got angel's wings, and their advert is 'the gates of heaven never close' which means that this place is always open, year in and year out, night and day.

We had a tremendous meal for a breakfast, a large glass of fruit juice first, then hamburgers with all kinds of pickles and coffee and chocolate cake! The American food is very difficult to get the hang of at first. One evening we had spaghetti and meat sauces, but the relish served with the meat course was peaches, sliced cucumber in vinegar, the peaches were the tinned ones in syrup, then cream cheese eaten with it too. I put a whole lot of peaches and cream cheese on a side plate and ate that afterwards as my dessert.

This girl Jean was very sweet, not young but terribly lively and so far the only person we've met who was critical of America, she is an American but has lived in almost every country in the world, England, Egypt, France, all over. Her husband is an architect from Yale who she wants us to meet. He has got so tired of clients and their bad taste that he is running a toy factory as well as doing some nice modern shops in NY. They seem a very good couple for us to know. Next time we are up in town they want us to get in touch with them. Would you thank Auntie Dot for her introduction to them, it was splendid to meet such a lively person.

Jean took us back to our hotel where we paid our bill nineteen dollars and fifty cents for two nights, and reserved a double room at their hotel in Boston, in case we had nowhere to go when we arrived. Our train left Grand Central at one pm light saving time. They have two times here you know, just to make life more complicated, so you have to ask which time it is always.

Grand Central is a phenomenon! You go into this tremendous hall, which we know very well from photographs, and from there go through separate double doors to each platform, and there are all the trains, spotless, all under NY and so artificially lit, all electric so there is no smoke. The one we came on is apparently one of the newest and poshest. All pressed aluminium and streamlined, with automatic closing doors, done by air pressure.

(Geoff writes)

Our detailed letter is getting so far behind with events that I think we must tell you the latest things now and finish this off and post it.

Roughly we have been in Boston since Weds. night, staying with Mrs. Weidenfeld's sister in a very nice room in their large house. We have met a number of people at Harvard and the 2 friends of Uncle Billy (Geoff's Father's brother) who were very charming to us (we are having dinner with them on Tuesday) but the great news of the evening- Sunday- is that we have taken a most wonderful flat! June is absolutely crazy about it, it is so beautifully equipped and complete. We shall move in at the end of next week I think.

Tomorrow we must see about jobs, that is the next thing on the list. Goodbye to everyone from me.

June wants a last word.

Goodbye from me too. This new apartment is a dream, I wish you could all come and see it. It's all modern, new. The bathroom is tiled right up in white tiles, new white bath, WC and basin, shower and electric extract fan.

Then the kitchen is yellow rubber floor, HUGE refrigerator, electric cooker and all one wall is white cabinets. It is centrally heated and free hot water and is on a wonderful wide street in Boston, like a lovely continental boulevard. The lounge has blue walls, a bright modern blue, and white trim, with a lovely white painted fireplace. The bedroom leads off the living room, has coffee colored walls. We have our own front door and we are second floor up.

Hope we can get a job now so we can afford it! I have just found my tea coupons so I am sending them, you had better use them. No rationing here!

As my letters on the whole are so long, I think I should read them through and then give you the important points.

Our third letter was written in our new apartment. Geoff explains that the furnished places we had gone to see were all rather depressing, so in spite of 849 Beacon St. being unfurnished (but it was cheaper than places in Cambridge near the University, only eighty five dollars per month) we had gone ahead and taken it, and with the help of the janitor lending us some furniture that was in the basement, and a flush door too that Geoffrey painted white for a low coffee table, we felt settled. We bought a mattress and got a very large jerraboam bottle from a restaurant which we made into a light for the coffee table, and made a big shade for it. We found a very good bright blue 'campaign chair' where the canvas is slung on a metal frame- it was two dollars in a second hand shop.

We had had several trips over to Cambridge to see the University, and we loved the style of the ivy covered buildings, brick with white columns and porticos, white painted sash windows and a very pleasant domestic scale. We had met Lester Collins, chairman of the School of Design, and he wants to take us out to see the country round Cambridge.

Since we arrived we've had a very good look at Boston in spite of the heat. Have you heard of the dreadful drought in the area? It's really been terrible and so humid too. Just after a shower you feel wet and so sticky again.

We've had several trips round all the shops, as you can guess, they are beautiful and so many big stores, it's amazing. Some are air-conditioned and some are not. Boston is very much bigger than you ever think, two million people. Very wide Boulevards, quite a complicated underground and transport system, very large docks and shipping areas, some fine parks and a very good Museum of Fine Arts. It has many more museums, but we've not seen them yet.

We went one day to the top of the Customs House which is about twenty six stories high, to get a picture of the whole of Boston, it's very surprising, there is a huge airport on land reclaimed from the sea, and lots of islands all connected by ferry to the town. Some of the buildings are quite old and very picturesque in timber. None of them is really old by our standards, seventeen fifty or so. The houses in all the suburbs are timber and very different from England. We had a good potter around the dock area, but it was very fishy and hot.

Today we decided to have a last rest before starting on our job hunting, and after all our moving, so we went by bus to a very lovely peninsula sticking into the Atlantic, called Nahant. We had the whole day pottering around there and sitting on the rocks, fortunately today has gone much cooler after some tremendous storms. It was a very pretty spot and lovely to go to a quiet beach. The University gave us lots of addresses of architects to try, and we decided that Monday morning first thing is the best time to start.

Last weekend we phoned the two ladies Uncle Billy (Geoffrey's father's brother) *met on the boat. They live in Cambridge and took us a drive on Sunday afternoon round all the lovely parts of Cambridge. Then on Tuesday evening we went there for dinner, they are both very nice.*

We've eaten in quite a lot and shopping is very different. Each person has a large pram type container, which they push around and pile stuff in, then as you leave it is all checked at rapid speed and you pay. You can get anything. (I am still amazed not to have everything rationed.)

The next letter is August 17th 1952.

Thank you for your letters, the first one to this flat came yesterday. It is lovely to hear from you and so good to find our first letter in our own letter box, in the hall downstairs. We each have a key to our own stainless steel letter box, which is built into the wall. There is also a buzzer, which guests press in the outside hall, then we press a red button by our door and speak to them on a microphone system. If it is someone we want to come in, we press a black button, which opens the door downstairs. Very Posh!!

Last Sunday I spent the whole day re-doing the lounge floor twenty one ft by twelve ft first washing it well and when it dried doing it with polish.

Geoffrey wrote his first newsletter for The Architect and Building News.
(Before we left London he had set it up with them, as we were one of
the first groups of architects to come over, and architects in England
were very interested in the architecture scene here)

I started on Monday morning with an armful of drawings and so
far must have gone to about 20 interviews. Everyone has been super and
terribly kind, going to no end of trouble to ring friends and see if they
needed anyone. One really nice old chap who knows the President of the
Royal Institute of British Architects wrote me two letters of introduction to
big firms here, and he gives my work tremendous praise in them. I've not
struck anyone who didn't try several friends, so I really was lucky, but the
summer is a very slack time and all the Harvard students are out at the
moment. There is no agency here that lists architectural vacancies, and most
of the firms don't take women!! (This amazed me as I had thought of the
states as being very progressive, but in equality of women it certainly is
not. When I had gone for job interviews in London no-one had ever
remarked on me being a woman, and I knew many successful women
in Architecture in Europe)

However I now know I am in for quite a search. It's just that it is so hot
and so tiring to keep on explaining every drawing, 20 times and then them
saying how lovely my work is but they haven't got anything.

Geoff got a good thing last week, to do some Harvard University posters
and arrange for printing and everything. He may get a part time architect
job, so we are keeping our fingers crossed.

Lester Collins asked us out to his home on Thursday, we went for a
picnic with his wife and little girl and had a wonderful time. He said it
was always hard to get a job straight away and he thought maybe I should
take a part time job until a good firm had a vacancy. Lester Collins met us
at Harvard in his car, an open SS Jaguar- a beauty. We then went to his
home outside Boston, in the country, it is very beautiful. Wonderful white
wooden houses and such lovely trees and grass everywhere, it's quite like
England.

JUNE: Roots of Steel

On Friday evening we decided to go to Cape Cod this weekend and take a tent and go camping, so we went to the International Union of Students at Harvard, to borrow a tent. There are crowds of folk go to this place for the evening, some people live in. It is run by a Swiss chap and his American wife they are only our age and are very kind and so helpful. Anyway while we were talking about fares etc. and which place on the Cape to go to, an American fellow came up and said he was going by car to Cape Anne, which is about one and a half hours away, and would we like to go, so we decided to go there. This chap Gordon ran us home on Friday evening and then called about 10 yesterday for us. I made a picnic lunch for us, bacon and red currant jelly, peanut butter and redcurrant jelly, and hard boiled eggs, with bread and butter, bananas and a bag of peaches. He was going to umpire a tennis tournament in Manchester, New Hampshire. We went to this Essex Country Club with him, it was a superb spot and a lot of the tennis players from Wimbledon were there, so we were able to meet them, Louise Brough, Nancy Chaffee, and Marie someone from Los Angeles, she is very young only about 18. It was funny to see them without their fans, and after the game they were all busy carrying cases and clothes on coat hangers to their huge cars, ready to move on to the next tournament.

This country club is on the hill above Manchester, with views along lovely parkland, with super trees and golf course and beyond to the sea. Manchester is the opposite of what you'd expect from its English name. It is a very small lobster fishing village. A wonderful harbour in a tiny estuary, with lovely yachts and boats and trees and lawns and white wooden houses coming to the waters edge. In the centre of the village is a picturesque green, with a white wooden town hall and white wooden church, and not one single thing to spoil the beauty. America is usually bad about that, and sticks neon signs, drug stores, rubbish dumps, just around the corner from the most beautiful spots. Anyway yesterday was the first time we'd found such an unspoiled part, and it was lovely. Just about five minutes from the harbour we found a beautiful beach a complete bay of white golden sand and at either end a promontory of red rock into the sea. Here we had our picnic lunch.

Gordon brought us home in a large Cadillac.

Next letter August 21ˢᵗ

Geoff started work yesterday, he heard on Tuesday, that an office in Cambridge would take him part time, but couldn't take me as they didn't want a full time person. I am still persevering but building work is very slack in the summer. There are a few offices doing Government work and only US citizens can work there. Geoff is getting paid a dollar seventy five an hour so on the whole week he gets seventy dollars or so. Last night I got quite a good thing. The University had a man who wanted a scheme for a large nursing home and wanted a young architect with hospital experience, so I got in touch with him, and he and another man came around here last night to give me the details. I'm going to do it here at home, at first he only wants preliminary eighth scale drawings to try to get financing. Keep your fingers crossed. I may get a job in Harvard Library, or I have been considering teaching Architecture to Art students at Mass. School of Art, but as I find it so terrifying to address a group of people, (even if its only my own twenty first party!!) I think the teaching job is out.

Auntie Dolly (Hakin) wrote and gave us the address of some friends of hers in Boston, Mrs. Brinnin, who has a beautiful home in Boston that's been illustrated in Life. Her son is a literary figure, a friend of Dylan Thomas, he is in England at the moment.

I have lots of terrible mosquito bites Mrs. Siggourney came with ammonia and things so they are much better now. Mosquitoes are terrible.

I have just been looking through last Sunday's paper again and wondered if you knew about these papers here. In the week we buy The Christian Science Monitor, which is excellent, rather like the Manchester Guardian. The general standard of the other papers here seems to be much lower than our low. They have so many horrific things in that how people can read them and still be normal, I don't know. I guess the size of the country is like all of Europe and if we had a paper that covered all the crime for that it would be pretty shocking too.

On Sundays we buy The New York Times, which costs twenty five cents and is a monster! We bought it when we were down by the river, and Geoff thought he must have picked up about ten copies, by mistake.

The TV here is amazing, all the shows are sponsored and in the middle of an exciting play, a little jingle will come on and advertise Pabst Blue Label or some other product. We see TV quite a lot, well anyway we don't ever look at it, but it's always on in restaurants and places. It is very bad here, absolutely monstrous. So far we have only met two people who had their own TV sets, no one we've met in Boston has one. The BBC should do much more to shout about it's high standard I think.

The radio here is so complicated too, of course it would be in such a large country. The standard radio can get I'd say more than fifty stations, with every single item paid for by some commercial firm, even the news is sponsored. However there is a really brilliant programme on the FM radios, lots of stations are owned by Universities, Harvard & Yale have large ones. One station has concerts non-stop and with no 'jingles'. We are busy saving up to buy an FM radio. All this talk came from the word 'advertising', which is the key word in America.

I've been looking through the paper, one point on the census, there really are the most fabulously rich people here, when we went to Cape Anne and Nahant, some of the houses there, country houses, cost fortunes to run and staff. In general there is this tremendous high standard of living. Every family where they are healthy and have a job has all the gadgets, and as you walk around in the evenings and look into rooms with lights on you can see one after another with new furniture, modern wallpaper, striped or bold coloured. Even typists earn fifty dollars a week and as long as they are working they have lots of new gay clothes and appear to have everything they need. We visited a house that is owned by a huge Italian family, all kinds of cousins, aunts, grand parents etc., and they all work, even the children have newspaper routes. They wanted to show us a gigantic restaurant size refrigerator they had bought for their kitchen. You can see how exciting it is for them, when they probably had no jobs in Italy, and therefore few possessions.

Most students have cars, school children have cars and as long as their Father takes full responsibility for them they can drive at twelve or thirteen years of age. Last week on the beach in Manchester there were lots of young boys twelve thirteen and fourteen, all driving up in large modern cars. They work in the evenings or one day or so a week, and with the money pay out for a car, or their gasoline.

Anyway on the absolute opposite end of the scale, any family who can't work, or who have a sick father and lots of kids, live in the downtown in the most atrocious slums. Downtown NY is a terrible area, our clerk at the Windsor Hotel had done social work in his student days in that area. He told us some of the most abominable conditions, maybe eight people sharing one room, and often not all the same family. These conditions seem doubly wrong when the rest of America is enjoying such a boom and has a far too high standard of living, compared with the rest of the world.

The strange thing is that apart from Mrs. Siggourney, Mrs. Thomas, and Jean Beckwith, oh and Gordon, we've not found anyone with any criticism at all. They never consider that all is not golden and wonderful here, and will not take any criticism at all of anything. We soon learned not to say anything about what we felt, other than that it was very nice. On the boat there were crowds of Americans who in very loud voices talked about our awful food in England and laughed about us and we were treated along with French and Italians as behind the times, old fashioned and having to be kept. We anyway didn't mind that too much, but found we must not say a word about them or they were really mad.

Don't think from this that we are at all fed up we came, we're terribly interested to see it all, and have found a lot of people who are really more intelligent and all the people we have met in Boston have been very kind to us. One chap said that we must think of the Americans as adolescents, they are so pleased with all their new toys, and like an adolescent, cannot stand anyone telling them they have got a lot of things wrong.

There is a tremendous amount to learn from the way they achieve things too. Around Boston there are huge eight lane freeways in all directions, and these now cover America. In the heavily built up areas of Boston they have 'clover leaf crossings', flyovers, double roads, one up and one below. They are just laying the last stages of a 3ft diameter pipe line bringing natural gas from Texas to Boston, over 2000 miles. Taxes in Boston are high and Boston is wealthy, Governor Denver has got himself nick-named 'road builder', as he has done so much.

Yesterday an amazing thing started a few doors away from us. Three police appeared with signs and shut off a large area outside a very big funeral home here. Then all day large cars kept drawing up and people going in and last night there were crowds lining up, just like a football crowd. Everyone in quite gay clothes, so I couldn't believe it was a funeral. Yesterday we found out it was Gov. Denver's brother, who was his henchman too. Gov. Denver has eighty eight thousand he is just about to spend, so that made the crowds even thicker.

Apparently when you die, you are taken to one of these funeral homes where they embalm you, and dress you up in the clothes your family liked best, they pad your cheeks and make you smile and colour it up and you are on show for some time before they put you in your coffin! Nancy Mitford's stories are not just invented we find. I was so horrified to hear about it, I think it's the most awful bad taste thing to do and apparently they charge you thousands for their services.

Mrs. Weidenfeld has not arrived yet so we haven't heard what the tourist class is like on the Ile de France. Must go and start work on this nursing home.

Aug twenty eighth

On Saturday we went up to Cambridge to the new Gropius Graduate Centre, Geoff wants to write about it in his 'letter from America'. Then we went to MIT to see the new student dormitories, by Alvar Aalto, when he was teaching there, which is another new and famous building, it is very good, students rooms right on the river. We then walked past the MIT buildings to a new twelve storey block of apartments, where Mrs. Brinnin (Wally and Dolly's friend) lives. Her apartment faces onto the Charles River and looks across onto Beacon Hill, which is the old English area of Boston, it is a very posh area to live in, and the streets go up steeply from the river, the nicest view of Boston. Mrs. Brinnin's son is still in London staying with Dylan Thomas, he also is a friend of James Thurber. On Sunday we went into the country with someone from TAC (The Architects Collaborative) office, Geoff wants to do an article on their work, so someone from the office took us out into the country to see some of their houses, they were great. Monday I went job hunting again, I am now wanting any job until an architecture one turns up. Tomorrow I'm going to a huge store 1 min. away from us, as a mail order girl. I will get seventy five cents an hour plus one percent of sales. I just sit at a counter and people come to me with their orders. What a hoot! I hope I can understand what they say! I've been to some amazing places, Tuesday I went to a trick shop in Cambridge, he sells glasses that leak and all sorts of mad things, but he had found someone already.

I've done a lot of work on the nursing home, and got my first check today twenty-five dollars, so it's about 10 pounds. This weekend is a real bank holiday and is the end of summer.

September fourth

We have been having a very busy time, first of all my job, it is very convenient at this store because I do part time, two evenings I have to work until nine pm, but other days eleven to four pm so I am able to go for interviews before and after. It is less than two minutes away from us and now I am getting the hang of it, it isn't too bad. It is quite an insight into the American way of life for a large number of people. We have discovered a lot of people have their clothes, house gadgets, cars etc., on the never never. (This is what buying on credit is called in England) *A lot of people have a three hundred dollar account for things they have got from us and they pay it off so much a week as they haven't the money to pay it all off. They have a little well-worn book, like our ration books, and they just keep adding to the purchases. Isn't it amazing?*

Anyway I am finding my way better with their language, they come in and ask for jeepers or creepers and they turn out to be gym shoes, and men come in and ask for a skirt, which turns out to be a front wing for a car!

We sell everything washing machines, car parts, furniture, clothes, they all come from the warehouses which means we cut our costs so much that the goods are near wholesale price. There are about eight of us on the counter at once and people give us the number from the catalogue and if we have it in the building, we have eleven floors of warehouses, we send up the order by compressed air tube and a gang of men put things on a huge conveyor system. It's quite amazing.

Today I bought our wireless set there, so we are very thrilled and we've been listening to the wonderful FM stations. We just heard Clement Attlee (English Prime Minister) on a BBC programme, it was wonderful to hear an english announcer!

Last weekend we had a very good time. I had to work until five pm on the Saturday of the holiday but when I got in Mr. Muse (the nursing home guy) phoned to say they were having a party. He is only 32 or so and he and his wife are both lawyers. They have five children and she is due for another now! We have met four couples with six children isn't it amazing? (It was very popular then to have these big families, but when we returned to America in 1967 with four children, everyone was telling us you should only have two- I pointed out that on our first visit we had been told you should have a large family- a quick change in planning!) *We went around to the party and had some lovely records on and talked, and about eight thirty some chinese cooks brought a delicious meal round to the house- pork ribs, slices of pork with mushrooms and soy sauce, chicken with mushrooms, etc., we had a really huge meal. A lot of the restaurants will bring hot food to the house, which seems a very good idea. Some people at the party were going up to New Hampshire for Sunday and Monday and asked us to go, but we decided we couldn't really afford the hotel expenses. We hope to go while we are here, as it is very beautiful. The nursing home for Mr. Muse is doing well, he came yesterday and collected my first drawings.*

On the Sunday we went with a whole party from the International Student Centre to the most beautiful beach we have ever been on. It is about an hour and a half away, we swam and lay in the sand dunes in the sun. We went back to Cambridge and went to dinner with some of the folk. Monday the weather was very dull, so we had a lazy day, we met Mrs. Brinnin in the Copley Sheraton Hotel for tea and then went to a news theatre and saw some very good films of America which once you are here you realise we just haven't seen anything yet. This friend of ours Henry Fournier who has the most delicious car, a Lincoln Continental, is going to Chicago in a week or two, we hope we might have enough money to join him. There is some tremendous architecture over there and it is like a different country from New England.

On Weds we went to the International Student Centre to hear a lecture on Boston town planning, and then we went to Geoff's office as he had a client coming first thing on Thurs. and had to finish some drawings. He is doing some interesting jobs. I had my first job offered me, the only architect in Boston who wants anyone, but unluckily the office is 20 miles from here and when I rang the station I found the only trains were one bringing folk into Boston in the a.m. and one back there in the evening. They had a cottage we could have lived in, but Geoff couldn't have gone back and forth.

Last week I phoned Mrs. Weidenfeld at her sisters. She was glad to hear me as she has been terribly poorly and thought she was about to die. She was in the hospital all the way over on the boat, I think it was very severe asthma. We will go and see her soon when she is better.

Tuesday ninth Sept.

Here is some good news. I have got a job! After about thirty eight interviews, I am due to start on Monday. Isn't that good? It's with a large firm but not one of the real old ones, thank goodness. They are just about to start a new hospital in the Virgin Islands, and they also do schools and another hospital here is quite well on. I start at eight thirty and work until five fifteen. I will get paid seventy dollars which is not too bad; our rent is twenty a week so we will have fifty to live on. It is quite a lot if you think of it being twenty seven pounds. (I was earning only 8 pounds when I first started work in London) *The cost of living here is about 3 times what it is in England. While Geoff and I both work for the next few weeks we should be able to replace our savings that we brought.*

We have just done a sightseeing tour of Boston, the naval dockyards and saw the old sailing boat, 'Ironsides'. The weather has been cooler these last days, in the seventies, so I have felt comfortable in my summer dresses. People here seem so nesh (a word used for steel when it is not hardened enough, a Sheffield word) *they were wearing coats yesterday with the temperature at 72, so what they wear in the winter, which is apparently terrible, I don't know. Mrs. Weidenfeld is coming around today for tea as I finish work at four pm.*

Weds seventeenth Sept

The third day in my new job. They seem nice folk, about fifty in the office. These first days I was working on the new Massachusetts State mental hospital. With my long days I won't be writing so often as I have very little time. I am working on the nursing home too. Tomorrow night we are going to Mrs. Brinnin's for dinner. Mrs Gropius has asked us out there so we may go on Friday or Saturday evening. That will be a really big occasion!

Saturday twenty-seventh Sept.

We have been very busy with Geoff starting at Harvard and meeting crowds of new people too. It's been amazing. Last Saturday we went to the International Student Center. They were having a huge barbecue, there were about 10 cars and each with about 6 or 8 people in. We went to a beautiful little lake in a huge wooded area near Concord. We sat and talked and swam in the lake. It is the most amazing thing the student center. The driver of our car was an American student, about 30 or so, next to him a boy from Israel, and next to him a boy from Iraq, and with us in the back a wonderful man from Egypt. He had a huge beaming face and a great sense of humour. All the students seem older as it is mainly post graduates.

We sat and talked with 3 Germans, and some Italians. One of the Germans had been in the Luftwaffe and had been shot down by the R.A.F. His face was terribly scarred, it made me feel very bad, what a senseless thing war is. Then we went for a walk round the lake and found an orchard with brilliant red apples in large twenty-five foot trees, and the leaves were a pale yellow. The yellow and the red were like a Chinese painting. We all wended our way back to the cabin and some people started the fires ready for cooking. About 8 of us climbed to the top of a hill overlooking the lake and the cabin, with it's now smoking chimney. We sat up there for an hour or more until we heard that the food was ready. We met two very interesting Italians, one the older man was a judge from Milan. He is here for 3 months and was such a fine sincere man and so correct. The contrast between the Italian behavior and the American boisterousness is very amusing to see, and also the difference in maturity of brains is very great too. After we had eaten, hamburgers, pickles, tomatoes, coffee and cherry and apple pie, we sat and talked and a boy with a guitar played, and a lovely girl from Hawaii did some Hawaiian dances and sang the quaint words to them. It is the most amazing thing to find such a group of people together, and all getting on so well. There were Chinese, Japanese, Scots and Welsh, such a mixture, and although you meet Americans who are really all different nationalities, as soon as they come to live here they just become Americans and lose all their national traits.

When we got back to Cambridge we went to the Centre and met an English architect from Gibraltar who had just arrived, so he and a friend of his and Geoff and I went to the Continental Hotel and sat and talked. It's really quite noisy in the Student Centre and on Saturday nights they have a dance. We talked to them until eleven thirty and then when we were just walking back to the trolley, to go home, a car of students stopped and this huge chap Chuck Fraggos an ex-wrestler jumped out and said he would treat us to a meal, they were all going to a café in Harvard Square. About 8 of us sat and ate and talked until one thirty pm, then they ran us home.

Sunday I did my last drawing for Mr. Muse and delivered them to him.

Monday Geoff started at Harvard and found he was in a group of about 16. He was rather disappointed to find from an interview with different Professors that he won't be allowed to work on his own as he had *hoped, and as you do in England for post-graduate work, but has to do different courses and attend lectures, which is not the same as the tutoring he was wanting. We had never had the Graduate Courses in the United States properly explained to us. The difficulty is that most of the students have never done <u>any</u> architecture, they have their degrees in every other subject, other than architecture. This is not the case in England, to get a Masters Degree in a subject, you already have to have a B.A. in the same subject. Otherwise everyone in a Masters course is working with different backgrounds and standards, and a two or three year course in Architecture leaves you very lacking in knowledge compared to the students who have spent five or six years for a B.A. in Architecture as we had.*

They have just got their first project, a large area of the Everglades Park in Florida. It is a national park, but so vast that people cannot see much, part sea and part land. It seems funny to be doing these school projects again but it's wonderful to be at a large University like this one. The atmosphere everywhere and the life now the students are back, makes Cambridge wonderful. We went to the Graduate Dining Hall one evening for dinner, which is very lively and in a Gropius building. Geoff has written an article on Walter Gropius, you know the very famous German architect, and he wanted to show it to him before it was sent, so Geoff phoned to see if we could go out to meet him. Gropius is away in Paris working on the UNESCO building, but Mrs. Gropius was there, and she said she would love to have us go out to see her, so on Friday evening. Henry took us out to Lincoln in his Lincoln car! We had a very interesting evening and the house is beautiful. We knew it all very well from photos of course, I even knew the 2 pine trees at the end of the drive, we had been lost once and Henry thought we were lost again but then I saw the trees and said 'there is the drive' Geoff and Henry were surprised. Mrs. Gropius is a beautiful woman and so lively we just couldn't get away. We kept saying we would have to leave and she went on with more wonderful stories so that it was 2 o'clock before we knew where we were.

Yesterday we were invited with the other students to Lester Collins house in Weston. He is chairman of the school. He had asked all the different professors to his party with their wives and Lester and his wife Petronella had got wonderful food. We came back to Harvard with one of the professors and his wife. He is about 36 and they have 6 children and she looks like she is having another! They are very friendly though, all the professors and lecturers. When we got back to Cambridge we went to a Chinese café with them and then we stopped at the Centre.

Sunday October fifth. 1952

We were invited this weekend to go out on a trip to New Hampshire with some people from my office. The hotel bill was going to be rather a lot and as we hope to go away next weekend, Columbus Day holiday, we had to say no, it's a pity as they were going into the real ski mountains and staying in a ski lodge by a lake and they said it is beautiful there and especially now at this time of year. Anyway we will go some other weekend. On Friday evening I met Geoff in town we went to see "Ivanhoe" It was very good and made us feel we were in England still! The Jew and his daughter were from Sheffield and the shots of their home in Sheffield at the time of the crusades were very interesting. We both enjoyed it very much, probably much more than we would normally have done. Yesterday we pottered around and had a late breakfast and then Geoff went to Sears Roebuck to find out about some cupboards for a kitchen he did in the office, and I went and got the groceries etc. we had lunch, and then headed to town to meet Mrs. Weidenfeld. Geoff hadn't met her here before, so was pleased to see her. We went for a walk in the park and around the lake, then went to a lovely Italian shop, Carbone, to look around. We bought an Italian milk jug, which we really needed, and also some Japanese split bamboo mats, they are big ones and a lovely green colour. It is a beautiful shop, I am hoping I may be able to sell them some pots when I get going. (I had started to go to a ceramics class) We then took Mrs. Weidenfeld out for tea to Schrafts a very nice continental tea place, and we sat there and talked until five thirty. We then had to dash off as we were going to a party, so we saw Mrs. Weidenfeld onto her underground. She is so different from her sister it is surprising, I can't decide whether it is the American way of life that ruined her sister, or whether it is being married to Max Weidenfeld that has made her so nice. He is a super old chap you know.

We then went to Harvard, to this party at Elliott House, there's a photo here of it. It was a boy we met on the boat, he had been in Oxford two years on a scholarship and is now out in Harvard doing research. We had a very pleasant time and met some interesting people there, one boy who is studying philosophy and has been two years in Oxford has a brother-in-law who ran the United Nations building in New York, he was the chief assistant architect on the job so we're hoping to see him, as well as Harrison, the architect, when we go back to New York next week.

On Thursday we had a real day for weather, the humidity was ninety five percent all day and was so uncomfy, everyone was just wet, then in the evening when we left the office there was a real storm coming in from the sea. It is a wonderful sight Boston in a storm as all the high buildings are lost in the low clouds, and every now and then you can see the red storm lights flashing on the buildings, and hear the ship's sirens and it is all quite eerie. They do not get a real fog, it's just this very wet cloud blowing off the sea, anyway Thursday evening from seven until eleven we had a real electric storm and torrential rain and the temperature dropped so rapidly and Friday was cold all day from it. You don't know what to wear when it does those jumps and so fast too.

I'm glad to hear Daddy and David are enjoying their trip in Ireland, all the men seem to have been busy, Father (Geoff's Father) *has been in Scotland and in London just recently. I just wrote to Rosa in Bergamo, Italy and had a long newsy letter back, she does envy us being here and would like to come herself for awhile.*

Lester Collins has given us some tickets for a concert on Tuesday evening, he just handed them to Geoff one day in a crit. (criticism of students' schemes) *in the Department. It sounds wonderful and Charles Munch is conducting. I'm glad your music lessons are so good Mummy, I bet you do enjoy it too.* (Mummy had decided to try to regain the high standard she had had on the piano, so was taking lessons.)

October the fourteenth

We have just had the most wonderful weekend, we went on Friday evening to New York, it is just over two hundred miles so isn't too far. A friend from the office took us and found a hotel with us when we arrived and would not let us pay for any petrol or tolls on the freeway. We found a good cheap hotel, five dollars a night for the two of us. On Saturday we went to the Lever House building, by Skidmore Owings and Merryl, which is brand new and very good, then to Fifth Avenue shopping, I bought some wonderful new shoes! About four-thirty we went to the top of the Empire State Building and it was just tremendous. When we got out at the hundred and second floor, the view just took our breath away, it really looks like a dream, quite unreal. We could see about sixteen miles around, out to sea, and over the East River and the Hudson River. They are the two strips of water that make Manhattan an island. Then we could see the various boroughs of New York, Yonkers, Brooklyn, the Bronx and over into New Jersey. We stayed there and watched the sunset and waited until the lights came on, it was so beautiful. Jean had asked us there for dinner at seven-thirty so we left the Empire State Building and hurried and changed and went by taxi to Jean and Jim Beckwiths. They are Auntie Dot's friends you know. They have a wonderful apartment on Sutton Place, overlooking the East River, with a garden in the back to the water. We had a beautiful dinner and a wonderful evening. Her husband used to be an architect but gave up in disgust at the American setup! Jean is expecting a baby in February so if Auntie Dot doesn't know, I guess she'd be interested. On Sunday we got up quite late and went to Central Park. It was a very hot sunny day and was just the weather for seeing Central Park. We walked pretty well over the park, and then lay on a bank in the sun.

We then went to look at the Guggenheim Museum by Frank Lloyd Wright on Fifth Avenue. It is very modern with some great paintings. The rooms are only small but beautifully furnished, with Bach music playing very softly as you look at the paintings. When we came out we got tangled up with the Columbus Day parade on 5th Avenue it went from two pm to six pm but was not very impressive.

On Sunday we went to a beautiful modern house in New York, a huge one for the Fairchild's. We just knocked at the door and told them who we were and they took us all around. It was so lavish, an amazing place to live in. Yesterday Monday we went around the United Nations building, it was all polished ready for the opening today, anyway we got in as Geoff had an introduction to the architect. It is all tremendous, and was so fascinating; all the delegates were in looking around so we had a super time. We left New York about three p.m. and went to Yale for four hours on the way home. That has another beautiful campus and it was so good to get the chance to see around. It was quite an outing!

Monday twentieth October.

The weather here has suddenly started jumping around the central heating goes full blast now, and today the temperature is thirty degrees and on Saturday it was quite warm. The temperature is given about every fifteen minutes on the radio so that's a help, though I still never hit on the right clothes. I don't know how I will manage this winter, they keep the buildings at about seventy five degrees all winter and at times it's down to zero outside, so that when you go in shops and cinemas and offices you just about die of the heat. Everyone has a perpetual cold in winter, from perspiring inside and then going into the freezing and raw wind outside.

Thursday twenty-third of October

We have been quite busy these last few days looking for a new apartment. We found we have been up in Cambridge, at Harvard quite a lot in the evenings, which means we have to eat over there, and then travel home late and although its only a little journey it still costs 15 cents each, any journey even a one stop ride is 15 cents, so that there and back for two is 60 cents which is about five shillings. We suddenly decided that we ought to try and save more out of my money for the trips we plan to make, so the best thing to do was one of us to live on the spot where they work. Well yesterday we *found a very nice apartment on Harvard Street, it isn't so lavish as this one but has a beautiful lounge with a bay window, a bedroom, bathroom and kitchen.It is unfurnished and is 70 dollars including central heating, and all electricity. Well we were paying $85 here and then a $5 or so electric bill. As well as this we will save on Geoff's fares and he will eat at home for lunch so we will save about $1 a day on that. Anyway we hope we'll be better off as we keep planning trips to Florida, California, Chicago and all around so we are going to need some money!*

I shall be just near the pottery I have been going to, in Cambridge and Geoff is five minutes from his department. We shall be really in the student atmosphere more too, I think once we move over we will enjoy it very much.

On Saturday we are going to hear Stevenson, which we're looking forward to. I went on Tuesday lunchtime to see Eisenhower arriving, and then went with all the throng to the common to hear him talk. It was the most amazing sight! For that time everyone went quite fanatical and there really seemed to be some election excitement, but it all finished straight after, and people were left looking lost and rather silly with their 'I like Ike flags' etc. He is such a likable character to see that I am afraid he will get in, because the Americans on the whole seem to be interested in the most peculiar things and seem not to be put off by a person not appearing very intelligent. On the party broadcasts on the radio people asked him how Mame makes her pancakes etc.! Truman is very unpopular, his mud slinging has done Stevenson a lot of harm too. Anyway we hope to be able to form our opinions on Stevenson's policy on Saturday (if he has one) We were sorry to hear people were put off Stevenson because he was being called an "Egghead" which I guess meant he was an intellectual, and they were out! We are both of us very well though it's a wonder we don't have colds, Tuesday morning the temperature was 30 degrees they had snow in New York, Maine and New Hampshire and now today it's been in the seventies all day, we just have to listen to the weather reports to know what to wear.

Third of November

Geoff had some good news for his birthday (October 31ˢᵗ) a letter from Lester Collins to say the committee had been considering his case and would now allow him to do his own research instead of the set course, so he is very pleased, he attends the lectures he thinks are good, and then spends all the rest of the time in the library, which is excellent, and probably the best architectural Library in the world. Every magazine article as well as book, is referenced to every person or building of interest. The course itself was very disappointing the people in the course were not very bright and it turns out they had all done their BA in another subject altogether, some in chemistry, geography and all sorts and Geoff had hoped he would learn quite a lot from the other folk, but of course he couldn't do it as they really didn't have any ideas about architecture. The English scholarship boys are so carefully picked and then put with these others, who of course pay the full seven hundred dollars but most of the English are very dissatisfied and some go home straight away. It should have been explained to students from abroad what a Masters course is in the U.S. Anyway there are no hard feelings between Lester Collins and Geoff although Collins is a very nasty sort of man to deal with. He wanted Geoff to write a letter to the committee saying he was leaving the course on health grounds, so that there would be no criticism of his course. Geoff didn't do that though. His wife has invited Geoff and I out there to Thanksgiving dinner the last Thursday in November. It is the party of the year here with turkey and all the trimmings so it should be good, but it's very odd for him to ask us I think, and not any of the others who have stuck to his course. Last weekend we had a wonderful time we went to a concert at Symphony Hall, with two people from Geoff's office, and then afterwards went to the Stevenson rally here in Boston. The whole election here is very interesting, but very complicated, we have enjoyed seeing one though, very much. Although Eisenhower is a favorite around here, it is impossible to judge the whole of America, this part is so unlike anywhere else. We are just going to be as surprised as the rest of the world by who gets in, but apparently the London bookies have 7:5 odds on

Eisenhower. They seem to be America's only guide! (Eisenhower did in fact get in, so the bookies were right)

On the Sunday we telephoned Henry to see if he'd like to go to the beach as it was such a perfect day, so he called for us and we went to Nahant and climbed all over the rocks in a lovely little bay, it was a beautiful day. In the evening the temperature dropped to below freezing and we went with some friends to see an old Charles Laughton and Elsa Lanchester film, and an old Eisenstein one at the Boston Film club. I think Geoff caught a cold on the Saturday but all last week he had a very bad one. Now the weather is hot again very humid so that one is damp all the time. How humid is it in England? I've never been so aware of the climate before, but I'm sure you don't have an 85 percent and 95 percent humidity do you?

Monday 3rd November (A letter to Geoff's Family)

Geoff had quite a good Birthday in spite of having an awful cold all last week. I bought him a tie. The main thing I'm buying him is a Remington typewriter from Mrs. Gropius. It is almost unused and Geoff is to get it today. He is very thrilled, it is a Remington portable, silent. He has been finding it difficult to type his articles and various things for Harvard too. We went out to dinner at the Copley Plaza Hotel, there was a floor show, and dancing and a very good dinner so we enjoyed it. The ladies were all given cases of lipstick and nail polish. (We were amazed to find that after all the wild cocktails that were served on a carousel bar, grasshoppers, dry martinis, old fashioned, Alexander's, sidecars, daiquiris to name a few, people were having a glass of milk with their dinner! Guess they had not got used to wine with food at that time.)

Last night we met Henry the friend from Geoff's office and asked him to come home for dinner. We went and did the shopping for the meal, then Henry, who used to live in Mexico, and has a taste for very strong food, suggested we buy some Armenian tortillas, they are made fresh in a small Armenian kitchen and you take them home and warm them under the grill and they are delicious. So we started off with tomato juice, then the kind of pancakes, which you roll up and eat, about 4, and then with them we had avocados, and a bottle of wine with it. Afterwards we had strawberries and cream and coffee so it was quite a meal. We were going out about 8.30 to a friend who was giving an election party. It was very lively, in fact there is a lot of excitement these last few days, with loudspeakers going all around and posters all over, and each group of politicians having a real go at the other. Tomorrow it will be all over anyway and I'll be glad about that.

A typed letter from Geoffrey from our new apartment, 358 Harvard St., Cambridge, dated twenty sixth of November 1952.

I am writing you a letter using my typewriter on June's orders as a birthday celebration, although it is now nearly a month since my birthday! We feel very ashamed not to have written for so long but moving into the new apartment and doing all our Christmas presents, has kept us so busy. After Thanksgiving (tomorrow) Christmas really starts, June says they have been busy erecting an eighty foot Christmas tree on Boston Common in front of the State House, and all the nice shops. In Cambridge Shopping Center they have fixed red candles on to all the lamp posts and garland festoons along one side of the road all round Harvard Square. It's going to look very Christmassy at any rate!

We had a surprise last weekend. Uncle Wally flew in to see us- he was visiting New England on business, and said that while he was so near (only two hundred or three hundred miles away!) He thought he would drop in and see us. Wasn't it good of him? He stayed with Mrs. Brinnin; she is the person who knew Wally and Dolly very well in Detroit, and later moved to a very modern apartment block in Boston overlooking the Charles River. By a strange chance I rang her up on Friday night to see when John would be back from New York, where he had been to make an appearance on TV-John is her son and, about 32 or so who is a literary critic and lecturer- and so she told me that Wally had phoned to say he would be arriving at 9 p.m.

He phoned us straight away and we arranged to meet him with Mrs. Brinnin at the Sheraton Plaza Hotel for lunch on Saturday. Saturday was the day of the great Yale versus Harvard football game, so was very busy and full of excitement-although the weather was very disappointing. Harvard Square was full of visitors. We took the Christmas parcel for you to the post office, as we had been busy packing it on Friday night. By the way June says you must definitely not open parcels until Christmas Day. Not even mothers (June says especially not mothers)

However would you believe it, the man in the parcels office picked up our parcel and shook it and there was a slight rattle, and so he wouldn't accept it for insurance, he said that unless things were packed absolutely tight everything would get broken. Of course we knew this, but one of the presents was quite unbreakable but in a small box, and it was this that made all the noise. So we had to undo the whole thing. June was very fed up. By this time when we left the post office -still with the parcel, we re-packed it on Sunday- it was quite late, but we had a coffee in Schrafts with an English chap we ran into, and then went home to change.

June put on her gray suit and white blouse and wore her blue hat and looked very pretty. We took a taxi and were not too late! I was very surprised after June's descriptions, to see Uncle Wally as she has always said how big he was. But he really does look very American now and he was very nice to us straight away and we were busy talking about everything we had seen, and he said we haven't seen anything yet! June thinks he has changed a lot, from her memories of him. Although this was only as far back as 1947 she thinks he has definitely altered since then. We spent all afternoon over lunch, and then went up to one of the private suites of the Sheraton plaza to see a very wealthy English woman whom Mrs. Brinnin knew and wanted Uncle to meet. She was very funny; she had composed a dance tune which the leader of the Sheraton dance band is getting published for her. She played for us, it was very queer. In the evening we had a lovely dinner in a Boston restaurant, and I had a thick juicy filet mignon steak.

On Sunday afternoon we showed Uncle round Harvard Yard and took him in the modern Graduate Center designed by Gropius, which he liked very much and thought it was very luxurious. We called in the International Center for tea and met a lot of our friends there, who we introduced to Uncle so we had quite a party. We were invited to Detroit for Christmas so June has been very excited about it and has been inquiring about plane and rail fares. It seems such a long way away. We are hoping to see Bill and Betty, (my cousin Bill Holroyd) on the same trip, that is even further away still, in Toronto—miles and miles!

The new apartment is beginning to look very nice and we are quite used to living here now. It is really very much more convenient to live so near to Harvard. It was really so dirty when we took it over, June was nearly in tears every time she looked at it. After our other one it seems such a come down. Fortunately we had a week to do all this cleaning before moving in, so by that time it had been transformed. It is in a very pleasant street, quiet and full of trees, and we have a huge corner bay window, which catches the sun. I have my desk in this and it is really quite delightful to sit and work and look around in all directions. Also we have a huge balcony in front of the living room and bathroom, which is very nice to see through the windows. It will be nicer still to sit out on it in the summer. The landlord is buying paint for us to pep up the colors in the bedroom, and shellac for the floors, which were very good once upon a time but have been allowed to deteriorate. June says that in the office people have told her that houses which had always been lived in by students, are usually in this condition, as the students do not stay very long and most of them don't bother too much about things while they are studying. Henry Fournier and Alison King were very good in helping us move. They arrived with their cars before 9 a.m. and Alison had borrowed a ski-rack to fix on her roof, so that we could fill it with the biggest things like the mattress. We were going to use the bedsprings that were stored in the basement of this house, but at 6 p.m. we went to get them and found they were hopelessly twisted. We went out to some second hand shops -still open-bought a spring for 4 dollars and carried it home ourselves! Tomorrow we are going to Lester Collins home in Weston for Thanksgiving dinner, so we are having baths and hair washing. I am really enjoying my work now at Harvard, and taking full advantage of opportunities not available in England. As a research student everyone takes a much greater interest in anything you are asking them about, *if they can help. I feel very sorry that June's work is so uninteresting although, as Uncle Wally told her, she's bound to get something out of it.*

A PS from me-

This housework when it is so dirty makes you black in no time, but the apartment is looking lovely and so cosy and warm, it's more like home than the other one, but not quite so modern! They are all students in the house, the ones below us have a baby but we never hear it, it's very good and quiet after Beacon Street.

Thursday, fourth of December

We have been very busy on the flat, we washed the walls and paints and floors with an acid cleaner, then painted the bedroom, three white walls and one lovely light blue one, and cleaned all the windows too and they look much better. We have 6 large windows in the living room that we gave a real clean as they were black. Last weekend I spent the whole weekend doing the bedroom and living room floors, cleaning them and then doing them with shellac. They now look so wonderful, the whole apartment does, it's amazing the change in it. We wanted to get it all done, as I have to work this Saturday and the next, so we get a longer Christmas holiday. These office hours are really tremendous and there is no break at all and you really have to work hard otherwise they throw you out pretty quick. Most people are in about 8.15 in the morning and leave at 5.15 with three quarters of an hour for lunch, it's quite a day.

We have been having our first really cold spell, on Monday it was 19 degrees all day and the cold just seemed to go right through you. As I walked down to the train (To go under the river to Boston) in the morning my eyes ran so much I could hardly see! The amazing thing is that inside our office is kept at 75-80 degrees all day, so that I can't bear to wear a winter vest, I just put on jumpers and scarves when I go out. The men wear thin summer like white shirts in the office and no winter underclothes. It is nice as I walk home in the evening to know I am coming home to a really warm apartment. We have 3 windows open all the time so it is not too boiling, but we have not yet bought a blanket.

Monday December eighth.

First I congratulate Geoff's brother Michael and his wife Barbara on the birth of their little girl Julia.

This last weekend has been just beautiful here. It was still a little cold but so clear and sunny with the most beautiful blue skies. Yesterday Geoff and I took a bus to Lexington and from there went a wonderful walk and then had tea at a little old coffee house on the sort of green of the village. It is funny in this area as there are little plaques up where a stray British bullet landed, and bridges where fierce battles were fought and so many British fell. They are all kept alive these tales and it is the only history of the area, that and the landing of the Puritans on Plymouth Rock, and the Boston Tea Party. Lexington is full of little figures of the minute men, who were the home guard and were ready to fight in a minute.

On Saturday of course, I worked. We had dinner out in the evening and then a friend, a metallurgist, came home with us. Yesterday evening we had an architect friend from New York State round for the evening. We have some beautiful berries, brilliant red ones, and bright green fir branches in the flat. We've also got quite a crowd of big bright witch balls in the flat so it looks very Christmasy. The shops are just a dream, I do wish you could see them. Each one is covered in fairy lights, candles, Father Christmas figures, Holly and wonderful figures moving around, and all the streets have fairy lights strung on the lampposts, all the way along. The Christmas trees on the islands in the middle of the roads, with the lights all over, it is really just so much, it's unbelievable.

Sunday twenty first of December

A Very Happy Christmas and all of the best of everything for 1953, to you all. We are now getting very excited about Christmas, the shops are wonderful and all the houses have candles in the windows, Christmas trees, and holly wreaths on the doors it looks beautiful. We had our office party at one of the hotels in Boston on Friday, we had two large rooms with dancing in one and food and drinks in the other. Good food too, lobster, pate de foie gras and caviar! It was just Friday afternoon but was quite nice. Better than working anyway.

Yesterday I had my hair cut very short and permed, it looks beautiful. It was a $20.95 perm as a Christmas gift reduced to nine dollars. I wondered about it, however it turned out very well. We fly on Wednesday evening to Detroit, and Dolly and Wally will meet us at the airport. We are keeping our fingers crossed for the weather as we have two changes to make, in Providence and one in Buffalo so we hope it is good flying weather for all the landings and take offs.

Mrs. Brinnin and John came round one evening last week, they were just off to Florida, to the hot sun and beaches for Christmas, so they came to wish us Christmas greetings, and I gave her some lovely french soap. Mrs. Siggourney and Mrs. Thomas came to tea today and brought us a homemade Christmas cake. I got Dolly a small bottle of Chanel #5 and Wally a wool scarf and a Chinese puzzle, and some lipstick and nail polish for Sally. She is a girl who ran away from home about two years ago and has lived with them ever since. (Dolly and Wally never had any children of their own.) *We brought Billy and Bobby, Geoff's nephews in Canada, some really American toys.*

We have been this evening for dinner and to a party at the International Student Center we had some films and carols and decorated a huge tree. We brought a philosopher from Belgium home with us for supper so now he has just gone and I am finishing this.

We go to Canada on New Year's Eve all being well. Hope you all have a wonderful Christmas!

Tuesday January 6th 1953

As you will see we are now back home after a really great tour of over three thousand miles! We had such a super time every minute that the days went so quickly. Dolly and Wally were very kind to us indeed. On Christmas Day about 12 of us went to a large hotel called the Whittier, for Christmas dinner in the evening, we could see Canada across the river! Wally and Dolly are very entertaining, Dolly was chatting away all the time and telling us all the funny episodes they have had, and they have had hundreds.

Our flight up to Detroit was beautiful and very exciting taking off over the sea like you do from Boston. I took a film of the first part so I hope it will turn out well enough for you to get the feel of flying over Boston. We went on Boxing Day to see the Lone Ranger do a program, all the children are Lone Ranger fans here. Wally and Dolly had a party on Christmas Day and the writer of the program was there with his wife so he asked us all out. We seem to have had a succession of parties. Wally and Dolly Christmas Day with about 18 people, then Boxing Day we went to the University Club with the writer of the Lone Ranger and some other people, then Irene Kent Smith gave us a dinner party. We spent one afternoon going round the Chrysler factory and watched one car being made completely, the whole assembly takes one and a half hours. Another afternoon we went round General Motors Laboratories which are new and Geoffrey has been asked by Edilizia Moderna to do an article. Geoff went to see the Finnish architect Eero Saarinen. He was very kind and Geoff was with him for ages, and he was very helpful.

Irene took us to Cranbrook Academy of Fine Art one afternoon. It was started by Eliel Saarinen the father of Eero, he came from Helsinki. Wally took us around the early skyscrapers that he did the steel calculations on when he was with Albert Kahn. Dolly took us to her favorite dress shops in Detroit, and I tried lots of beautiful dresses and gave them both a fashion parade. One evening we went a drive to Grosse Point, where all the big mansions are, to see their Christmas decorations. They are on the shores of Lake St. Claire and looked so beautiful.

We went over from Detroit to Canada on the ferry, in the train on a boat, on New Year's eve, and Bill and Betty (Bill is Geoff's cousin) met us in Toronto; even that distance is quite a trip, from 12 noon to 8.30 pm anyway it was by the lake and we had a very good dinner on the train. When we arrived they were all there to meet us at the station. We went to some friends for a New Year party, and they took us on New Years day to Niagara Falls, they were wonderful. It was so freezing that the spray froze *on us. It was a lovely drive there and back these lakes are just like seas you know, you can't see any land at all.*

We had to leave on Saturday evening as we were still far from home, so we traveled by train all Saturday night to Montreal and arrived there for breakfast and to see the town. It is just like France, everyone was speaking French but the temperature was 6 degrees below zero and the wind cut right through you. We came home Sunday a 10 hour train ride through Vermont in very deep snow, it was just like a dream. Really beautiful villages with white timber buildings all grouped around a circular village green, with a church and a white painted spire, it looked wonderful in the snow, from a warm train!

January 20th 1953

Christmas is all well and truly over here, I'm afraid there was never very much Christmas spirit as we would think of it, the tremendous·effect that is achieved is only a commercial thing and all the shops vie with each other to do the most fantastic things, but the actual shopping is very unpleasant. The shop where we bought your food parcel is a very good one and that part of the shopping was great. I do hope the food was all good, but S. S. Pierce is the best food store in Boston so I think it would be all right. Did you have to pay duty on our gifts? I was surprised when our gifts came to find we had a duty to pay on them I thought gifts and especially Christmas ones could come in all right. Do let me know if there's any food that you would like me to send, we can send ham or meat parcels, steaks and joints, or fruit, or sugar anything you need, or a tin of butter. (England still had all the food rationed at this time.)

We have been very busy recently Geoff met a boy from Norway, Chris Norberg Schulz, who has studied architecture in Switzerland and came to Harvard to work with Gropius, who of course is no longer here (Gropius was supposed to be here this year, it was to have been his last year but he and Dean Hudnut had had a row and Gropius resigned a year early) *Chris said he didn't find the Masters course at all interesting and has dropped out and is now working with Geoff. They are visiting various professors for help and taking all their work, and last Friday I was asked too. It was to see the Dean of the school of Architecture from Athens University, Professor Michelis. He is over to give a few lectures here and is staying with his wife Effie in a hotel in Cambridge. He and his wife were very charming and we had a wonderful evening, they're quite old and so very Greek too. Geoff and Chris spent quite a few visits talking over different things and all these professors are so friendly and generous with their ideas. Last night we went to a lecture in Harvard to hear Professor Michelis. Tonight we were in town looking through the new summer dresses. Tomorrow I am going to pottery again, I wonder if I will have forgotten all I knew? I hope not.*

Last weekend we did a very exciting thing we went on Sunday to New Hampshire skiing for the day. We went to a place called Mount Sunapee it is about one hundred and seventy miles from here so was quite a trip. Anyway, we left home at 5.30 in the morning and were in the beautiful mountains by 10. We went with the students again and three cars of us went. Ours was a shooting brake with 9 of us in and full of skis and sticks and boots! We took a picnic lunch and had it there in a lodge so the only expense was a dollar each toward petrol and then two dollars and 70 cents to hire skis boots and poles. The chair lifts were quite expensive, so Geoff had one ride while I was busy learning how to stop other than sitting down! We did enjoy it, the sun was out and was so beautiful on all the new snow, skiing was fun too, you'd be amazed how awkward you feel with those long things on your feet, and when you first start at the top of a hill you are racing down in a few seconds, stopping is one of the difficult things! Geoff did famously too, he thought he would twist his ankle or something. However he didn't and was on his feet more than I was. New Hampshire is very beautiful and to see unspoiled snow was such a treat as ours in Boston is so dismal. It is snowing again this evening though the last few days have been very nice weather for a change. We left Sunapee about five, feeling so tired after all the mountain air, and got home about 9.30 after some wonderful skids on the road. On Monday we were so stiff we could hardly move and my shoulder muscles from pushing with the sticks, were just terrible. However it's better now and we're all ready for our next dose. They go out each weekend if we just have the time to join them. Last Saturday we bought some good ski togs, Geoff got a huge sweater about one inch thick and very warm and I got a bright orange red ski jacket with a hood and its nylon so is very light weight but very warm, and looks so smart with my black trousers.

Sunday February 1st.

We have had a wonderful week really the weather has been good, about 35 degrees most of the week. Last weekend we went on the Sunday with Henry to see some new schools near Boston, and then we returned to Boston for 3.45 to the Conservatory of Music to see Andre Segovia play his guitar. It was wonderful, nothing like a Hawaiian guitar at all. He played some beautiful Bach pieces, and didn't strum his guitar but played each note separately and it sounded like a harpsichord. We have been to 3 or 4 of the concerts at the Boston Symphony here with Munch conducting they are terrific. The seats are $2 so if it is cold we find it better to stay at home and have the concert on our FM radio. The BBC is on each night so we hear lots of your talks and plays. Last Saturday we heard Bronowski's play "The face of Violence" which was exceptionally good, done by the BBC.

On Monday we visited a boy from my office in the new apartment building where Mrs. Brinnin lives. In one of the corridors we met Gordon Kirby who was talking to an Englishman he'd just met in the elevator. Gordon was the boy we met at first who took us to Manchester by the sea. The chap he had just met was so English, in funny english clothes but so amusing and pleasant. He was one of the editorial staff of Punch magazine so Geoff and he knew a lot of folk in common, Roland Emmett one of them and he also worked on the festival of Britain; so I could hardly drag them apart. He is over here for a time working on the editorial staff of Christian Science Monitor. It is surprising how interesting any lively person from Europe seems here, there's just something that clicks as soon as you meet them, of course there are a few odd queer ones, but Christian Norberg Schultz this Norwegian friend and professor Michelis and his wife and several other ones we've met are wonderful people. When you first meet the Americans you think how good they are going to be, because they are instantly so friendly, but then you find they are the same with everyone they meet, they seldom seem to have a good friend and having once met one, and had a very pleasant evening you think that perhaps they may be a good friend, then you never see them again, and perhaps if you do, they have almost forgotten who you are, so you never get to know anyone well, in fact I don't think there's any more in them to get to know, other than what you first see in them.

Yesterday we had another wonderful day, we went down to explore old Boston, that is all the tip of the main headland, with the docks and the old houses. It is a fascinating part and we had lunch in the Blue Ship on T wharf, which is right out in the sea with fishing boats all around, and large steamers too. The sun was brilliant and it is just like another world from Boston, that I am in everyday. The Blue Ship has low ceilings and beams and the pianist was playing Beethoven, and it was so peaceful watching the boats bobbing in the sun. We then walked up to the Old North Church and the old burial ground on the Hill, we were amazed at this area it was all Italian, shops, people, chatter and even the dirt! It all looked lovely on a sunny day with the very narrow streets and everyone buying from little carts in the street. We bought some artichokes and were tempted to buy some salami, but wondered about carrying it around all day! The Old North Church is one of the typical old New England ones with a Wren type spire built in 1723 by the early immigrants, anyway we took photos all day so we hope we should be able to show you what we saw. We walked down to the old dock where H.M.S. Constitution was built against the British and we hoped to go across by ferry to the airport. However we found the ferry was closed for good, two weeks ago, so we had to go under on the underground, under the sea to the airport. We went onto the roof of the airport and watched the planes coming in and out and loading. It made us quite excited to see all the activity. We watched a large BOAC plane take off for England and then a Trans World Airlines leaving for France. They are beautiful things to see and the idea of people going to so many different places so quickly is very intriguing. We went out for a quick walk this afternoon. Today is particularly cold, ten degrees with an icy wind but beautiful sun. It made our eyes stream so we did not walk far.

We had a real shock last weekend, we called into the architecture department to see one of the lecturers and found that Lester Collins had been fired. He had been told on the Thursday to leave on Friday. We were surprised to find out the Dean knew what he was like. The department is now left high and dry and the students are annoyed to have paid six hundred dollars and to lose their lecturer. I think they'll be better off without him. Geoff and Chris are now attending some very good lectures, not only architecture ones, and are up to their eyes in work. Geoff comes home for lunch each day as we are so near and it saves our money for other things. One day last week I had left him a cauliflower cheese to warm up and when I came home it was still there and lots of burned-out matches all round the oven! He is a comic, he doesn't like the gas oven, because you have to light it.

Sunday Feb. 8th

We have just had quite an exciting week! One day, Monday we got the oven on fire, and on Tuesday we had burglars in the house. The first mishap, we were having pork chops and I was busy grilling them and they caught fire, so I pushed them back into the oven and turned off the gas. Anyway next time I opened it up the flames were higher than ever and all the fat in the bottom of the pan was on fire too, so I came in to tell Geoff and he came to see what he could do. We tried blowing and it was no good, so I got a pan full of water and threw it in the oven all over the pork chops, and then when we closed the oven the flames went out. So we just had vegetables to eat for dinner. It took me all evening to clean the kitchen walls, they were black from the smoke, and then to clean the oven!

On Tuesday evening the girl from the flat above us came in to see if we had heard anyone around the house during the day as she had had her radio, record player and gold jewelry from her grandmother stolen. Luckily Geoff had been in our apartment so we were quite O.K. Geoff heard someone go upstairs about 10.15 in the morning, but thought it was someone who lives here as there are always people in and out, but the girl on the ground floor saw a man she'd never seen before, coming at 10.15 so that must have been the one. I told Geoff if he hears anyone else when he is working, not to go out and see who it is, as so many of the burglars here are armed, so it is not worth risking anything! It must have been someone who had been watching the house because there are students in all four apartments except that top floor which two girls have, and they go out to work each day.

Wednesday Feb.25th

This last weekend was a holiday for Washington's Birthday so we had another long weekend. We had Prof. and Mrs. Michelis round for the evening. They are very entertaining as you can imagine. She is having an exhibition of her paintings in one of the art galleries. They are older than us but very interesting to be with. On Sunday morning a boy Alfredo Della Paolera, (isn't that a great name?) who is an architect in my office came around in his car to pick us up. We went first about 50 miles to see a new school by Gropius and Partners, which we have been wanting to see, then we went from there to Newport, Rhode Island. It was a fantastic place. It is that headland into the Atlantic where the Vanderbilts and many wealthy people built summer palaces at the beginning of the century. Now empty, they stand very dramatically on the cliffs, and on Sunday the waves were crashing onto the rocky coastline, and the Vanderbilt's house, which is probably the biggest of them all was like some wonderful film set. They are like huge hotels and all are perfect copies of French or Italian Renaissance, and some in English style architecture too. We were amazed. We had some lovely runs on the beach with Fred's little dog.

On Monday we went out to Wellesley to see a man called Irving Fine. He is the head of the music department at Brandice College near here and Roger Fowler our musical friend in London, gave us an introduction to him. Roger met him when they were both in Paris and later in Salzburg, Irving was lecturing there. He is only quite young and a very good chap, he is about 35 and has a wife and two little girls Emily and Claudia. We had a wonderful time with them and he is such a sympathetic person to talk to.

Yesterday- Tuesday we went to an excellent lecture by a Danish architect, and tonight we have been to a concert in the Music Department. given by an English composer pianist playing contemporary British sonatas.

March 5th 1953

We were so pleased to get your letter with the photos, Elizabeth seems to be getting so big, she looks as though she has grown a lot since we left. Jolly (her dog) looks sweet too, I like the way his ears go straight up for such a long way and then just curl over the last bit!

We have had another very busy week, on Monday we went to one of a series of lectures we have been going to by a modern poet, and on Tuesday we went to hear an architecture lecture by Professor Fisker who is head of the Copenhagen School of Architecture and he's just visiting here. We went afterwards to have a glass of wine with his daughter and her husband, who are living in Cambridge and who Geoff knows. On Wednesday evening Geoff met me in town and we went to see "Moulin Rouge" which is an excellent film about the painter Toulouse Lautrec, Jose Ferrer played the lead character and he was brilliant, it was very good. On Thursday I went to my pottery and Geoff to a lecture, I glazed about 6 pots so had quite a busy evening. Effie Michelis wants us to go on Sunday to see the exhibition of her paintings with them, so if we don't go anywhere else, I guess we will go there.

We had a wonderful surprise today a check arrived from the income tax people for one hundred and fifty dollars so we celebrated by buying a joint of meat! It's our first one since we came to America but they are so huge and so expensive that we always buy steaks and chops and veal etc. This joint is rump steak of beef, just over four pounds of it so I shall cook it tomorrow, and we will have it cold for quite a few days. It was the smallest joint they had so you can imagine what they're like! We thought we would buy a bottle of California wine to go with it, as a real treat.

Last Sunday Geoff and I went down to the old harbour here in Boston, and down to the fish pier. It was so cold I thought we'd freeze to death. It was about ten degrees, but felt so much worse as there was a tremendous gale wind, however it was brilliant sunshine so we took some cine film of it. It is the most fascinating part of Boston, we were watching large ships loading and unloading, planes coming in across the harbor at the airport and huge aircraft carriers and submarines (like queer sea monsters) in the Navy yard. On the fish pier there were some boats covered in ice from mast to stern they must have been out in the rough seas the previous night. I was hearing on the news about a 25 foot high wave, I remember once telling you Daddy, about a wave that size towering over a small boat and you not believing me Pa, do you remember?

My office work is the same as ever, it is a tremendous size, chronic diseases hospital that I'm working on, it is up to about the 5th floor and is a 15 million tender price, so you can imagine the size of it. All the construction and planning is very lavish and wasteful so I have nothing to learn from that, but as far as the gadgets are concerned it is just unbelievable. We are having coloured television of all the operations, which the other doctors in the hospital can turn on and see the operation, and the camera lens is so fine that on a thing like an eye operation you can adjust it so that the eye is about 20 times normal size. The screens are very large and so you see it probably better than the chief surgeon. I've been busy working on the television equipment and fixing of cameras and microphones etc. and now I am working on a revolving altar in the hospital. We have a large Chapel and it has a revolving altar with three different religions served. A Jewish Ark, a Catholic and a Protestant altar. It's really like a small revolving stage and runs on ball bearings. I am quite pleased to be doing these sort of things as they are the only things to be learned in the office, the ordinary detailing and over building every part is a shocking waste, but then there's a lot of waste in everything, paper, food, and all building.

We have had one or two letters recently from people in London, working on the coronation, they sound very busy, I guess it will all be exciting. There's always a lot about it around here, with films on television and posters to travel to Europe, but all the passages were booked up last June for this spring, so if folks haven't already booked they have had it I should think.

Well must go now I feel very dozy, it has been snowing a little but it is very warm in our apartment I can never remember how cold it is outside.

March 15th.

Last Sunday we went with Prof. and Mrs. Michelis and some other Harvard professors to see Mrs. Michelis' exhibition of paintings. The museum was the most wonderful spot, a huge house that has been redone inside with modern interiors, it is in the country and stands on a hill looking down onto a lake, and trees in every direction. The paintings were lovely, very charming Greek ones with the most beautiful little houses and blue skies, it looks a lovely country. After we had spent the afternoon in the museum we were asked to a cocktail party at one of the Harvard professors who teaches architecture and lives next door to Gropius in Lincoln. He has a wonderful house, a modern timber one set in a silver birch wood, very attractive. We met a Greek architect there so about six of us found a small wing off the lounge with a huge coal fire in it, so there we sat with Professor Bognor, talking about American architecture. We came home with some Cambridge people, professors, and the Michelis's and then went to these people in Cambridge for supper, so we had a very good day.

On Thursday I got about six pots so was very pleased, three of them are beautiful I think I shall try to sell them. On Friday evening we went to a concert given by the Harvard Choral Society. A huge choir, well, really three choirs, and the girls University in Cambridge, Radcliffe, took part. It was really wonderful, they sang 16th - 18th century French and Italian motets, chansons, and the main works were Giovanni Gabrieli's music written for the Church of St. Marks, Venice- very powerful music too. When we got into our seats we found we were sitting next to some friends so they came back here for a glass of wine. On Thursday when I went off to pottery I left Chris and Geoff busy working on some new scheme, however about 9.45 Geoff came down with Henry by car to call for me, and Henry had been here all evening as he was going off to New York to work the next day so had come to say goodbye to us. The two of them had had a very lively evening of course with no work! Yesterday we went with Chris and a friend of his from

Oslo. The friend is a typographer who is at present working on the New York Times, and he had come down to stay with Chris for the weekend. We all went a walk around downtown Boston in the afternoon, it was beautiful and warm and sunny and I wore my gray summer coat for the first time. It was a very rapid change as the beginning of the week Boston had its coldest yet this winter a steady 8 degrees, yesterday was mid fifties.

We went to the top of the Custom House to see the view, and then walked in the old Italian area and had some delicious Italian pastries! We went to eat at a very famous Greek restaurant the Athens Olympia, where T.S. Eliot used to eat when he was at Harvard. We had a super Greek meal with wine. When we got halfway through, the Michelis' came in! He is going to lecture in Washington tomorrow so they were leaving today, but want us to see them next weekend as they return to Athens at the end of this month. After our dinner we went and saw the neon lights of our downtown area around the cinema district and then came home here to chat. The two Norwegians have a wonderful sense of humor so we had a very amusing evening. Today we have been in the Boston City Library working. Our large joint was a good idea, it was a real money saver, I had it in sandwiches three days and Geoff had it each day till Thursday and we had it each evening, hot, with barbecue sauce, once in gravy and finally on Thursday evening as a stew! We were quite glad to see the last of it though.

Sunday March 22nd

We have just had the most wonderful spring weekend, very pleasantly warm with brilliant sunshine and blue skies. Yesterday we set off down to M.I.T. it is the other large University here in Cambridge, but it is mainly technical and Sciences, and Harvard is more Arts. It is a huge place with lots of modern buildings, and we were on our way to see a new dormitory block designed by Alvar Alto, a Finnish professor when he was here lecturing. We had been to see it before but were going for a second trip. On our way down we saw a film star, Magda Gabor landing by helicopter in Harvard yard, the center of the campus, to give a pint of blood in the campaign that's going on here. What a thing to suddenly come upon! We *met a chap down at the dormitory, who took us around everywhere and in to see all his friends rooms. Afterwards we went to see the swimming pool, also new, and then we went to a wonderful cafe they have there on the campus where you can get the hugest wonderful ice cream for only 15 cents, which is very cheap here for ice cream. The students do the serving all dressed up like cooks so they give everyone about three scoops instead of one. I could hardly eat mine. The ice cream here is really amazing as they have so many varieties and Howard Johnson's, that is a chain of restaurants all over America, prides itself on having 60 kinds of ices. After dinner we went down to Harvard to the Brattle theatre to see the 9.30 showing of a very good French film. It is only cheap, 80 cents, which is a student price, most films are $1.20.*

This morning Allison King a girl from Geoff's old office came, to see if we would like to go into the country as all the office were going out, to lay out a new house they are doing. So we went to this place, Peacock Farm it was wonderful and such a perfect day. We went a walk all round, and then helped lay out the site, it was quite amusing! Walter Pierce asked us back to his house to tea so Alison, Geoff and I went, and some other folk from Harvard, Walter and Marianne Fauburg were there too, when we arrived. (This was the first time we met Thais Carter, who turned out to be a very good friend until she died about 25 years ago) *We have been to Walter and Marianne's before, she is Danish and her father and mother are over here for a six month visit, he has been lecturing here at Harvard. Walter and Marianne have a little baby about three months old, a sweet little thing.*

Saturday 28th March.

This week we had a good thing happen, we sold all the furniture in the apartment, for July. I decided that as lots of students were looking for apartments, that I would let Harvard know that ours would be vacant, and tell them we wanted whoever had it to take all the furniture pots and pans etc. we immediately had about ten phone calls and sold everything very quickly, to a student and his fiancee who are being married in June.

Our plans for July are still very hazy, I am writing to Wally to see if he can see a good and fairly cheap car for us, I think we should get one for seven hundred dollars, and then we shall tour around for awhile, leaving most of our things here in Boston until we return. We had an offer from a friend to take us to Mexico and share expenses with her, but if we can possibly get our own car we would be much better off. So far we have seven hundred and fifty dollars or so and Geoff will take a job again in a week or two, so will be able to earn eight hundred dollars in two and a half months. We are now very anxious to see the rest of America as we really have no idea of it, from this New England area, I think it will probably be better too in California and out in the farming country.

Geoff is now busy with his Edilizia Moderna article and then after that we will start our plans going. Last Sunday we had a lovely afternoon in the country, and Monday Geoff came and had lunch with me in town as he had to go and see the editor of the Christian Science Monitor, we went to the top of the courthouse, which is the highest building in Boston, and it was so clear we could see for miles, you aren't really allowed up, but as we are English, they took us. Every time we open our mouths we get asked where we come from in England. We had chosen the most perfect day for the view and the sea looked wonderful, it is such a pity that you don't have the feeling of being near the sea at all, until you go down near the harbours.

On Tuesday we went round and had the evening with Professor and Effie Michelis, our last one for a while as they left yesterday to return to Athens. Anyway we have their address in Athens and they often come to England so we shall see them again for certain. They were a very nice pair, we were sorry to see them go. On Thursday I went to my pottery and made two more bowls, I am getting quite a collection of things. On Friday Chris left for Chicago for two weeks on a visit to see a wonderful architect, Mies Van der Rohe, a German architect who at the moment is one of the most famous in the world. We hope we will be able to visit him in the summer when we go to Chicago, we shall hear soon from Chris how he got on.

Last night we went to the Brattle Theater here in Harvard to see a great French film "Les Enfants du Paradis" it was super, Geoff had seen it before, but I hadn't, and we both enjoyed it tremendously. We went with a friend Christopher Wright who is a philosophy lecturer here, then when we came out we met Bob Nealy and a girl Mary, and Bob asked us to go for coffee. He is living in the same apartment building as Mrs. Brinnin we had a lovely evening and night, it was three by the time we got through! It's so beautiful to sit and watch all the neon lights and the skyline of Boston reflected in the River, I would love to live near the water like that. Today we have spent the afternoon in the Lamont library in Harvard. Geoff is working on his article for Edilizia Moderna and today we got some excellent photos (they are very expensive) taken by a photographer in New York. The article is to be a description of General Motors new research buildings in Detroit, that we visited at Christmas. Have you seen any of the articles in the Architect and Building News? The last one was the March 5th issue so if you are in the library David, or Brian you may like to read it through, it will be like having another letter from us as they are very news filled as to what we've been doing and seeing. (Geoff had been asked before we left London to contribute a diary of our travels and interesting modern buildings, for the English magazine Architect and Building News)

April 6th

We have just had Easter weekend. Went to see two films "High Noon" and "The African Queen" both excellent. One of the days we took the trolley to Winthrop Beach, which reminded me of the pebble beaches in Llandudno. (Where Granny Whitham lived.) *We went to Mrs. Brinnin's for dinner one night, her son John was in New York, as he runs a poetry centre there, and he always has poets from England over, last week he had Louis Mc. Neice, and last weekend Osbert and Edith Sitwell, Elizabeth Bowen the week before, and Dylan Thomas is coming to stay with them for one or two weeks.* (Dylan came over on one of the few flights and had spent the whole time in the air, drinking at the bar. I think when John met him in New York he had to go straight to the hospital. He didn't live very long after, as he was a bad alcoholic.)

The English fellow who was with Punch, and is now editor of Christian Science Monitor, phoned us to ask us to go to dinner. We really ought to have people back to dinner more here, but I only have 3 plates and table settings, and by the time I get home it is so late to start to cook.

Friday April 10th

Tuesday I went to my pottery class and left Geoff home busy finishing his article as it had to be done the next day. I decorated two deep bowls, they are not fired yet of course so I don't know how they will be. On Wednesday evening I phoned Harvard to find out what films, lectures and exhibitions were on, and found that there was a choral concert given by the glee club of the University of Puerto Rico it was free too, in the Sanders Theater. It was the most wonderful thing, in the first half they sang the old European classic works, Palestrina, di Lasso, some 13th century Spanish, French and Russian and in the second half they sang Latin American music, some old and some new, they ended up with contemporary Puerto Rican songs.

Last night Thursday we were to have dinner with the Henniker-Heaton's at 6.30 so we went first to Bob Nealy's, who is a boy from my office who lives in the same luxury block of modern apartments where they live, and also Mrs. Brinnin. It is on the Charles River, right on the water's edge looking onto the skyscrapers of Boston. We sat on Bob's balcony for a short time and watched the Harvard and MIT rowing crews have test runs up and down the river, ready for the race this Saturday. At 6.30 we went up to the 11th floor to Peter Henniker-Heatons apartment. We haven't met his wife before, she was very nice, a very big woman, she is a singer. They had asked two more English people for dinner John Allan May and his wife. He does an editorial each day for the Monitor, they're quite young and have been over here just over a year.

Tomorrow we are having Chris round for dinner, he's just got back from Chicago where he's been to see Mies Van der Rohe, so we're dying to hear all about it. Geoff got his article off O.K. with all the photographs and drawings, it cost three dollars 15 cents to send it! We are now waiting to see the next stage, and see it published. We will ask them to send a copy to you.

Mr. Biagnani the one who took us out in Milan is now gone, and they have a new editor, Mr. Romanini.

I imagine how you must be looking forward to your trip, to the south of France. Somewhere among our maps at home we have the most excellent map of Provence and the Riviera if you can find it.

Next week we are going out one evening with Roger Fowler's (our musician friend in London) cousin and her husband, he is a post graduate student in psychology here at Harvard. Roger is hoping to get a scholarship to study in America next year, in New York. We would be thrilled to meet him here, really it would be excellent to have your friends travel around with you all the time! Places would never seem bad if you could be cheered by some good friend! We are very surprised at the American ideas of friends, they are so friendly with every soul they meet, and never seem to see one person more than a few times. They seem a very unstable crowd, with a phenomenal rate of Mental illness. The girl upstairs went insane two weeks ago and is now in one of the many mental hospitals, it is very interesting to see the difference of people here from the ones in Europe and try to decide why it has happened. I think as we travel west we shall probably find saner people where there are more country people, farmers and less ambitious for all the material things. We are getting very thrilled by the prospect of our trip, last week I got a huge scale map of all America, so are going to plot our route, and then wait to hear from Wally if he's got us a car yet.

Sunday 26th April

This is just a quick note to wish you all a good holiday. If you telephone the Gilmaires in Paris give Sylvie my love. I sent her a Christmas card, but don't know if it was the right address. We have been busy as usual, last weekend we had a great trip to New York. It is a very exciting place to visit and our sail down the Hudson to Staten Island was very good, the views of the downtown skyscrapers seen from the water are wonderful. I'm glad you liked the photos of our apartment, the furniture was quite easily assembled. All our things we will be able to sell when we leave as they have not been used much we will be selling everything for the prices we paid for them. We will sell the lamps that we made as well. I will be quite sorry to sell everything, as it is very attractive and so comfy too. We have no idea what we shall do in July, there's so many possibilities so that we don't pin our hopes on anything. There's quite a lot that we must see somehow, before we come home. Whilst we are here we may as well see as much as we can because it's quite a long way to come, and in such a huge country you really do have to travel around. We have met Roger's cousin and her husband who are here at Harvard, they are American and are very interested to hear about Roger. We had a letter from him on Friday he sounds much happier he's teaching French for three hours, music for three hours and taking a madrigal group for two hours and this 8 hours work gives him five pounds a week and the rest of the week he can devote entirely to his music so he is very happy. He now thinks he will be in Paris next year, not in the U.S. which is a much better thing for him too. On Friday evening I made a baked Alaska, which is ice cream covered in meringue and cooked in a 450 degree oven, it was wonderful. (You have to put it on a wood board, to insulate the ice cream from the bottom. The meringue insulates the rest.)

Sunday May 3rd

Lectures finished last week at Harvard so the year soon seems to have come to an end. We were due to go to New York again this weekend as a friend was going in a brand new car, however the weather for the past five weeks or so has been so depressing we have had just cloudburst rain every day and its been cold and wet one day and muggy and wet the next, we have both felt horrible! I have never seen such rain, on Friday I got drenched to the skin going to the office, you know the rain in the film "The Rains Came" well it was exactly like that. We therefore decided to stay home this weekend and at least keep fairly dry.

We had an invitation to Durham, New Hampshire one weekend, it is a small university town and sounds very pleasant. The invitation is from one of the English speaking union members and they live in a beautiful 17 hundreds House, a large farm house. We are waiting until the weather improves a little and until Chris Norberg Schulz, our friend from Norway has gone home. He is only here for two more weekends so we feel we want to see him and not go away. Everyone is planning leaving and all the students in our house are going off. The two we know upstairs, one is an architect, are off to Paris to study for next year! On Wednesday afternoon I went with Geoff and Chris to the last of the lectures on philosophy of science, I heard all year how good they were so I felt I must go to one. I did enjoy it, he was a wonderful little German fellow, Philip Franck, with huge black boots, and very amusing.

On Friday evening we went to hear Dylan Thomas reading English poetry here in Harvard, he was <u>very</u> good. We've been reading in the Listener how excellent he is on TV The Listener is really the most wonderful thing, we always enjoy reading it, also the Observer which we see most weeks, it seems so sane after the papers here. We still get shocks from all the things here! We are just going out for a walk by the river, Chris is coming for the evening. Geoff had a letter from Edilizia Moderna the other day saying what a brilliant article he had written for them, it was the most flattering letter all the way through, I felt so thrilled about it.

Joseph Raymond McCarthy, Witch hunting. Anti-communist Period. A bad time to be in America.

At this time in America there was a hysteria everywhere about Russia and the Communist Party. Oppenheimer was the chief scientist who had worked in Los Alamos, NM. Inventing the atomic bomb. He was persecuted by the insane witch hunters, and was abandoned by all his fellow professors, too. Teller and Strauss who were working under Oppenheimer, were both attacking him. Probably from jealousy, as Teller was wanting to produce a hydrogen bomb, and Oppenheimer said it was too dangerous. You could destroy a whole continent with a hydrogen bomb. It was not possible to express any socialist ideas, or even concerns for your fellow men without being labeled a communist.

I was working at the time in the office on the Massachusetts General Hospital for mentally ill patients, and the office was designing rooms that you expect to see in an abattoir. The walls, ceiling and floor were all the same glazed brick, like the old parts of the London underground, with cove base, corners and ceiling which was apparently done so there would be no maintenance, there was a large drain in the middle of the floor and they could be hosed down easily! The windows all had a hideously designed metal screen to cover them, and I felt if you were not mentally ill when you went in, you would certainly be after a period in these cells.

We had had a friend, John Satchell, from our university days in England, who was very sweet, and gentle, he had to have a period in a hospital near London for a mental breakdown, they gave him shock treatment, and at the weekends, when we lived in Chester Square, he would come and stay with us. Because of my sympathy with John, and any other person who became mentally ill, I was always trying to push our hospital design into a warmer, more humane building. I pointed out that the intention was not to use it as a slaughter house, and that any one of us could find ourselves in there.

The office was a very odd assortment of people, I think the highest paid members were permanently based in Washington as lobbyists. They were not architects and had no ideas on that subject, they were there to get our big office more jobs. The boys who worked in the office were mostly MIT students, they were nice enough fellows as long as you stayed off any serious discussion. They all wore the same uniform, clean white shirt every day, gray pants and the brown and white saddle shoes that were very popular then.

I guess I tried to talk them into having more sympathy for their fellow men, especially the poor souls who were going to be in our insensitive hospital. One day the boss had heard about my ideas and sent for me, saying he wouldn't have communist ideas in the office, and that I should leave the next Friday. I think by the time I wrote the last letter I had already left but as we were about to leave on our trip it was not too inconvenient. People were really confusing any sympathy with fellow men, with their fear of Russian communism. It was really a terrible time and the witch hunts and the McCarthy hearings in Washington were on TV every day, in all the bars and restaurants. I was horrified that people didn't defend their friends when they were in trouble. I thought the English people would have stood by anyone who was put on trial and labeled a communist; they would have even given support to someone who was not a particular friend, that was just in trouble. Our second year in America the whole thing was much worse, and made me determined to return home to England. It was a very bad time in the U.S. I think I got some idea of how the Germans had been brain washed by the Nazis to vent such hatred on the Jews. I would really like children to learn much more history and sociology in school, as I'm sure that mass hysteria is always a possibility again. In 2006, I saw an excellent film, "Goodnight and Good Luck" Edward R. Murrow's exposure on TV of the Mc Carthy period, made by George Clooney, which is about the Mc Carthy witch hunting. It is not as strong a protest as it might be, as the 50's persecution of film people in Hollywood, was really frightening, and everyone was so afraid at the court hearings, that no one dared to support the people on trial, as they themselves would be labeled a communist. Many very talented people left the US at that time.

Once I mention school education, I must add that the type of tests, SAT's etc. that were given to my children in the US were ridiculous. It is no use wanting a child to make a black mark next to the answer you have taught them, you do not find out if they can write, spell or even think. My idea of developing a person's brain is to spark enough interest that they will read, discuss other people's opinions and then come up with an essay of their own ideas, based on many books and many opinions. You have to trigger a young brain to start forming its own opinions, and be able to discuss and back up their ideas. The debating and arguments in England that I find so invigorating, sharpen your thinking. Argument is very disliked by people here. I guess they are not secure enough, and feel they're being attacked by other ideas. Maybe the government wants to limit the extent of learning and individual thinking, so that people can conform to the useful worker types, and won't rock the boat by disagreeing with the government.

The present craze for political correctness is a very worrying thing to me. Everyone has a different set of ideas depending on their whole upbringing, experiences and education, and to be telling people what ideas are correct or not is the first stage of brain washing.

Back to my letters.

May 11th Cambridge

We are tidying up here and we now think we may go to Chicago at the end of the month. We wanted to get there before the school of architecture closed and before it is really too hot. We will let you know as soon as we know ourselves, there are so many deciding factors.

Chris goes home on Thursday to Norway so we had our last dinner with him on Saturday. We hope to visit him in Norway so we don't really have to say goodbye.

On Saturday we had the most amusing thing happen. We were down in Cambridge shopping and we met the wife of an architect Geoff worked with. She said did we know the Cambridge Association was having a sale of paintings etc., so we said I had some pots I wanted to sell, she said she would ask the people running it, if I could take them, and they said yes. So I came home and chose four of my best pots and took them back. As soon as I unwrapped them, three were sold immediately for five dollars each, then I noticed all the money went to one large box and everyone started to say how good I was to give such beautiful pots. Then it dawned on me that it must be for charity! I went outside and looked on the posters and there was no mention that it was for charity so I went inside and asked one of the women and she said "Oh yes it's to help the Art Association next year!" I was just horrified and said I had no idea it was for charity as Mrs. Compton had never mentioned it, so they were all very apologetic and gave me the money from them, and would not even take any commission on them, which I had been quite prepared to pay!

Sunday 17th May

I have left my job now, and have got a hospital to design for a professional fund raiser! Have you ever heard of such a man? I wanted to do something at home, while I'm busy getting things washed and cleaned and packed. It *is quite a large five storey job that doesn't have to be detailed so won't take long and I get $2.50 an hour. I got 40 dollars for two days work last week so it's very handy and more enjoyable work to do. I am also supposed to be lettering one thousand four hundred cards if I get time, Geoff will help me on the lettering too. I think we shall be off in two weeks to Chicago. We have a lift offered by one of the architects here, so we have to store our trunks and can just take a few things. We're waiting to hear definitely when he's going over, so when we do I will let you know. Next weekend we are going to stay on the farm in New Hampshire, it will be our last look at this area.*

Last week we sat down by the river one or two days when it was sunny, and got really brown, we went to an open- air concert here in Harvard and a lecture. One evening we went out to a party and I went to pottery to finish glazing some pots. It was really my weeks holiday so I got 70 dollars from the office, I came to the end of my color schemes for the large hospital so I was glad to be able to finish with that place. Geoff and I did some help on a UNESCO project here in Harvard, Geoff had done a lot already, so we got paid for all that, and also my forty dollars it was a real windfall week. Today we are having a lazy time and I am relaxing from the hospital, I have two more frantic days on it and then it has to be flown to this chap first thing Wednesday morning in Atlantic City. We've just had a real Sunday tea, and then we are going down to Harvard to see two comedies, Charlie Chaplin and W.C. Fields it should be very good.

Sunday24thMay

We have just come back from a super weekend in New Hampshire. We stayed on a farm, two hundred years old, which is ancient around here, the house was originally a garrison against the Indians. The walls are huge hemlock logs 5 inches thick by 1 foot 6 inches wide, it has later farm buildings and has one hundred and sixty acres of land, it was a beautiful spot. Mr. Skeele was in the Navy, and four years ago when he came out, didn't know whether to try business in Boston or to start farming. They've only been farming for four years but seem to be doing fine. Mrs. Skeele's father has his own apartment in one wing of the House, he is a splendid old chap who was 90 last birthday, and he is still English, he came from Liverpool about 1883, and came over on a five thousand ton boat, the first one ever to have electric light, and it took them eleven days! When they arrived in New York it had no skyscrapers and you could see Trinity Church (on fifth Avenue) from the river. He came to represent an insurance firm. He is such a lively man and so amusing and witty, Geoff and he got on so well. *He was talking all about hiking around Llandudno* (which is where my Granny Whitham lived) *and he was very thrilled that we knew it so well, he seemed really delighted to have some more English to speak to! He was just chuckling with delight all the time.*

Yesterday we walked through the woods, which are very wild and down to the river. It is actually running through their property and is beautiful with waterfalls, unfortunately the sun was brilliant and had brought out the mosquitoes so we each got bitten. We also saw our first snake! There are lots around here but so far we've managed to avoid them, it was about 3ft long and I just stepped into some long grass to smell some blossom and it came slithering out at great speed. There are only one or two poisonous types round here, one which kills you within about ten seconds! However we haven't seen any of them. Mrs. Skeele's dog killed one last week apparently and took it home, it seems unusual to have these pests, we are really so lucky in England. One day the wife of a boy in my office rang him to see how to get rid of a snake which was chasing her round all the time she was trying to weed the garden. The other thing to watch out for is poison ivy, which is another dreadful thing and makes you ill with fever and puffed up all over with the poison from it. We haven't met this yet!

Now we are back home and lettering these 1,400 cards at $2 per hour. We are packed up and ready to go on Weds. or Thursday.

<u>Note.</u> Somewhere during our Harvard stay we went down to see Philip Johnson and some other houses in New Canaan. Geoffrey was doing an article on Johnson's house, and he asked us for dinner, which was a special treat, the house was newly built and very like Mies Van der Rohe's style, this was the period that Johnson was doing all Mies type buildings.

University Hotel, Chicago. May 31st.

Well here we are in Chicago as you can see, we had a very busy last few days seeing friends and doing our last packing, then we took the trunks to our friend Thais Carter and she will store them for us. Elliot Deutsch, the boy who was bringing us, decided he wanted to leave at lunchtime on Wednesday so he came and we packed all our things in his car, a huge Buick. Then he and Geoff did his packing which was tremendous, he was taking everything from Harvard so the back of his car was crammed. We left Boston about 3.30p.m. Wednesday afternoon and drove through Connecticut where we went to see some very good houses, Elliott is also an architect. We got into New York about nine o'clock I guess, it really looked a dream city, we drove in through the Bronx and down the Palisades which is a high elevated highway next to the Hudson River. The Washington Bridge was all lit up and the skyscrapers were too, against a deep midnight blue sky with the fullest yellow moon dangling behind the skyscraper's silhouette. The road is 8 lanes wide all going one way and the other half is at a lower-level on the cliff, going the other direction, this road goes the full length of Manhattan about six miles, and under it is the road next to the docks, so that we could look to the right and see the Queen Elizabeth and all the large liners and to the left this dream like skyline. We suddenly burrowed down under the Holland tunnel, which goes under the Hudson and into New Jersey. We found a motel about midnight.

On Thursday we left about 9am and were then on the Pennsylvania turnpike. This is a road that you go through a toll at the beginning and for two hundred and eighty-eight miles you just drive on a six-lane highway. I drove on this stretch of road, it runs through beautiful scenery, through the Appalachian Mountains and wonderful wooded hills. It is supposed to be the best road in America. The second night we stayed in a motel about halfway through Ohio. On Friday morning we set off into Indiana across that state, which is very flat and just goes on and on, with farms and trees, we had lunch in Warsaw. We were soon in Illinois, and Chicago. Elliott brought us in on the Lake Shore Drive, which is like Paris or some huge capital, but by the sea. The lake is exactly like the sea of course, you cannot see any land, and it is very blue with waves and sand and rocks.

We went first to his mother's apartment, a modern one near the lake and there we had showers and recovered a little from the heat, then we had dinner with them and came around to this hotel about ten o'clock. It is near the Chicago University and about four blocks from the beach. Elliott called for us the next day and took us for a drive around Chicago we saw the downtown area and the Loop which is the center of the business area. It is a very lively city, and has a population of about three and a half million so is quite large. He dropped us off on the beach. We sat there enjoying the breeze until about 7.30 then went and had dinner and went exploring downtown. I phoned Dolly's niece who lives in Skokie, one of the suburbs. She wants us to go to a Coronation (for Queen Elisabeth) luncheon there on Tuesday, she's having 60 people including the British consul's wife and she asked us to stay on for dinner and see the coronation on television so it will be good. Tomorrow we are seeing friends of Chris, the boy from Norway, he is an architect here.

June 6th Chicago

This last week we've had a wonderful time, people have been so kind. On Monday we went to John and Jano Wally's. They are the friends of Chris from Norway. John teaches Design, at the University of Illinois and Jano makes jewelry and pottery and they have a very large workshop with a showroom and an apartment over, this is right in the center of Chicago, near the loop. We went and looked at two buildings that are very famous in the Chicago School of Architects, and also an early house by Frank Lloyd Wright, which is not far from where we are living. Next week we hope to go and see some of his recent buildings one is a very large factory for Johnson wax, which I think will be excellent. On Tuesday we went to the coronation luncheon at Dolly's niece, Joan. We saw the films in the afternoon and evening, the first film was shown here at 3 p.m. When we woke up about 7.30 a.m. we switched on the direct broadcast from London of the Queen's speech, so we really heard a lot. The films were good, but I was sorry it wasn't sunny for it, we had a temperature of 95 degrees so could easily have spared some sun.

On Wednesday we went to the Institute of Design to see a German, Konrad Wachsman who is the head there, and is working out some beautiful structures and space frames for colossal hangers. There are only five parts in the construction and it can all be fitted on the job by any workman with no building experience. He took us out to a very good seafood restaurant where Geoff had fish chowder and we both had hot lobster with cheese afterwards. He again is a friend of Chris. Chris is going to teach in Oslo, and he has his own practice there, he met Conrad and John and Jano Wally and quite a group of Chicago designers and architects and painters, when they all went to a design congress in Oslo last year.

Thursday we went to Illinois Institute of Technology, where Mies Van der Rohe is the head of the architecture school. His work there on the new campus buildings and in Chicago is just superb. We saw him briefly as he was just off to Germany for the whole summer, but then the other professors were so friendly and were fixing up for us to see some of the many fine buildings there are here. We are going to Mies' assistant professor Reg Malcolmsen's home for dinner tonight. Thursday evening we went to Elliott's, he had some friends in. Yesterday we went to see an exhibition of students work at the Illinois University and the school of design and then to a painters, for cocktails and then to John and Jano's for dinner. What a week! Chicago is a very exciting city, but has lots of slum areas although for 22 miles the Lake Shore Drive is perfect.

Next week we may be leaving for California, a group of students are delivering a car to Los Angeles, it will come across from Detroit on the ferry and then we drive it (five of us are going) and deliver it, all we have to pay is the gas- it's really a wonderful idea. It will take us five or six days to go there as we hope to stop at the Grand Canyon and any other real sights and in the desert areas we shall probably have to drive at night as the day is too hot.

Monday 15th June, Yellowstone National Park

I do wish you could see us at the moment, we are in a little log cabin about eight thousand five hundred feet up in Yellowstone National Park.

We have just been busy getting our log fire to burn for the night as it will be very cold, it's huge logs which we lit with kerosene and on this we have to heat the water for washing. It's really enjoyable for an odd night or so, Geoff and I have a little cabin all to ourselves. We were given quite a pile of logs and I guess should have stoked the fire much more. We woke about 3 a.m. and were absolutely frozen! It had been <u>so cold</u> that the spring in my watch had snapped. We took all the bed clothes and wrapped them around us while we got our fire going again.

We have been up in Yellowstone all the day, it is quite a fantastic place. It has snow mountains of thirteen thousand feet around us, a large lake, and then of all things, geysers and what they call mud volcanoes --they give off tremendous sulfur gas. We visited one area that has about 40 of these fierce looking bubbling cauldrons, they are all boiling and steaming and every now and then throw up in the air great jets of water. I think it's the noise that is so grotesque the earth sounds hollow and you can hear this roaring and tremendous hissing as gas, water and steam shoot out. We have rarely been aware of the centre of the earth, and what it is made of. The largest geyser throws a jet of water about 60 feet high. We are going to see that tomorrow we hope, it's called 'Old faithful'. Today too we went to the Grand Canyon, its not the same one as the Colorado one, but is very huge anyway. I took lots of film of everything we've been seeing so I hope you will see them OK.

This area has black bears, mountain lions, elk, wildcats and deer. Today we met a huge black bear and as we were in the car, I was able to film him and he came very close, about two feet from us. Last night we were hurrying across the plains between the Big Horn mountains and these Rockies that we are now in. We were pursued all the way by the fiercest thunderstorm, I was never so glad to be away from anything. The whole land was so flat and our car hurrying along seemed to be the only thing for this lightning to jump to, it was just one jagged line after another, and all round us, and the sky black as ink! The night before last we stayed in the Black Hills, they were wonderful too, such long-distances of pines and mountains, and we stayed at our best place so far, the White House Game Lodge; we were very thrilled to find Eisenhower and his fishing pals had just left that morning, there was still the air of excitement all around and press offices set up there too. Calvin Coolidge had had the lodge built in 1927 it was a wonderful spot.

On the plains we have had temperatures around 98 degrees but in these hills it is beautiful air. Most of the towns here are so amusing, the large ones have a population of five hundred and some are just a drugstore and gas station. We went to a very exciting town called Greybull (they are all Indian names around here) they were just closing their two day rodeo. It is a yearly event and all the Cowboys from the district come in to compete. It was so exciting and so amusing to be sitting in this little café with real live Cowboys all around, with their high-heeled fancy boots, suede jackets and huge hats! The road in these little places is just one wide one with little buildings on both sides, sometimes just a dirt road. You cannot imagine until you start crossing such a large country as this, what distance really is, from Boston to Chicago was two and a half days hard driving, and now this is our fifth day of real driving and we still have a good step to go. It was very hard to think of this whole 'West' existing until we came. After this we go to Salt Lake, the Nevada desert, the Mormon's country, then on to Reno, and so on to San Francisco and the Golden Gate.

George Thorpe is the man we are traveling with, he is a friend of John and Jano's. He is going back home to Sausalito. He offered to take us just the day before we were leaving and as we were going to be five in the car that we were ferrying, which means it's very hot, we thought this would be much better. He also has had the time to show us many places.

Before we left Chicago, George wanted me to get an American drivers licence, so I could help him drive. I got the booklet for the test and got all my questions right, and then went outside with one of the DMV guys, and we stood on the steps, I was waiting for him to show me the car we would take the test in, and he asked me which was my car, so I said I did not have one. He looked at me like I was crazy! I did not get my licence, so George had to drive all the way.

Geoff wants me to tell you he's had buffalo steaks with orange slices, he ate it at the game lodge we stayed in. We had a marvelous trip through the Badlands in South Dakota, they're quite fantastic, huge pinnacles of red earth and white dry plains. We crossed the Missouri and Mississippi rivers, you can go right down to New Orleans by boat from Illinois. The plains at first were very rich with cows being fattened there for Chicago slaughter houses, and fields of crops, and now the plains are dusty and sandy with wild sage growing and tumble weeds blowing around. We climbed from this plain up a pass eight thousand nine hundred and fifty feet high and we just twisted up all in one steep climb, the view was a real air view and was wonderful.

San Francisco June 23rd
A letter from Geoffrey
Sorry we have been unable to give you much information about our travels and that it made you worry, but you will be pleased to know everything has been perfect. The car we were originally taking with the five students, would have been fun but at the last minute a much better thing turned up. John and Jano Wally, in Chicago rang us up at the Harvard Hotel to ask if we could use a lift to San Francisco-because they had a friend staying, who was going back there by car and would like to take us. Of course we jumped at this offer and have had the most wonderful guided tour of everything without anything to worry about ourselves. George Thorpe knew everything very well and was in no hurry, so made many little detours to show us something special. Also he wouldn't take any money for the gas so we have had a very cheap trip. George said he had to make the trip anyway to get home and was glad to have our company.

It was unlike anything we have done before, to travel through so many types of country-Mountains, Prairies, Ranges and one Desert -all on the most perfect roads. There is a stream of traffic doing the same thing of course and regular gas stations and restaurants and motels, far from the old ideas of pioneering! Yellowstone National Park was almost too organized in fact. When we were waiting for the "old faithful" geyser to play there was an audience of dozens of people. It was still impressive though to see the fountain of water spurt up to two hundred feet, with all the steam. It does this every 65 minutes on average so people know when to wait around.

One of my favorite parts was when we climbed up through the Black Hills before going into Yellowstone. We wound up a zigzag road into the snow level with magnificent views all around and blue and yellow flowers thick on the slopes. Coming down we followed a rushing torrent through deep gorges. Yellowstone has the bears, which June liked very much. Black ones and brown, coming up to the car for chocolate or cake-they are likely to be dangerous though, so you have to be very careful. Wyoming was a wonderful state, mountains and valleys covered with wild sage for miles and miles. The mountains here are the Rockies and they go right behind Salt Lake City giving it a wonderful setting. We both swam in the Salt Lake- or rather floated. The salt prevents you from sinking and you can just lie like a log with feet and hands in the air it is quite impossible to sink! It was not cold at all, June enjoyed it very much.

The next state was Nevada, after all the drive through the White Salt Lake desert, where Malcolm Campbell's Bluebird trials were. The road is dead straight all the way across. (Now 2006, I just saw a great film, "The World's Fastest Indian" It is about Burt Munro a New Zealand Motorcycling legend who bought an Indian Scout in 1920 in NZ, and spent years modifying it to become the world's fastest motorbike. His dream was to race it on the Bonneville Flats, and set a new world record. He worked on it for half a century, and in 1967 when he was 68, broke all records, by pushing it to 190.07 mph. This was on a machine whose top speed had been 55mph. His record has never been beaten. It is a true story, and if you missed it, it is a great film and well worth seeing) *In Nevada the law allows gambling and they make a big thing of it with tourists- it is perfectly safe and well organised. The most amazing thing is to see old ladies and family parties working the machines for all they're worth! Playing 21, or rummy with silver dollars instead of matches like we used! There is always a restaurant and soda fountain in every place. At night the neon lights are fantastic in Reno, which is the main center.*

After this we had one more range of mountains to cross, the Sierras and on the other side of these was California, with palm trees of all kinds suddenly entering the picture and fruit orchards on both sides. We thought that it was going to be an anti climax to actually arrive in San Francisco after eight days of travel, but it was not at all because it is so fascinating. George took us for a quick trip around before taking us to a hotel (the Hotel Beresford) and we were just amazed at every new thing we saw. It is all on hills so steep that they have to use cable cars. Motor cars seem as if they're going to slide back, the streets are so steep, steeper than the top of Brooklands Crescent (where Geoff's family lived) *and quite straight. Of course the houses are very picturesque, with balconies and flowers taking advantage of the marvelous views across the bay. At night it is like fairyland-we went across the Bay by ferry boat last night in the sunset and it was almost unbelievable.*

June and I are both very well and have been since we left Boston, very brown with all the sun. We heard today that the temperature in Chicago was 108 degrees June was glad we were here, as it is very much cooler. Men wear their English sports coats and flannels because it often gets cool like England. We seem to see English people everywhere. We have managed to find people- architects usually- who introduce us to friends in towns we are going to, and we always have someone to see. This is very nice and useful because we get a lot of ideas on architecture.

July 1st. San Francisco

We are still here and very busy looking around. Everyone has been terribly kind. John and Jano Wally in Chicago gave us a list of their friends in this area, they are all painters, photographers (Morley Baer) designers, and architects. Connie Moran a Russian friend of John and Jano's gave us the name of a designer with Schumacher in San Francisco so we made a visit there. Reg Malcomsen who is of one of the professors at IIT in Chicago and works with Mies van Der Rohe, gave us some friends of his to visit, architects Campbell and Wong, so we have been taken around to the most beautiful modern houses in the San Francisco area, they are all surrounded with palms and cacti, lemon trees, eucalyptus trees and wonderful brilliant flowers. They are always on hills as the whole district is steep hills, and they have views out to the sea or over the Bay.

Last Saturday we went to a party of architects and on Sunday a girl called Emmy Lou Packard who is a painter and whose husband was an architect but was killed recently in an accident, took us into Marin County, which is over the Golden Gate Bridge, to see lovely homes and we had a picnic lunch in Muir Woods. They are tremendous redwoods and are so huge and the oldest are one thousand eight hundred years old. The climate here is quite unusual, it is never really boiling, the last week it was 86 degrees but with a sea breeze all the time, but it never goes really cold, the winters are 40-45 degrees and the sea mists are perfect for these huge redwood trees. You would love San Francisco more than anywhere we have seen in America so far, it has an Italian picturesque-ness about it and the sun has a tropical brilliance, all the buildings are white or pale pink with palms and cacti at every corner. The people are quite English too on the whole, and we have seen Coronation Picture Post and stacks of newspapers from England with photos, they all followed it very closely. Quite a few got up at 2 a.m. in the night to hear it on the radio! We saw a superb color film last week of it, it was a very long one and the colors looked beautiful.

We have been on some marvelous trips on the beach here, we went down one day to Seal Rocks, which were covered with tan colored sea lions, then we clambered right around the main headland on the rocks, and the waves were just smacking up to a great height. We have spent quite a lot of time in Chinatown, it is the largest group of Chinese outside the Orient and is most fascinating, we got some lovely little dolls for Elizabeth, one about two inches high and you twist off the head and out comes another and then another the baby is about quarter of an inch high!

At first we thought we would stay here until September if we could find a job, but the A.I.A. have a list of architects wanting jobs here so we shan't stay. We plan to leave this Friday and go down to Carmel first in Monterey Bay, and then on to Los Angeles, and then back to Chicago to look for jobs there. We have now been traveling for six weeks so it will be nice to stay put again, in spite of the heat in Chicago. If we don't hear of a ride by car going back, we will take the Greyhound bus, which is the cheapest, and drives the whole three thousand miles across America in two and a half days, day and night driving. We are hoping to stop in Santa Fe and also see some of the Indians in New Mexico and Arizona. We are going back on the south route so shall see entirely different areas and we can get off the bus where we want and get a later one.

Thursday July 9th – Los Angeles

We are now back into tropical weather it is a steady 90 degrees in this area, but that is cooler than Chicago where they had a hundred and four degrees last week! On the desert areas Arizona and New Mexico (where we have to travel through on the way back) they get a hundred and twenty degrees in the shade all the time! The heat and cold of the center of America is of course the reason so few people are there. Most of the population is on the two coasts. This area where we are now is tropical and would have no vegetation other than the palms and oak trees if it were not for the irrigation. There are lots of eucalyptus trees, they smell and look beautiful, and great varieties of brilliant flowering shrubs.

We had a very good ride down by Greyhound bus. It was four hundred and fifty miles and we left at eight a.m. and got into Los Angeles at 7.15 p.m. The buses are air conditioned so as long as you stay on, the heat is not bad. People have air conditioned cars too, very often. We came down on Sunday, not on Friday as we had intended. On Thursday we went over to the University of California in Berkeley to meet Vernon De Mars who is one of the well known architects in the area, we had lunch with him and talked over Geoff's work with him, then we were met by a friend of John and Jano's an architectural photographer called Morley Baer. He lives near the University of California and so took us to his home. He is not much older than us and is married to a photographer, they worked together until she recently had a little boy, who they've called Joshua! They have three houses in Berkeley, they had just bought one and are having it altered for dark rooms, etc., and they were living next door to it in a friends house that had just been built and was wonderful, with views right over the bay to San Francisco and the mountains. They also had a house they were renting before the new house was finished, it was theirs until August so they said why didn't we go up and stay in it, as they knew how tired we would be of hotel rooms. It was all furnished with their things and wonderful books all round so we really enjoyed it, we were higher up the hill in Berkeley than them and had a superb view. It was a new timber house, with the living room all opening up onto a balcony with views of the water, the ships and the hills. It was very good.

Saturday was July the 4th so we could not have traveled really that day, we went to Chinatown for dinner and were nearly deafened by Chinese fire crackers. They were just like bombs and were making all the children cry, I didn't think much of it as no one seemed to really enjoy them except the silly lads who were setting fire to them. We never saw any pretty fireworks. July the 4th was really a sell! We had a large box of chocolates to celebrate it.

We have found a good Little hotel here in Los Angeles, owned by two British people and we have a room with a breeze for 12 dollars per week so it is very cheap. On Monday we just looked around the downtown area which is where we are staying, Los Angeles is a huge sprawl, you go for miles and miles from one part to another. On Tuesday we phoned a designer of sets in Hollywood, Les Marzolf, who is a friend of John and Jano (He used to be part of the WPA in Chicago, where he did all the sets for the Theatre there) *and he came in an open car, a Thunderbird, to fetch us, and took us around to show us some houses we had wanted to see and we went to a little modern one, perched on the hill above Hollywood, on Cahuenga Pass, which was his house. We stayed there all day and went to meet two more friends of John and Jano, Fritz and Eula Long. All these people are friends with one another they were all in Chicago during the depression and were in WPA together. They are all splendid people, and seem very European in their way of thinking which is a wonderful thing, we really enjoy them. Fritz and Eula have been so good once again, introducing us to all the architects of the area. Yesterday afternoon we spent with John Entenza, who is the owner of the magazine called Arts and Architecture.*

He is the most lively man and has some great stories of all the world famous architects. We are having dinner with him this weekend.

Los Angeles, July 22nd.

As you see we are still here, we were asked last Friday to come to stay with Ed and Viola Spolin in the hills above Hollywood, they have a guest suite, living room, kitchen and bath which is on the floor below the House and opens out directly onto the garden. (In fact it was in the process of being built, and had no walls. Our first night they told us we may get a visit from a possum! But not to bother as they were very timid) *Viola has her sister coming at the beginning of August so we shall have to leave before then. We were planning to go at the beginning of this week so it is very good to stay longer, in spite of it being such an awful town, the weather is just perfect now the real heat spell has just dropped a little and it is 85 degrees to 90 degrees now and goes so cool in the evenings so we can sleep, very refreshing sleep. The people here are probably kinder than in any of the other places so far-they're amazing. Last week we were taken one day by an architect and his wife to see some of the lovely houses here, they took us out for lunch and then dropped us at a wonderful beach where we stayed for the afternoon, then we had dinner (this was just Geoff and me now) and then we went with Les and Ed and Vi to the opening performance of the Hollywood Bowl, which has concerts in the summer and is a fantastic place, set in a bowl of some hills. Bruno Walter conducted and they played Wagner and Beethoven, we did enjoy it. Another day we had dinner with Charles Eames and his wife Ray. He is a very famous architect and chair designer. They have a wonderful home just on the cliffs in eucalyptus trees with the sea below them.*

On Friday we came out here during the afternoon, we met Ed and Viola Spolin through Les Marzolf, they are all friends of John and Jano's. Vi is a very vibrant person, she is Russian and very involved with theatre. She finds theatre is a perfect medium for teaching children, she says she can find something important for every child, even if it is just raising the curtain. Geoff has had some really interesting discussions with her because of his days in theatre. (We learned later that her son was a very progressive theatre producer in Chicago, and very well known)

We had a barbecue in the garden and they had asked another architect who we wanted to meet, a very interesting man called Gregory Ain. Their home is perched on a 60 degree hillside with tropical plants and trees all round. We eat upstairs with them and sit up there too, but it's nice to have our own little room and we have our radio with us so we're fine. We are down here now as Geoff has an article to write. We had steaks cooked over an open fire and baked corn it was delicious and then a large green salad. On Saturday we went in the morning to see a famous modern landscape architect Garrett Eckbo, who was trained in Harvard and wrote one of the main text books. He was very nice and we had a good chat with him, he asked us there for dinner too last night. Ed and Vi went and Les and two other people as they all knew him.

Through Gregory Ain we got introduced to several Case Study House architects. The Case Study houses were designed, one a year, by the best architects in the area, and then they were built. Many of them were very innovative. One of the most warm people we met was Raphael Soriano, who was born in Rhodes, in Greece. He took us to several of his houses, and his case study house was lived in by a film star who had just made a film with Tyrone Power. She was very beautiful, but had a dumb little poodle dog who kept jumping up at Geoff. At one stage the dog had his teeth through Geoff's best jacket and was swinging by his teeth. Geoff was just trying to brush him off without looking at the problem, but of course the dog needed lifting up to get his teeth out, it was very amusing! Raphael is still so very warm and typically Greek/Italian. I remember he picked up lemon eucalyptus leaves and rubbed them in his hands, he was really into sensual things like feelings and smells and touching everything.

People here are so different from Boston and that area, they are very humble compared with the east coast and are really much livelier, and are very kind. We have had so many invitations to homes to dinner we should have to stay a month to accept them all. Even people in some of the houses we've been to see, have asked us to go for dinner! Folk who don't know us from Adam. On Saturday we went to about four houses by good architects and then we went to see a man called Richard Neutra. He is a German architect and is the Gropius equivalent on the West Coast and along with three others is one of the big men in America. Geoff rang up Mrs. Neutra to see if he was well enough to see us and she said sure, that they were going for the weekend to one of his best country houses to stay, so why didn't we go there to see them. It was a wonderful house, one of his earlier ones with a moat all round. It used to belong to Von Sternberg, one of the top producers of the time in films and is a fabulous place. Neutra has just had a heart attack so we thought we'd stay only a short time, however he was fascinated by Geoff's work, which he took to show him, and kept saying 'do go on I'm so interested'. Mrs. Neutra sang some German songs to me while we were waiting for them. These brilliant men from the continent are really very sad to see as they seem like a fish out of water, they've never absorbed the American way of life and don't seem to be a part of this society. As we sat with them in this German Modern House I suddenly felt very sorry, they would have so many friends and equals to discuss things with in Europe and here they are lost. We stayed for three and a half hours and had a wonderful time he is a very interesting man. We have done so much I can't tell you here. I'll try and write again in a day or two. I went swimming today and it was super, so warm.

Les Marzolf took us to Mexico for the weekend before we left, it was the most fascinating country and the Mexicans are so beautiful. They ride horses over these very arid looking hills with scrub and cactus plants everywhere, and the Mexicans wear brilliant clothes with huge straw hats. We bought some beautiful little Mexican things.

NOTE. The reason we were able to meet so many famous architects in the US, is because Edilizia Moderna asked Geoff to make appointments and see them, so he could write articles for their magazine, which he did, at regular intervals. He got great photos of the buildings, from

Julius Schulman. Geoff was also writing a diary Letter from America for The Architects Journal in England.

6 East Kinzie St., Chicago Tuesday August 4th

We arrived here on Sunday after a very good trip back. We left Los Angeles on Tuesday last and went to the Grand Canyon first. We got off the bus at a place called Flagstaff and went by local bus to the Grand Canyon. It was a very impressive sight as it is so huge, we walked a little way down into the canyon for about two hours but it is so hot down there so we came up fairly quickly. You can go down to the bottom on horse-back, but it takes a day and is really killing too. At the bottom of the canyon is a very wide river with a bridge over it, the actual crack in the earth is about one mile across and very long. We had planned it so we could travel by night on the bus and have the days seeing things. Our main luggage we sent on to Chicago to collect when we arrive.

After the canyon, we traveled Wednesday night through to Santa Fe, which is in the center of the Indian area in New Mexico. We phoned a friend of Les Marzolf's in Santa Fe, an old lady who had made costumes for Les at the theatre in Chicago where Les had been putting on plays in the depression, and before Les moved to Hollywood to work on sets for films. He has known her for years, and she was so glad to see us and took us all round in her car. Santa Fe is an incredible place, the streets are red-brown dust and they are all rutted with the rain, as it is the rainy season now, they have rain every afternoon without fail. Most of the buildings are built of mud bricks, they call adobe. The town had lots of Indians strolling around, and all the poor people speak only Spanish. This whole area New Mexico, Arizona and California used to belong to Spain as well as Mexico. It was funny to think of us still being in America! We went to see sand paintings in Santa Fe and had a very good look around in the museums and the quaint little streets.

In the evening Geoff and I went to see a potter that John and Jano know, he had a beautiful house with a Spanish patio in the center and the house all around. He has made some wonderful pots, and also has a marvelous collection of Chinese Sung dynasty ware, they were very beautiful. We stayed the night in a hotel in Santa Fe and the next day left early by bus for an Indian pueblo called Taos. These pueblos (or towns) are reservations given the Indians by the government for which they pay no rent, and are self supporting, they receive no financial aid at all. No one except Indians can live in them and they have their own style of architecture, which looks wonderful set against the hills. We got some photos of them so we hope you will be able to see how interesting they are. They wear wonderful gay clothes and brightly colored blankets. We spent the whole of Friday in Taos and then in the evening got a little bus to Raton where we caught our Greyhound bus line again.

We got on the bus Friday evening and stayed on it until Sunday, mid-morning, when we arrived here. It wasn't too tiring really as the bus was so cool inside, like a refrigerator. One place we got off for a meal, Salina, it was just like being cooked in a pan! They have temperatures of a hundred and ten and a hundred and fifteen degrees most of the summer I really can't understand why people go to live there at all. Kansas City and all this area is just so flat and this glaring sun and dead air. Just unbelievable.

We were glad to sleep in a bed when we got here, after four nights in the bus. It was the most wonderful trip though, I can hardly explain how much we enjoyed it and in each place, John and Jano's generous friends, always so kind. We are now at John and Jano's for the next six weeks or so, they're going away for a month on August the twentieth so told us to stay in their apartment which will be wonderful. Do write to us here.

PS Although it is hot here in Chicago we are so near the lake we just go over and swim and last night had a picnic supper there with John and Jano.

Chicago. August 11th

We are just beginning to settle down again after our trip, it seems ages since we were living quietly in Boston though! Since we came here we have been busy sorting out clothes and washing things. Geoff has been trying to get all our trip condensed enough to put in one article, but I think it will have to be in two articles though, as there is so much news that you can't miss out. Last week we caught up on some of our sleep, and went swimming most days in the lake. It is wonderful you know, just like the sea and so huge you cannot believe it is only a lake, it has waves and large ocean going ships. We had two picnics down there with a crowd of John and Jano's friends. On Friday evening we went out to dinner with some friends of theirs, and they had a barbecue in the garden, it was very good.

This apartment of John and Jano's is right in the loop, it's just a short walk to any point in town from here, and 5 minutes from the lake. It is a huge apartment (actually was a whole house on 4 floors) *and we have a floor to ourselves, Jano has a workshop on our floor, she makes lovely jewelry and John makes exhibition stands and furniture. He is a lecturer in architecture, at the University of Illinois, they are an incredible pair, they always have the house full of students and friends, and they are so kind. They are going off in about ten days to see John's father in Denver and will be gone a month, so Geoff and I are going to stay and look after their cats, they have two Siamese, and they're so amusing. John and Jano have gone out to help Jano's nephew and his wife paint their first apartment. He is only about 21, and just got back from Korea. Geoff and I went one night with them to help paint. Tonight Elliott Deutsch, the boy we drove from Boston with, came around and we went to a very good Italian place to eat, it had tables and chairs out on the pavement just like home! We then went a walk, along the beach and have just come in from an hour's sail in a motor boat. Chicago looked wonderful from the water, like New York, and it was so delicious and cool and the spray was refreshing.*

We are now busy looking for jobs, and we must also start looking for an apartment before the students start returning. John and Jano won't take anything for our stay here, so we must get somewhere of our own. I wish we could have seen you when we got back from out trip, we had so much to talk about and it was all so fresh, it is almost impossible to know where to start as you can guess, and in a letter it is hard.

Viola, who we stayed with in Hollywood has a son here, he is only 26 or so, runs the Playwright Theatre, so we have to go and see him, he has been getting very good reviews, so we must give Vi a report on his productions.

*My next letter August 19*th

I have just had a job, from a friend of Johns, measuring up and drawing a multi -millionaires apartment, as John's friend is redesigning it. I have just finished drawing it up for him today and now we are both on the job hunt. Geoff has written his articles, and then yesterday I found an apartment. It is here in town fairly near to John and Jano, and we should be able to walk to any of the offices, so this will save on transport costs. The couple who had been renting the apartment, are furniture designers and have done quite a lot to the apartment, it has a large living room, a small bedroom and kitchen and they have installed a lot of built in book cases and cabinets and everything in the kitchen they have put in, new sink, exhaust fan, cooker, refrigerator and they want to sell us all this plus the bed, dining table and two chairs and a settee for 300 dollars, then when we leave we will sell it again. The furniture is all new, that he has made, so it is very pleasant.

August 30th 1953

John and Jano left last Monday so it has been lovely to be on our own. We have had temperatures of 98 degrees every day cooling to 80 degrees at night! We have really felt it this week, I don't know why, as it has been this hot before. We have had a few interviews and on Thursday Geoff went for a second visit to a world famous firm of architects, Skidmore Owings and Merrill, they have offices in New York, San Francisco, Japan, Europe and in Istanbul and do some very good work. They have a huge housing scheme and had been working on some maisonette housing, but didn't feel satisfied with it so have asked Geoff to go in and work on the design of that, for two months anyway, so we were very thrilled. We were down to the bottom of our finances, 20 dollars travelers checks left and I got 30 dollars for the little job I just did.

We have been down to the lake to swim and cool off for three days whilst it has been so hot, the lake is really a vital thing to this city. Last weekend we borrowed a projector to see all of our films, they are really very good. We will keep them until we come home as they need to be explained.

(My cousin Desmond who was teaching in the University of the Gold Coast in Accra, the campus I had been working on in London, had written to my mother that the University was not pleased with Harrison Barnes and Hubbard, their architects) *I was so pleased as I felt the University people might be so dim that they wouldn't notice the architects inefficiency. If only it meant that Harrison Barnes and Hubbard wouldn't go on getting all these large jobs, they and hundreds of architectural firms are a real menace to have around. Desmond would not be surprised by it all I guess, as I wrote to him what archaic wasteful buildings we were doing.*

September 1ˢᵗ

I just had a real windfall of mail, wonderful. Ten letters all at once, 9 were sent on by George Thorpe from Sausalito and one was your wedding anniversary letter Mummy. Thank you very much, we really are so happy together we never stop to think how lucky we are, and it came as a shock on our trip, to only meet two couples who were not divorced. It's really incredible, and very sad this country, people are not really happy I am afraid, and there seem to be several causes, mostly it's having too much of everything and being very selfish, in spite of being generous to strangers.

Geoff and I were sitting last night by the lake and thinking what cheap thing we could do on Wednesday (our wedding anniversary) we decided if it was still so hot we would go for a sail on the lake. Today is 99 degrees again and the humidity is high. Last night the apartment only cooled to 90 degrees during the night so you just lie in a damp pool. It won't go on so much longer I hope.

We had a letter yesterday from Edilizia Moderna saying they were very pleased with the recent article Geoff had done, and they would like him to do more on our trip to California-also the magazine Arts and Architecture which is the best American Magazine, want him to do one, and he is writing one for Architectural Review, in London. We got a letter from Philip Johnson who runs the museum of Modern Art in New York, he had read Geoff's article on his house in New Canaan, Connecticut and wanted to compliment him on his article, and wants to see him in New York sometime. Isn't it good? I feel very thrilled. Geoff enjoyed his new job yesterday but he has rather a tricky thing to work on, so I hope that will be OK. I must go and have a swim now as I am dripping!

Thursday Sept 10th

Last weekend was Labor Day so we got Monday holiday, we went to see two interesting professors here. In the afternoon we went to see Hilberseimer who teaches town planning at IIT. He is a very good old chap with interesting ideas on planning, we talked to him so long we had to take a taxi afterwards to see Konrad Wachsman. He is an engineer, (we had visited him briefly on our way through Chicago, before our trip west) *and is doing some huge space frames, for hangars, for the very largest US planes. They are beautiful things, very delicate and simple, and consist of a number of prefabricated joints that can be connected in different ways, and by unskilled labor. He is a lecturer at the Institute of Design, and Chris in Oslo introduced us to him. He is about 55 and another interesting German academic. He took us out to Riccardo's for an Italian dinner, with chianti, and we talked for ages.*

Last Tuesday I started painting our new apartment as we hope to move in next weekend, John and Jano will be back. It has a very nice pale gray carpet, which has to have a good clean and the nice modern tweed couch. We are painting the walls and ceiling all white so things will show up well. I am looking forward to moving in now as it is a muddle with our things all in cases.

We had a lovely day on the 2nd (our wedding anniversary) *Thanks for all the good wishes, Geoff came home with a huge box of Frango mint chocolates, they were all wrapped up and when I undid them I couldn't think what it was, they had all run to liquid and formed one box of glue.*

Anyway I put it in the fridge and we cracked pieces off, it was lovely. Geoff's face was even funnier than mine when I opened the box! It was one of our over 100 degree days, so we went to an air conditioned show at night.

September 20th. Sunday- New address #8 West Erie Street.

We are all settled now in our new apartment, we got it all painted before John and Jano came home and then last Saturday we washed the carpet and did the cleaning around and moved in on Sunday evening. A friend of John and Jano's ran us up in his car with all our things, so it was very easy. Wonderful to be here in a place of our own again, and it looks very good, walls white, and the door is yellow, just a flush door with a plain anodised aluminium knob, and the carpet we washed came a beautiful light gray. It is the largest room we have had.

The people in the house are very nice, while we were painting they asked us in for a glass of wine and a cup of coffee. They are all students or ex students from the Institute of Design so we have a lot in common with them. We had two of them in for dinner last night as I had a large melon, and a three and a half pound piece of beef, some ears of corn and fruit and cheese, so we had a lovely dinner. Geoff tossed us a nice green salad which is supposed to be his thing now, and he does it very well.

Last Monday I went for an interview to the Chicago Planning Office, the architect in charge is a young fellow called John Cauldwell, he is English and was a partner of Maxwell Fry and Jane Drew, in London. He was in Africa working for them, so we didn't know him in London. When we first came to Chicago Geoff met him with John Wally and he said I should go in and see him, and he gave me a job. I was so glad as I wanted to fix one up now that we are all moved in here, so I'm starting tomorrow morning. The work sounds very unusual so I hope I will be able to cope with it. I went in on Friday to get the feeling of the office, the first job I do is to reorganize and re-plan the office, so that will be quite easy, but after that we should be preparing schemes for slum clearance and re-planning. It is so new to me that I'm quite worried how I will fare. John Cauldwell says they really need an architect as he is the only one. All the rest are town planners, sociologists and psychologists and when any buildings have to be designed John has to take over all design, as they have no idea.

His mother is over from England at the moment, and he's taken her to New York today, and then goes to Washington, and will be away for two weeks so I will be floundering a bit while he is away. Geoff and I work about two blocks from each other, so we will eat together each day for lunch. I finish at 4.30 though and Geoff not until 5.30 so I will be able to have dinner ready when he comes home.

John Wally had proposed Geoff as a lecturer at the University of Illinois for next term, to give a series of lectures in the evening to all the architects there in a large class, however Geoff feels he could not do it, and he is not really thinking of architectural education at all, if you're really a teacher like John Wally, then it has to be the main job of your life and you have to concentrate on that. These articles Geoff writes already take a lot of time and we have too much work to do, so I was glad he said no, but was very pleased John proposed him.

John and Jano had a wonderful party to celebrate coming home last weekend, we had a really good time. Then on Tuesday we went out to dinner with Elliott Deutsch, and after that we went to see Adlai Stevenson on TV with John and Jano and friends. Stevenson was excellent. (I think he was too intelligent to ever be voted President. They were all calling him 'an egghead')

I went to see an exhibition of Japanese art on Wednesday afternoon and I saw a notice of a lecture by Sir Leigh Ashton from the Victoria and Albert Museum in London, so I went to see him, as Geoff knows him through James Gardner, who Geoff worked with on the Festival of Britain. Leigh Ashton was helping us on our Brazil trip planning. Today we have had a perfect day, Geoff and I went to the Japanese exhibit this morning and went to the yacht harbor this afternoon and sat in the sun, and then to see a very amusing French film.

October 8ᵗʰ 1953
Geoff is very busy on his huge housing scheme, he's going to make a model of it too, so he has a lot to do. Last Sunday we went down to the site

near the lake, it is in the center of the 'black belt' and we spent the whole day looking around that area, some incredible slums still, in spite of all the clearance. It is really an amazing part, we walked all the day and never saw any white people, even the busmen and police are negro, and the little bright faced children are so cute, its really like being in another country, they keep perfectly to themselves and so do the white people, it is really a difficult problem. My scheme for a new hospital is in the same area so we went to see that site too.

Last night we went to the Institute of Design to see some films. We saw Oliver Twist again and a Swedish film, which was very good. They have films every Wednesday and the program is excellent. We are only about six houses away from the Institute of Design. Tomorrow we are going to see a Gilbert and Sullivan opera, 'Pirates of Penzance' Chicago has about eight legitimate theaters as compared with about two in Boston, it is really a much livelier place.

The man that owns this House would like me to start making lamp shades as a business for him, I've been seriously thinking of it as he is the sole agent for some lovely Japanese papers and that wood shade of ours is one of his imports to Britain. I would be able to continue on my own when I got back to England too. I'm not sure yet what I will do.

October 30th Friday

Last Saturday we went in the afternoon with the Jamaican dancer in our house to watch him dance, then in the evening John and Jano came for a real slap up dinner. I bought a beautiful sirloin steak over three pounds in weight and cost three dollars. It is amazing the cost, over 1 pound for meat! (Poor England still had rationing) *then we had baked potatoes, squash, peas and green salad, fruit salad, cheese and biscuits and coffee, it was very good. We had invited the Alschulers and Jim and Naomi in later, so we had a very good evening as everyone knew everybody else. Sunday we went with John and Jano to a photo exhibition and then to see two designers they know. We came back to Chicago about 7 in the evening and then had a Chinese dinner in town with John and Jano, and then dashed to see Jose*

Greco, the Spanish dancer, it was good, but not so exciting as Antonio and Rosario who we saw in London.

Geoff has had a wonderful visit to Mies Van der Rohe, the architect we really came to Chicago to see. Mies was very friendly, I wish I could have gone but I was working.

On Tuesday evening John and Jano called with a little English chap, he has been back and forth for the last 20 years, he is a theatrical fellow, has played with Stanley Holloway in England, and plays the back end of a horse here! He was making us die with laughing. Yesterday Geoff and I went to the Good Design Exhibition, of furniture, pottery and textiles. We bought 2 chairs, they are lovely ones designed by Bertoia, an Italian. Currently they are only available in the U.S. We have admired them a lot and if we have used them we shall not have duty to pay on them, when we bring them back to England.

We are getting ready for our Halloween and also Geoff's birthday party. (He was born on October 31st) We are going with Neville, the boy from Jamaica, and Naomi and Jim. It is a large house with parties on all floors so it should be good. I was busy last night making Geoff a bright green wig out of rug wool, I sewed all the strands together and it looks wonderful! He has bought over 100 candles and is going to fix them on somehow, so folk will see he is his own birthday cake! My costume is a wonderful red wig, that I borrowed from Neville, it is really crimson. I got all my jewelry on at once, a very dark skin colour and huge theatrical eyes, I just look like Cleopatra, so that's what I am going as. It should be a wonderful party as most of the people are designers or painters and are very imaginative. We saw a film of one of Neville's parties and it's like seeing a modern ballet!

Next Tuesday we are taking John and Jano, and Jano's Mother, who is staying with them, to a concert of Temple ritual dances given by Frank Lloyd Wright students from Taliesin, and he himself is giving the commentary - He is 87 and quite crazy, so it should be very amusing.

November 6th Friday

On Sunday we went to John and Jano's for dinner after a whole day cleaning ourselves up, after the fancy dress party;(it was a great success.) John had to go out and give a lecture in the evening so Jano, Geoff and I were sitting chatting and I suddenly noticed big sparks going past the window, we ran to look down and there was a huge fire started, a great pile of garbage was blazing and it was setting fire to the timber entrance at the back. Geoff phoned for the fire brigade and they were there in a flash, it took them quite a time to put it out as it had really taken hold. We were so glad we had stayed at home and not gone to John's lecture. They have had 4 fires in that building and the reason they say is that the building next door makes fire- fighting equipment and has lots of oil coolers or something. Last year they had all the plaster down with the water they pumped onto the fire. They say the worst worry of the fires, is that the firemen pinch anything that is removable, so it is a real mess once they get in your building.

You know this country is incredible for the fires it has, every evening the fire trucks are out to some fire, and in our street there have been fires in nearly all the buildings. For one thing they overheat the buildings so that in winter the timber is just ready to ignite, and also the wiring in most of these houses is terribly bad, it was poor stuff when they first put it in, and now it is old. (On reading this now I remember that whilst we were living in Chicago several shops were mysteriously set on fire, and several dry cleaners had acid thrown on the clothes. People said it was because they had not paid the local Mafia for protection. I wonder now if someone who had a grudge against John, some student perhaps, who knew he would be out, had set the fire?)

Yesterday we had our first snow! It started a little on Wednesday evening and then yesterday morning there was quite a covering, we went from 80 degrees to the 20's in a week! I don't know if I told you last winter of the tremendous electric shocks you get here in cold weather, I had almost forgotten them, until this recent cold spell, and now I am off again. I have very bad ones too because I wear rubber soles so don't earth any of the static electricity. Last winter when Geoff used to meet me, he would forget and lean to kiss me, and get a terrific shock through our noses or lips! Every time I touch any metal after I've been in the cold, you can hear a crack of the spark, and boy can I feel it! The other night I touched one of Jano's cats and sent it right up in the air and it spit at me too! When I first started doing it Geoff told me it was just me, and it was quite a time before we asked folk and they said it was quite normal and they all did it. Poor little Professor Michelis from Athens, had a terrible time in Cambridge every time he shook hands with people, he'd give them a shock right up their arm! I get all on edge when I go into a building trying to avoid touching metal or people, and I always forget. I think I will trail a wire from me, and earth it as I go. In the design of our hospital operating theatres, we had to be very careful to earth the operating table and provide a bracelet type earth, for all the operating room staff. The anesthetic they used in surgery then, was easily ignited by a spark.

Many articles of clothing were a synthetic fabric that built up static, and several patients had their lungs blown up during surgery, so it was an essential point in our design.

November 15th

We had a very good week again, last Sunday we went to Chicago University to meet a friend of John and Jano's, who is the carilloneur there. We climbed right to the top of the bell tower and watched him Play for three quarters of an hour. The bells are the second largest and finest in the world and were all made in Croydon! (A suburb of London) *He himself was in England for 3 years and thinks it is perfect. He played Jerusalem, and God Save the Queen to finish! Afterwards we went down into the church where a boy who was with us, played the organ. He has studied in Paris and given recitals in America, and played very well. We went and had dinner with them in the International Student House, and then about 8 came up into town and went to see 'Singing in the Rain' and 'Kind Hearts and Coronets'- both very good of course. Wednesday I had a holiday so managed to get the washing and ironing done. I redo the cuffs on Geoff's trousers* (the turned up cuffs were worn then and were always wearing out where they touched his shoes) *and press them. If I move them around I can stop them wearing and fraying and the crease from the cuff doesn't show. In the evening we went to a film at the Institute of Design "Life Begins Tomorrow" which we saw 4 years ago, but it is very good.*

Friday I had a hectic day, I went to a film on modern dance in my lunch hour, it was free at the library, then I had to go and see an architect about a scheme I am doing in the office. He has done the same sort of scheme, so John Cauldwell thought I would get some tips from him. Then at the last minute Councilor Merriam phoned to say would I go down to Chicago University to a council meeting to explain my scheme for re-doing his office, so I had to dash home and change into some impressive clothes! Then rush down there, it went quite well and they seemed to like the scheme very much, if it goes through I will be very busy as we are going to use a group of students as free labour, and I have to buy the materials and oversee the job- which will be tough for me.

We just bought Geoff a beautiful shirt last week, a new material Dacron and cotton, white, no ironing, you just wash it and hang it up to dry. Everyone wears white shirts in the offices. Yesterday we bought two beautiful fine wool dresses for me, one is gray and is a soft cashmere wool, the other a very gay blue one, so I am set for the winter.

Friday evening we had a Norwegian boy and his fiancee from Copenhagen round, he is in Geoff's office, they are a very nice pair. Last night we went to a bird watchers party with John and Jano, and tonight we have some complimentary theatre tickets with Neville, the Jamaican dancer.

November 21ˢᵗ Saturday

Today I have to work, but as I am only here to answer the phone, I thought I'd try to write a few letters. We take it in turns to work on Saturday and this morning there is just a coloured boy from IIT and one other chap and me. We have quite a few coloured boys in the office, and of course Neville the Jamaican is a beautiful tan colour. It's really a funny thing that the problem they have set up here of segregating whites and blacks in the south has made the relationship difficult for them, and the whites feel they're being condescending to talk and treat them as equals. Of course they are completely the same once they have been given the same chances and education, if anything they are better! (Very interesting to see the recent election of Obama, an African American from Chicago. We could never have dreamed of this in 1953) *The girls wear very good clothes and they don't overdress as many of the whites do - we were amazed when we first came to Boston to see people at 8 in the morning going to the office in tafetta dresses with diamante sewn all over, and lots of jewelry, stockings with butterflies up the backs, in fact the clothes you would expect for a party at night! There are some coloured judges in this building and they seem to be about the most respected folk in it.* (I think this paragraph was aimed at Daddy, as when I was at University there was a really beautiful Jamaican medical student, who was very tall and elegant, and a great dancer, and he asked me to the dance at the Student Union. I felt really special as everyone I knew would have jumped at the opportunity, but when I got home Daddy was sitting in the Hall waiting for me, and he said "we didn't even know who you had gone out with, what was his name?" I said Simon Ramassar, and he went berserk! I remember Mummy cried when she heard!!)

It is an incredible place you know this City Hall, they have a large number of courts here and our elevators are always full of judges, and jurors. One day when the man next to me in the elevator walked out I saw he was handcuffed to men on both sides of him! There are always lots of mafia type little guys, chomping on fat cigars.

We had a very good week again, last Sunday evening we went to the theatre with the free tickets that Neville had, it was at Vi Spolin's son's theatre, you know Vi who we stayed with in Hollywood. It is a very lively theatre, it's a sort of repertory company. On Monday evening Vera the girl who used to live in our apartment came around, she lectures at the Institute of Design and often pops in, so Naomi, Neville, and Jim all came too. We listened to Truman's broadcast which was really excellent, he was about the first person to warn of this terrific fascism which is here. Stevenson has hinted at it but never been so outspoken as that. All the evidence against White was given by this woman, who was herself a self-confessed Communist spy and she said she had burnt any papers which would incriminate him, so in White's trial later nothing was ever proved. Truman must have been warned of hundreds of such people in his administration, he'd have had no staff if he fired them all. Some of the Harvard professors who were sent to Washington for trial, among them was a great scientific hero, Oppenheimer, who was a highly respected scientist who had worked on the atomic bomb. While we were in Harvard, folk with social ideas, or people who'd had them at one time, were arrested, and the rumour and bad name that they got, ruined their lives. We have heard of one or two here in Chicago who never became American citizens and because of their criticism of some part of life here, they had been deported to England for anti- Americanism! That is the beginning of another German fascism.

On Wednesday evening we went to our film show and a few students came back with us for a beer and popcorn. You buy the corn you know, pop it yourself in a covered pan and have it hot with salt on. On Thursday evening Ruth the girl in our house who has been in Toronto for six weeks holiday came home, so we had to have another party for that, we had a real week of them. Last night Geoff and I had dinner in town and then went to see "Captains Paradise" the new Alec Guinness movie, it is very amusing, have you seen it? Today Geoff is working at home and I'm going to do the cleaning and wash my hair when I get in. John and Jano are coming for dinner tomorrow, we are going to a new exhibition at the Art Institute in the afternoon and then home for dinner.

Thursday next is Thanksgiving so we are getting a holiday. John and Jano asked us there for the day. Jano's mother, two sisters and husbands and nephew and wife are all going it's a real family thing you know. Friends in our house, asked us last week if we would like to have the Thanksgiving dinner with them, they have one each year, they are all old friends, so we are lucky to get in with such a jolly crowd.

November 29th

We had a lovely Thanksgiving with Jano's family. I had made the cranberry sauce which was worrying as it was hard to get it to gel. I had my Fanny Farmer Cookbook as I had no idea what I was making, (it is something we never have in England) *I followed the instructions carefully and everyone said it was delicious. There were about 16 of us, Jano's mother was there she recently moved to Chicago where her 3 daughters live, she had been living near her 3 sons.*

We have had a freezing cold week in the 20's all week, and after we had eaten at Jano's we looked out and everywhere was white with snow. Today it has snowed ever since we got up but it has now gone warmer and is about 30 degrees so that's better. The difference between summer and winter, and indoors and outdoors is phenomenal here, this week the outdoors was 20 degrees, we try to keep our apartment as low as 75 degrees but in our office it starts at 82 degrees in the morning and finishes at 87 degrees by late afternoon! I can't wear any wool underclothes and in fact haven't worn any vest at all as I am just dripping in the office, I have to wear cotton blouses, no jumpers and a heavy cotton dress that I bought. It really seems as bad to be too hot, as it was to be too cold in some of the offices in London. Really heating is not solved at all yet.

We went down town to the French line office, anyway they were closed so I will go next week. We want to transfer our return passage to the SS United States, as it would be interesting to travel on a new boat and the French line has such class differences that we wouldn't be keen on another trip with them - though the food was very good.

We have just had an architect over to see us, he is from Norway and is marrying a Danish girl next week they are borrowing our cine camera to film the wedding, which is in Boston. We went with him to some friends of ours to see Verdi's 'Macbeth' opera on television - it was very good Geoff and I stayed for dinner, at our friends, Harold and Mary's. He is a furniture designer and has a factory of his own and is having pretty hard times with it, this is not a country for the small man in any line. They have a dear little girl, Jano, named after Jano Walley, she's almost one year old. Today we have *been working and listening to Howard K Smith reporting from London on European politics - he is excellent, on each Sunday at 12 noon.*

December 8ᵗʰ

Thank-you mother for the House and Garden magazine we were very pleased to see it, as the furniture seems to have improved since we left, we shall be able to buy some good things when we get home and get somewhere to live.

We had a really busy week once again, this last weekend we hired a projector and had film shows. On Friday evening for Naomi, Jim, and Ruth and then on Saturday evening for Irene and a boy she knows, then Sunday afternoon Neville came in and he'd been dancing all afternoon and hadn't eaten so he helped himself to our 4 pound leg of lamb and we showed the films to him, Mary phoned to say that little Jano, her baby was teething and so she ought to stay in with her, so could we take the projector and films there - so we did. There were four other folk there too, an architect just back from two years in Paris. We had a very pleasant evening and were talking wildly until early morning! On Saturday Mary's husband Harold who designs and makes furniture, had a sale, so we bought two very nice tables, they each take down to a very flat package so we can bring them home.

Tonight I was going to do so much and as soon as we finished dinner little Billy Mc. Nichol came in and has only just gone- 10 o'clock so my evening is lost. He is very entertaining and was telling us about playing with Albert Modley in pantomime in Leeds, and another pantomime in Bath. He has some amusing stories of the music hall people, though the really good days are all over in America, they require nightclub acts more now.

I have been in touch with our shipping people, the French people will transfer us OK to another line, now we're just waiting to hear from United States shipping line in New York that they have vacancies. They didn't have anything in July as that is the heavy booking time so it would be the August 6th sailing and we would be home around the 10th or so. It is probably as well for us to come then as it will take quite a time to close up here, we have to sell this apartment and pack up here, then go to Boston and re-pack the trunks that are left at Thais' there, then go and have a last look at New York, which will all take quite a time. It will seem very exciting when it gets nearer. We just had a letter today from Professor and Mrs Michelis in Athens, they had a wonderful summer back home, touring round Greece, Europe sounds very attractive whenever you read or see anything about it.

Sunday December 20ᵗʰ

Very happy Christmas and a Happy New Year to you all, the time has gone so quickly that it was only about Thursday that I realised Christmas Day was next Friday!

We had an amazing week with the weather, it started last weekend snowing everywhere and then suddenly it got much too cold to snow, it went to 20 degrees then down to 10 degrees and eventually to zero, which just froze us! It stayed cold all week until this weekend and now it feels really good, as it is warmer again. We were so cold walking to town, it's about three-quarters of a mile each way to the office, so we bought all sorts of things to wear, Geoff's ears nearly froze in his hat so he bought some fur ear muffs, I had a wool hat already but my legs were so cold, so I bought some very nice fawn wool knee socks, then the top part of my legs was cold, so I bought what they call snuggies, these are like the old fashioned bloomers and they come right down and tuck into my socks so the only exposed bit of me is my nose!

On Wednesday I had such a headache though in the office so came home at lunch time, I think it was the great difference in office temperature and outdoors 86 degrees to 0 in three or four steps! On Friday I woke with a sore throat, which was the beginning of a cold, so I had the whole day asleep in bed. We got all our own American cards off last week so that is the end of those. We made a beautiful Christmas tree last weekend, it is very gay, and then John and Jano gave us one of theirs yesterday, a light aluminium one that they make for the shops. Our room looks lovely I wish you could see it, we have a little tree from John and Jano for our table that has witch balls on, and I have some earrings from Jano with five little witch balls made like a mobile so they move round all the time. We bought them a book of photographs of Switzerland, a beautiful one so I hope they will like it, they loved Switzerland, when they were there. I bought Geoff some Clarkes shoes, they are most unusual but look wonderful on, and he bought me some walking shoes, which I needed as we are always walking. I bought Naomi, Ruth, and Vera some Italian gloves in bright colours.

We are going to Jano's sisters on Christmas Day, all Jano's family will be going. I am supposed to take 50 mince pies as they don't know our little ones here, and Geoff happened to mention what good mince pies I make, so he's let me in for making 50 of them. On Christmas Eve we are going to a party at Vera's so we shall have quite a gay time. On Christmas morning I want to have breakfast here in bed on our own and listen to your three o'clock programme, it is broadcast to us here direct you know. I wish we were going to be home with you all.

I have been busy this weekend making my mince pies. Last night John and Jano came to dinner and we had mince pies with whipped cream on the top. Then we went down to their house as they were having some friends coming from Sioux City, and about six other people came too so we had quite a party. This afternoon we went to see Neville dance they were giving a Christmas show. The night club where he dances each night, is too expensive for us to go to. We have managed to save $800 or so and as we gave Harold and Vera $300 and spent almost a hundred on chairs and my dresses, we have done quite well in three months.

January 3rd 1954
A VERY HAPPY NEW YEAR TO YOU ALL!
We have been having a wonderful time over the holiday. We decided last Tuesday to have a party on New Year's Eve, so we started very hurriedly phoning people and I asked about 20 people and Naomi and Gay, upstairs asked more. We shared the preparation of food, and had wonderful things salami rolled around chunks of pineapple, Neville made that, then huge trays of hors d'oevres sort of things, and crisps and pretzels, lots of nuts, and

things on little biscuits, then we made rum punch and gin punch with lots of fruit in it. We had a fun evening people popped in and out going from one party to another, John and Jano came with Bill and Roy who are staying with them, they came about nine for an hour or so and then came again about 1.30 and stayed till 4.30. Jano was dancing and we all seemed to enjoy it -about 12 people stayed to 4.30.

On New Year's Day we went to a party at about 4pm which was at the home of a painter John Stenvaal, and he had a combined party with another couple. He has one every New Year's day, about a hundred people go and he serves a wonderful buffet supper about 6.30. The food was delicious and so much of it. We met crowds of interesting people there, I met a lot of the dancers from Sadler's Wells Ballet, they are in Chicago at the moment and seemed great people, there were some B.O.A.C. pilots there too, it was funny to have so many English contacts at once! About 8.30 we went to a composers party, he has a wonderful apartment not too far from us, and there were about 10 people there, he was playing some of his music for us, it was very good. He has written lots of very witty songs, that people like Beatrice Lillie sing. He just writes them to order, and some were so funny and he sings them very well and had us crying with laughing! Yesterday, Saturday we went with Neville, Jim and Naomi to see Sadler's Wells Ballet, we have had our tickets over two months as they sell out immediately. It was wonderful, one ballet 'Daphnis and Chloe' had me in tears it was so beautiful, they had a large choir as well as the most marvelous Ravel music, and the modern colours, as well as the perfect dancing were just too much. I don't think I ever saw anything so good.

Last night we had an Italian architect Angelo Mangerotti from Milan to visit us, he is lecturing at the Institute of Design for a while, and seems to love to talk with us as he can talk in French — he speaks almost no English - and none of his students speak anything but American. He's only young about 40 and a very lively person. His wife Maria and their little girl Anna are here, but Maria couldn't come as the little girl is only three and they don't have a baby sitter. We hope to see a lot more of them before the summer. American students and architects never talk about their ideas *and it so good to have people like Chris from Oslo, and now Angelo to talk to, even if some of our ideas are different.*

This evening we are supposed to go to Connie Moran's but I want to try to see Sadler's Wells again, it is their last night and they are doing a new ballet 'Sylvia', so we thought we'd walk down and see if they have any odd seats. (Connie was a very colourful writer from Armenia who had been married to an attorney in Chicago. She lived on the top floor of a very tall house and had a basket she lowered to the street on a rope. She would lower the front door key when you arrived, and also haul up her groceries to save carrying them up so many stairs. We went to wonderful wild parties at her flat, I remember one where everyone had to write some poetry, one of the lines "there are sequins in my beer" sums up most of her parties! She had taught school to Eskimo children in Shishmaref Day School, Alaska, and as her Christmas card she gave us a little book of eskimo recipes that the children had brought in to her from their mothers. We still have it and most of the recipes start with reindeer tallow, bear feet, oogruk meat, and seals)

We had some very good Boxing Day parties, we went first to one which was a German architect and his wife who is a doctor, it was very formal, they had a real Christmas tree with proper wax candles on it which we lit, and then they played the Bach Christmas Oratorio while the candles burned. Geoff and I were very amused as we had to have a large bucket of water, in case any of the branches caught fire! Afterwards we went to John Cauldwell's, the fellow I work with, and he was having a real English party with the consul there, it was quite a contrast to the first one.

January 9th Saturday

We have just received your letter about the Christmas gifts, I am sorry! (apparently the Customs had opened their packages and put everything into the wrong wrapping paper so that the scarf present for Geoff's father was given to someone else, all the presents were mixed up and went to the wrong people. They had also had to pay customs duty on everything!!)

On Tuesday evening a professor from Boston called Buckminster Fuller was visiting John and Jano. Geoff had heard him lecture at MIT and we both think he is a very interesting guy and were dying to meet him - last week he flew in for the evening to give a lecture and went to John and Jano's for dinner as they have known him for about 20 years. When he was working on his dymaxion car, in Chicago, he had been staying with John and Jano on the ground floor, and the landlord had seen the contraption he was making, and asked John and Jano if he was OK, and they explained he thought he was inventing a new car! We had a wonderful evening with him he was showing us slides of all his work that he's ever done, and then at 11 he had to fly off, to go to South Carolina to lecture the next day.

Sunday evening we had a dinner party for Naomi, Jim, Neville, Ruth and her husband, who just came home last week from Korea. The party was in his honour as he's been away for a year, we had never met him before. Ruth was nearly crazy the last few days before he came as she was not sure when he would arrive. Each time the bell went we were all bobbing out! We each prepared one course for the dinner it was very good. Afterwards we all went to see Beatrice Lillie, she is in town at a theatre and was very entertaining, singing some of the songs of the composer we had just met.

Last night we took John and Jano to see Cinerama, it was very exciting. Have you had it in England yet? It was so much like real life, that banking around in a plane over New York, Chicago, and down in the Grand Canyon, actually flying way down by the river in the bottom, it was just incredible. We were all delighted with it!

January 20th Weds.

Today is a really dull and miserable day, it was supposed to snow a lot, but it hasn't done so far, and the skies are very leaden gloomy grey. I am in bed with a sore throat and temperature. In the office yesterday I felt hot and queer so I came home about 3.30 and have been in bed since. I had arranged for Angelo Mangerotti and Charles Faubourg, Walter Gropius's son-in-law, to come and see the Planning Commission this afternoon as they had said they were interested in what we were doing, and now I'm not there myself. The rest of this letter is not very interesting, talking about the contrasts in weather and the inside of the buildings. I think this flu took me ages to get rid of, each time I went out I got sick again!

*January 27*th

I am still sick in bed, I have been here since I last wrote a week ago. By the weekend it was no better, in fact it seemed worse and I had been inhaling every few hours so on Sunday Geoff phoned Jano to ask about her doctor as she and John had a good treatment from him just before Christmas for bad colds. On Monday morning the doctor came to see me and said it was the flu and gave me an injection. He came again today and gave me another injection and says I must stay in all the week and try to go and see him on Saturday if I feel well enough. Jano has been popping in and out shopping for me and preparing food for us, she is coming to have dinner with us tonight and she said she would come and get it all ready. John is away in Denver as his father had to have surgery, so John thought he should be there.

I really wanted to get back to the office this week, as the number of architects calling in there looking for work is very worrying and the offices here are not too scrupulous with their treatment of staff. If you don't pull your weight a few days you are out, and some smart man who is not sick, takes your place, until he gets sick. I don't like that way of going on, but it seems to run through all jobs here.

Because of being in bed we had an uneventful week, Geoff bought me a wonderful book of Provence with photographs of Avignon, Arles, Aix, Marseilles, and even Cassis, all those lovely places we went to on our honeymoon. He also bought me lots of plastic straws and pipe cleaners, I cut up the pipe cleaners to use for the joints and have made wonderful constructions with them. I made a lovely dome and some tall skeleton frames and Geoffrey has been experimenting with wall panels on them. They look beautiful.

The folk in the house have been popping in to see me, Eileen Yarovich, the girl upstairs that we go to films with, came in last night with a present, it's a group of little Japanese figures all in bright satin clothes. Naomi, Jim, Ruth and her husband Don from Korea all went to see Neville dance last night at the Blue Angel. He dances there every night, it's a nightclub. It cost them 30 dollars for four dinners and the entertainment, so I felt rather glad my cold had prevented us from joining them!

We have been having amazingly dull weather and today it has snowed all day. Last week some place north-west of Chicago had a temperature of 40 degrees below zero! The lake is the thing that saves Chicago from temperatures like that.

February 5th Friday

Well I am much better now, last Saturday I went with Jano to the doctors and he gave me a last injection and looked at my throat, took my temperature and blood pressure again and said I could go to the office on Monday. I felt fairly tired all week so have gone to bed early each evening as soon as we have eaten. Tonight John Walley called in for dinner, Jano is away in Iowa at the university lecturing, so I asked John to pop in for dinner. It was nice to see him and chat, we seem to have been stuck in such a lot, on our own, and when you know you can't go out, it doesn't seem such fun to stay in, as when you choose to stay in!

We have now heard from the SS United States and have got a wonderful looking cabin and it is towards the front of the boat not at the bumpy, over the propeller back end, like it was on our way over. We sail on August 6 and although the boat can and did at first do the trip in three-days it now takes it slower and does it in five so we arrive in Southampton on the eleventh.

We had a letter from Henry Fournier who we knew in Harvard, he is in New York and asked us to go and stay with him, so we may spend 10 days with him and see round New York before we sail. Couldn't you come down to meet us in Southampton anyway? It is such a short trip and it will seem quite sad to actually arrive in England and yet not have any one of you there, the real excitement of arriving in countries is when you first see land again. We have often thought of our last view of England it was an incredible picture, early evening with a low sun over the sea, and lots of yachts hurrying back to Cowes before dark.

*February.14*th

We have been reading in the papers about your very cold weather, and heard from Joan and Granny too. I have felt much better this week really, I have had a chill on my bladder I guess it was, so have had some pills for that and yesterday went to the doctor and he gave me my last injection (I hope) for my throat as it was still a little sore. It is so maddening I feel really cross with myself for not throwing it off quicker, as I feel so worried when the weather is really cold that I might start all over again!

We haven't really had much snow at all, it has been far too cold most of the time. Last Sunday we walked in the sunshine to Oak Street Beach and it just looked like an iceberg the water had splashed up and up and frozen, to the height of 15 feet or more above the water line and had frozen in great white peaks so you could climb on to the top and watch the waves crashing up on the other side, it was just like cliffs and was quite a gradual slope up from the land side. It was very exciting. The river always has large iceberg pieces floating in it or else it is frozen solid.

Last Wednesday we went to the Institute of Design to hear Herbert Read give a lecture, he is from London you know, and gave a very good clear lecture. I don't think Americans have quite the talent for talking, lecturing and debating that we have. We went afterwards to a small party for him at Hugo Webers, it was nice to go out again. We met a very lively girl there, a Miss Kris from London, she is a psychologist and is studying at the University of Chicago and Illinois Institute of Technology, she's getting two PhD's one from each place at the same time, one in pure mathematics as well as in psychology. She's also lecturing at ID and she seems an incredible girl, we had heard about her before, but hadn't managed to meet her. Geoff was busy yesterday with a boy who was a photographer from ID. He is an excellent photographer and he was taking some black and white and colour photos of these models we made. They had huge lights and cameras and wires all over the apartment and it took ages to get all of the photos taken.

We are going out to dinner at 5 today to Franz Lipp's, he has an English girl over from Milwaukee for the Day and wants us to meet her.

Feb 23rd Tuesday

Last Friday I went to the dentist as I have had toothache, and I have to have the nerve canal removed from one of my top teeth, next to the front one.

We had quite a busy weekend, on Saturday we went with Angelo Mangerotti to some films at the Art Institute and then to London House for tea. In the evening we went to John and Jano's for dinner, they had a Norwegian architect a friend of Chris in Oslo, staying with them. We had a good evening. On Sunday Geoff and I went out a walk in the afternoon and found an amazing studio area, like Port Merion in Wales, or an Italian stage set. John and Jano had to go out of town on Sunday to a wedding so we had their Norwegian architect friend to dinner.

Yesterday was Washington's Birthday. I got a holiday but spent from 8.30 until lunch being drilled at the dentist and then came home and read a book and drank warm tea while my face undid from the anesthetic. In the evening we went to see "Gilbert and Sullivan" which we quite enjoyed. Tonight we went out to the drug store to get a tonic prescription made up, and while we waited the tallest man in the US came in, he was at a circus in town. Geoff and I had huge chocolate ice-cream sodas and it's just floored us, Geoff says he just feels like having a sleep and I'm going to bed anyway as its 9.30 and last night we weren't too early. Last week I was in bed by nine every night, I was trying to fight off a cold, so I think it did me good. (I remember while we were in California a very popular thing was to go to a drug store and sit at the soda fountain and have a "knicker-bocker glory.")

March 3rd Weds

We have just had the heaviest snowfall of the year, and of the past few years, it started snowing yesterday morning and snowed all day and all last night and today, it looks beautiful. We had 13 inches of snow in Chicago but the drifts were up to seven feet and on Lake Shore Drive two hundred cars got stranded yesterday evening - we had real fun walking to the office as there were so few cars around, and all the snow was unspoiled.

We have had Hans the German boy in Geoff's office, in for dinner they are translating a Swiss article on architecture. My dinners have really improved, Jano is a wonderful cook and has given me a start in new cooking, and I bought lots of herbs, garlic, wine vinegars etc. and am really enjoying it, and Geoff loves them so much.

Last Monday I went to have the nerve taken out from my front tooth, I had anesthetic and it wasn't as bad as I'd been preparing myself for. (As we had no insurance for dental work and the price of the surgeon and the surgery was going to be so high, I went to the large teaching hospital to have the work done. The professor did the work and a group of students all stood round watching) *It took ages to do of course. The final thing on the tooth now is that the roots are curved, and he can't fish out the remaining nerve from them, so I have to go and have some surgery and have the end of the roots cut out through my jaw and then my gums stitched. I have been debating whether to have it done, but I would be liable to get an abscess from the small bit of nerve left, so I guess I really have no choice, but to get it done.*

Last Friday we went to see "Hamlet" and it was very good. On Saturday Angelo came round in the morning to talk over a competition to rebuild the Loop area here in Chicago, he and Geoff may go in for it together. I won't be able to, as Planning Commission members are not allowed. On Saturday afternoon we went down to see the Malcolmsens for dinner. They have a sweet little baby. He is a professor at IIT and works with Mies Van der Rohe. We just talk and talk when we see them, he is Irish and enjoys talking. On Sunday Miss Kris came for the evening.

*March 13*th
(Letter from Geoff.)
We have both been going through it at the dentist recently, particularly poor June. Her big day was yesterday, she was on the 10th floor having this

piece of root cut-out, and I was on the eleventh having a filling. We came home by taxi, it's a good job I was there as she had been given a kind of laughing gas drug, which prevented her being worried by the ordeal. It didn't wear off all evening she said. We had previously arranged to go to the opera house to see Gershwin's Porgy and Bess with John and Jano. We all thought it would help take June's mind off the soreness and so didn't bother to cancel the seats. The operation was very successful and they will take out the stitches on Wednesday. So after a light meal I went out for a cab and off we went.

American theatres have lifts to get to the balconies and we had front seats so there was no trouble. It was a wonderful show, we were just engrossed all the time. It is an all Negro opera, very lively. The daily lives of these people living in Catfish Row, as it is called. June was absorbed by it and quite forgot her aches and pains. This morning June's face was a little swollen but she has now gone down and she is going about as usual.

A bad storm hit Illinois in the night, tornadoes did a lot of damage - blowing down the huge screens of drive in Cinemas.

*Sunday March 14*th

I feel so pleased to have saved my tooth, Daddy you shouldn't want me to have it taken out so easily, the new idea here is they take real pleasure in saving all your teeth, especially the really tricky ones like this - and now the only chance of an abscess is very slight, whereas the curved roots and a little nerve tissue left, the chances were almost certain for an abscess. You remember when Cliff Hardwick our dentist took out the nerve in my front bottom tooth, after it was broken, to crown it, well he never filled up the canal, because when my crown came off in school the flesh had grown up through the middle of the tooth, so I naturally had that trouble at Armathwaite in school, and had to have the whole thing out. This tooth will look perfect when it gets its plastic filling in the back of it.

Last Wednesday Angelo and Charles Faubourg brought three students from the Institute of Design to see the Planning Commission, so at long last I was able to show them around, it was funny because when I got back after

*lunch there were three older chaps from France waiting for me to show them
around the office, as no one here speaks French, so I acted as interpreter,
and after a few minutes with them, Angelo and crowd came so were able
to join in too. Charles and Ati Faubourg came round on Thursday evening
with an Italian architect who is just visiting from Naples, he's having a
six-month tour by car and covering the whole country and Mexico. Ati is
the daughter of Walter Gropius, and she is a visual designer and Charles is
an architect, they're a very nice pair.*

*On Saturday we went to dinner to some people in Evanston, he and his
wife are psychiatrists and they had some other people, an eye surgeon and
his wife there for dinner. We had a delicious meal and a very interesting
evening. We met them through John and Jano. Neville is closing his show at
the Blue Angel and going to see how the dance world is in New York, it will
be sad to lose him from the house as we all get on so well at the moment.*

March 28ᵗʰ Saturday

*We have been so busy, Geoff and Angelo and I, working on the
competition, so every spare minute we have had we have been walking
around Chicago and looking at the present buildings and reading all we can
and studying maps. Last weekend we spent the whole weekend at Angelo's,
Maria his wife cooked for us and we were doing some transport studies.
Angelo popped in one or two evenings in the week and came for dinner and
to work. This weekend we have a projector and we've been studying films of
Chicago buildings, taken from the top of the highest building last summer.
Today we spent all day walking around in the area of Navy Pier it is really
a wonderful site near to the lake and looking back on to the panorama of
Chicago business district, we've been considering it for the site of the civic
centre. At the moment it is full of rail yards, dumps, warehouses and small
factories and is not good land use. Really it is very lucky that I am in the
Planning Commission, as I have been able to help, on all sorts of things.
It is certainly a huge project though, the first prize is 20,000 dollars so you
can imagine they don't give that for nothing. Tomorrow we are going to get*

an early start and then Maria and Anna (Angelo's little girl) will come for dinner in the evening and we shall see all our films.

April 7th Weds.

I have just come in from seeing a film at the Institute of Design and remembered I hadn't written to you for a time. We have been terribly busy of course as you know, with our competition, and then in the office we have a large project on and have made one model already, and are now making a large one to a larger scale. There are three of us working on it and I've had to stay each evening, and I guess will have to work over the weekend as it has to be finished, for a meeting on Monday next.

This evening I came home about 6.30 and Geoff was working on the competition so when I had eaten I went over to see a comedy film with Irene, the girl upstairs. Angelo was there and came back with me to talk over some new ideas with Geoff, and he's just left. The film was one we've seen a lot already a silent French one "An Italian Straw Hat" which is beautiful and very funny too. I was amazed to find the students didn't enjoy it, I guess it's not slapstick enough for them.

Last Friday we saw a wonderful film called "Beat the Devil" with Humphrey Bogart, Robert Morley, Peter Lorre and Gina Lollobrigida, which was very good. I hope you can manage to see it, it was filmed in a beautiful part of Italy and was very funny. On Sunday afternoon we went walking and to an exhibition at the Art Institute and then went to the top of the Tribune building to study the plan of Chicago from the air. Fancy you seeing Chicago, the beautiful street you mention- Michigan Avenue is where we live Erie Street goes off it and our nearest shops just on the corner are all the good ones you'd see, Bonwit Teller, Peck and Peck, Saks Fifth Avenue etc.

We were also round the corner from the Allerton Hotel, they had a very good place to eat on the top of the high building, with great views right out on the lake and then looking north to Oak Street beach. The lake was very fascinating and unique for the City. You were always aware of it from the downtown area, we often went down on warm evenings with our dinner, as the air was so much fresher. Quite often we saw Mies van Der Rohe sitting on one of the benches outside his new apartment building, 860 Lake Shore Drive, studying his latest work, for ages. He had waited a long time to get such large and important buildings to design.

My office used to get very hot and when the temperature got above 100 we were told to go home as the drawings started to crinkle with our sweaty hands. I would always go straight to the beach, outside Mies' new apartment building, and after a swim would play Scrabble with a very amusing German woman who was a wizard at the game, and she used to take a thermos of Gin and Tonic to the beach, to get people to play Scrabble with her!

While we were in Chicago there was a tidal wave, very early in the morning luckily. There were always lots of people on the beaches but that morning as it was early, there were just people fishing. Suddenly the pressure in the middle of the lake increased tremendously and a huge wave came onto the shore and swept a number of people in, and several of them were drowned.

Back to my letter-

On Sunday evening John and Jano came to dinner and Angelo came in later on. Saturday we worked all day and stayed home as it was very cold, 20 degrees. The last three-days we have had fantastic weather temperatures, yesterday and today in the mid- seventies and so humid we have been so uncomfortable and then tremendous thunderstorms at night. What a crazy place!

Geoffrey adds a note- *Hope you are all well. This afternoon from my office* (Skidmore Owings and Merril) *Chicago looked amazing - I can see the lake all the time, but about 3pm a thick fog suddenly obliterated it. Just like a pea souper, except that at the same time it was raining very hard. Then it suddenly disappeared and the sun came out. From high buildings these weather effects are very exciting I think.* (Geoff's office was high up in one of the downtown skyscrapers.)

April 16th Good Friday.

I hope that it was a lovely surprise to get a phone call last night, I guess you'd be quite amazed to wake up in the night for that!! I had done quite a lot of checking on the time, I phoned the British consul and the British Information Service and they each said you were not on summer time yet and you are therefore only six hours ahead. Geoff hurried over the river to John and Jano's when he left the office, and I put the call in about 5 20 pm which should have been 11.20 your time, they said there was no delay, the New York people, so we expected it at any minute. I thought it would be exciting for you to just pick up the phone and it to be us. Well we waited to get through for a couple of hours until 7.15, by then we had just started dinner, Jano said she knew that would do it, if we started the meal. Geoff ran down to their downstairs phone and I was upstairs, so we were all 4 on at once. It was lovely to hear your voices after such a long time, could you hear us well? John and Jano were quite excited with it all and wanted me to send all their best wishes, when we got back to the table they had a glass of wine poured to drink your health, Daddy. They said they would love to have had a tape recorder to get the whole thing. (It was my father's birthday and that was why we were phoning. Nobody was phoning to Europe then, as it was very difficult to get through, and very expensive. Poor Daddy by the time our call got through they were both fast asleep, it was 1.30 am, so he sounded very perplexed!! There have been tremendous advances that have been made in all forms of communication. Now it is so easy to fly to anywhere in the world, and it is even easier to telephone anywhere, I can now telephone or fax a document to anyone in England at any time of the day or night for 2.09 cents a minute.

I have been sending via Email all these pages of memoirs to friends in Italy, Lithuania, Sweden, New Zealand and England and so for no cost at all. I can have 179 pages on their desk instantly. My grandchildren will never really appreciate the phenomena of all these miracles, and I have to remind myself of how far we have advanced. Our grand children are so easy on the phone and chatter on, whereas

Geoff's Mother was never used to the phone and would put it down so quickly, like she was handling a hot pan!

It had been a terrible hot day 80 degrees, and very heavy and humid and then last night it freshened a little and all the huge lights and neon signs were just starting blinking in a very rich blue sky, when we telephoned you, there were tremendous City noises, crowds of cars just going down to theatres and the evening just starting all round. The contrast between us in time, setting, and everything, made us suddenly aware of the distance. It was a pity it was not clear enough for you to hear all the City noises as we had all the windows open with the heat.

27th April Tuesday

We have had such amazing weather these last few weeks that I suddenly felt so tired and decided to have today at home pottering about. Last week midweek was very hot, then by Friday it was very cold, winter overcoat weather, but then on Saturday the temperature was in the Eighties with brilliant sun. On Sunday when we had planned to go for a walk it was about 40 degrees and clouds of steam rising from the ground and a real thick mist. The reason I think was the sudden change in temperature and then on Saturday night starting about 6pm and going on through the night we had a tremendous thunderstorm, just continuous lightning and torrential rain. Large areas of Chicago were flooded as it is flat as a pancake around here. Yesterday I went to the office in a suit and ordinary shoes and stockings and by about 11.30 the temperature was 86 degrees and so humid, everything was just damp and sticking to me and I was so uncomfortable. I will enjoy the rest. The weather in this area is really awful, worse than Boston's, we've had no spring at all and the hot days are so humid that you can't do anything but feel miserable.

Last week on Tuesday and Thursday we worked on the project with Angelo and again on Saturday and Sunday. They have been trying to get their scheme planned by the end of April, so we can start the drawings in May. There are so many different aspects to plan, express road ways, trucking, bus lines, rail lines and terminals, before you even start to re-plan the centre, gradually it seems to be shaping up very well.

Three of us in our office are making a huge model 6 ft by 4 ft of a shopping area, it has to light up and is quite complicated. We have to make it in our own time as it is for one of the Chicago banks, so we are hoping they will pay us well. I have been doing quite a few of the buildings at home but once we have the base made (we shall get a carpenter for that) then I will have to work down there at nights. John Cauldwell and the other architect in the office, are working on it too, we only have about 10 days more before the electrician has to do the wiring and it has to be complete by then. I have four buildings to work on today and will have to work all next weekend.

Last Friday Geoff and I went to see the Theater Ballet Company. We had the cheapest seats but when we got in we found a group of ID students who were the ushers so they gave us about the best seats in the house, the ground floor about 20 rows from the front! We have been able to do this every time at the Opera House and as the good seats are so expensive it is very convenient. We should have been on the fourth balcony and it's a huge place so it was really lucky. Tonight we're going to Angelo's to dinner and to work as Maria gets tired of being in on her own, and she has to stay with Anna her little girl. (This was our first experience of Italian Mothers, every night when Anna had to go to bed, Maria would go too. She always slept with her. Angelo was such an attractive man, I would never have left him alone so much. When we saw Angelo in Italy several years later he was no longer married to Maria. I think she was not intellectually equal to him, which was sad, but Anna their daughter, became an architect.)

P S. Look in Architect and Building News for April 8ᵗʰ Geoff has an article on Chicago. He's just had two more magazines ask for articles!

May 8ᵗʰ Saturday
I've been working so hard on this model that I feel quite dead from it, we have just about finished it, and so it is done on time - the Bank that

we've made it for, is having a party on Tuesday to show it off so I'm glad we got it done as they've sent out all the Gold leaf invitations! I hope we don't get any more to do as it's such exhausting work - we used plastic for the buildings and I made all the buildings while Ezra made the base, so I was using the electric saw a lot and it nearly drove me daft, the noise! It looks very good all the buildings light up from underneath and Rathje- the bank owner- was very impressed.

Today we were going round the student work at IIT and ID there was some wonderful work to see, so we have been out all day - it was a very pleasant change anyway. On Thursday I had an offer of a job with Pace Associates, they are a very good firm that I tried to get in with last summer but they didn't have too much on, but now they have a hospital and so wanted me to go. I felt very disappointed to have an offer from a really good office at last, and then not to be able to take it, they have done some wonderful work.

We got a refund from the income tax people last week of almost a hundred dollars. Our savings are slowly mounting, another two weeks we should have saved our $3,000 which was my goal -and we still have June and July to go, so it's good to have done it so easily.

It's very funny to think of Elizabeth, my little sister, *going off to* my old boarding school *Hunmanby, I really have very mixed feelings about it, although I loved it while I was there. Looking back on it, it seems to be such an unnatural thing to go and shut a group of girls off with one another, and to be so strict about separating them from all the life around. It seems to me now that it is such a difficult time for children, to suddenly have to start facing up to all the realities and that by postponing it or trying to, you make the shock of leaving school and mixing with all the thousands of different types, so great, because it all comes with one blow and not gradually. You impose much too great a strain all at once. Perhaps if you could find a really good coeducational school you would be much kinder in the long run. I don't know how David feels about his schooling, perhaps they weren't kept so strict, but I feel it was rather an unpleasant thing really- though at the time of course I enjoyed life there very much. We must talk about it when we come, as it is such an important thing for Elizabeth, and is difficult to discuss all the pros and cons in a letter.*

Last weekend we went to the General Motors show Motorama. It was held in the amphitheatre which is right in the centre of the stock yards! We've never been in this area before as it is really so unpleasant and the smell is just sickening. Ever since we had first arrived in Chicago, when the wind was in a certain direction the whole town smelled of the meat slaughter houses. *It is the hugest area of Chicago too - it seemed like another City. We had a very good meal there though at the Stockyards Inn - it is just like an English Inn and very pleasant inside - and it is supposed to be the best meat in the US. The sirloin steaks are $4.95 each, it really seems incredible for people to spend 2 pounds (sterling) on the meat course alone! We had a very pleasant evening though, we went with Angelo and were shown around the kitchens and cars of the future by the press representatives - it was just amazing. They had a large floor show with these cars just gliding on, covered with girls and after a few turns, going off. The climax was when a rather ugly Cadillac came in and everyone just gasped and applauded! It was such a funny thing to see - the Cadillac is just the last word here you know.*

P.S. Can you make us a dentist appointment for when we arrive home. The dental student I knew at University is called Peter Dryland. I would really prefer him or the young chap at the bottom of Ringinglow Road, Chester Burnham. Reg Parkins and Fergy Bishop are too keen on taking teeth out - which seems to be the older idea and Geoff and I both have had really amazing jobs done on the remnants of a tooth so it would be terrible to have to have it out, after all the work on the roots of mine to save it too. If you already made the appointments then perhaps we should go and if they suggest taking anything out we will go to someone else. You should watch out for Elizabeth's teeth as a dentist like Cliff Hardwicke can ruin your whole mouth!

My parents having lost their teeth in their Thirties and still thinking it was the best thing they ever did, to have got rid of them, it was very hard to convince them of the importance that people stress nowadays, about keeping their own teeth for all their lives, at almost any cost. My sister had the same very small mouth as me, and as she is 19 years younger, she should have been part of the generation to have orthodontic work, but I think Daddy would have thought it was throwing money away.

21st May Friday

You sound to have had a wonderful trip to Ireland, I'm so glad as I know you'd both enjoy seeing all the folk there. We have neither of us been to Ireland, and some time we must go. It always looks a fascinating country and Dublin has such wonderful architecture I know we would enjoy it, perhaps when we get home we will be able to make a visit there. We are planning on buying a car straight away, a little new Morris I think, and then we shall have a run around, go and see Granny in Wales, and go up to Cumberland maybe and call in at Grange as John Satchell lives there now. He was our good friend the ecologist from university days who had to spend a short time in a mental hospital and stayed with us in London on his weekends. *Is there any delay on new cars now?*

We have been terribly busy still, we're trying not to think of coming home as we both of us have so much work, and it is very unsettling. The competition is coming along OK, we've had lots of offers from folk to help us out on the drawings, so maybe we can get it all done. We have worked every night this week and we hope to take one day off this weekend. Bill Holroyd, (Geoff's cousin), *is coming down from Toronto tomorrow to a colour TV conference for a week, so we hope to get time to see him.*

I got paid three hundred dollars yesterday for my work on the last model, and as well as my regular office pay this is very nice to have. No tax deduction! Last weekend we took a break to visit John and Jano on the Sunday, we hadn't seen them for quite a while. I would like Bill to meet them if we can arrange it, as they are such a great pair. John and Geoff love to talk, I shall feel very sorry to leave them, they are such sympathetic people and have been the main reason why our stay in Chicago and our trip to the west coast have been so good. They have been very kind to us and are such fun.

Angelo just bought a new camera, sixty dollars worth and only had it about two weeks and some student at ID stole it from his desk! He was very disappointed. We are going over to Detroit next weekend to see some of the new buildings there, we may stay with Dolly and Wally over one night, but we're going with Angelo, Maria and Anna in a car with a student from ID.

We've been having very odd sort of weather, either cold or hot, apparently spring here is like that, no warm days so you go straight from winter clothes to summer. John and Jano are going off next month to Mexico for 12 weeks, which means we'll have to say goodbye to them before they go. John gets long summer vacations being a professor so they're able to take a really good trip. Two summers ago they were in Europe, re-organising the School of architecture in Oslo, which was when they met Chris Norberg Schultz, and then touring all around afterwards.

*May 30*th *Sunday*

We have just had a lovely week seeing Bill, it seemed almost like a new town as we visited lots of the places we've thought of going but have never gone. Last Saturday we met him in his hotel and then we walked up to our apartment and then down Rush street, which is like Montmarte in Paris and is all nightclubs and amazingly dressed people, we just looked at the spectacle, Bill found it quite amazing he said it was the first Capital City he'd been in since London. On Sunday we went with Angelo to see the new colour television show that Bill had come down to, it was very interesting and they are perfect technically.

In the evening Bill came to John and Jano's with us for a gourmet dinner - Jano is such a superb cook you know. He thought they were wonderful people and we saw lots of them in the week. We took him to Cinerama and then he came to us for dinner first - if you could see Cinerama I am sure you would think it was amazing, it is so real you cannot believe you are not really there - to Venice, Spain and then flying over America.

JUNE: Roots of Steel

Bill took us out to a very expensive French restaurant for dinner, and we had a bottle of Vouvray, chateau bottled it's my favourite you know, it was a lovely meal, a great treat (Vouvray were the caves in the Loire Valley I visited when I was a student and everyone had too much wine, the worst case was a professor who we had to leave in the hospital) *on Friday evening Bill came around and we went for a walk and then called at John and Jano's to say goodbye to them as Bill was leaving at eight the next morning. One evening we went to the Tip Top Tap with him, it is a bar on the top of the Allerton Hotel, with views over all Chicago and the lake, the lights were wonderful.*

Last Saturday when we were going out to meet Bill there was a note for us in the hall of the house, to say we must be out of our apartment by June the first! It was such a shock I felt just like I did when I smashed Daddy's car! We were very worried all weekend as we didn't know anything about American law and so we imagined we'd have to leave. They know we are leaving soon anyway from the other people in the house, and I guess he wanted to give the apartment to a friend or something - they're very unpleasant people anyway and we have never gossiped in the hall with them, as some of the folk do, so maybe we should have done. Anyway on Monday I went to the court in the City hall where they deal with all these cases and they said to ignore the note and to stay as long as we want, if he wants to evict us he has to take it to court and it will take him a long time and cost him a lot of money, and the court often gives 90 days time to find somewhere else, so he really can't do too much. I felt so cross though as it is going to be quite unpleasant and he's a very loutish sort of fellow to have to deal with. People here are so selfish though, he would never consider any difficulty it might give us, to move all our stuff out for six weeks. (I remember one strange thing in that building, one evening when I was waiting for Geoff to come in for dinner, the doorbell rang, so I went down and there was a policeman at the door, and he asked if he could come in. When I said what for, he said "To sleep it off"- He was totally drunk, and on duty!)

June 12th Saturday

Thank-you very much indeed for the letters and cards etc and the gifts, they will be very useful when we get home (I had just had my birthday on June the 10th) *I just worked in the office all day on Thursday and then in the evening Geoff and I went to one of the very nice Chinese restaurants for dinner, and then we went to see an excellent film "Three Coins in the Fountain" the film was all shot in Italy, Rome and Venice and the views were so fantastic it made you almost weep to see such beautiful things - America is really very ugly even their good things like California they have spoilt with oil wells on the beaches and all over, and bill - boards on every inch of the country. This film anyway was beautiful and the cinema was air conditioned too of course* (we have been having a humid heat wave, yesterday was 97 degrees). *After the film we went to John and Jano's, they had been to the doctors earlier in the evening to get their vaccinations and typhoid shots ready for Mexico. We went for a little stroll down Michigan Avenue and then they treated us to a delicious drink in the Tip Top Tap.* (It was very popular then to have all kinds of cocktails, daiquaries, alexanders, grass hoppers, dozens of different ones and you had to buy huge numbers of bottles to be able to make them, but they were so delicious.) *Jano gave me some lovely copper earrings that she had made. Geoff bought me some rum Frango chocolates and a book on Europe and last Saturday he bought me silver earrings.*

We went sailing with Charles and Atti Faubourg on their yacht (Atti you remember is Walter Gropius' daughter) there wasn't too much wind but we had a lovely dinner on board. We watched the sunset over Chicago and from the water it looks wonderful. Geoff and Angelo have worked the other evenings but it is really so exhausting this hot weather, you can't sleep or eat too well, and because you sweat continuously the whole day you feel like a rag by 4 o'clock. We were sent home early from the office yesterday. I have hunted around all week to find an air conditioner for the apartment, I really feel it would be worth it when we have so much work and packing to do. If you just get a refreshing night's sleep you can tackle the heat much better the next day. The air-conditioners are still expensive though, the one-third ton GE model I want costs 229 dollars but with the architects discount I could get it for 186 dollars, I could probably sell it to someone in the office for 146 so for six weeks coolness it would cost about 40 dollars. If I can get one without delay I think I shall, otherwise we're going to look dead when we arrive home.

I'm working in the office this morning, Saturday, then going to Angelo's where Geoff and he are working. Tomorrow we're going to the art fair on the northside and then going on a picnic with the Grossowsky's. I'm afraid Geoff is far too busy to write any articles for a while.

June 21ˢᵗ Monday

We just got your letter written last Friday about the car. What a wonderful surprise it was! Thank-you very much indeed -it will be just marvelous to have it, and such a beautiful present. We shall so enjoy using it - I don't know how to thank you enough in a letter, we were both so thrilled. When Geoff came home I was just near to the door waiting to tell him! Geoff thinks gray would be nice but if we can get it quicker we don't want any particular colour, we'd rather have it as soon as possible. We are still in the midst of our sweltering heat it's been 97 degrees for almost two weeks now, it apparently is a record for this time of year. - I will certainly be glad to leave the heat and this high humidity.

We went on Friday evening to John and Jano's as they were having a small pre-Mexico party - we had some beautiful colour slides of Mexico that a friend of theirs had taken and all the six going on the trip were there. It was lovely. Angelo phoned there about 12 o'clock to say how about going to Detroit at 5.30 am Saturday, so we left Jano's soon after and came home to get about three hours sleep. We got to Detroit Saturday about 2.30 pm its three hundred plus miles. We went to see a wonderful dome made of light aluminium at the Ford plant then we went on to see a new shopping centre, north of Detroit. About 11.30 at night we got a hotel in the downtown area and I went to sleep in a second it was very cool for the first time, as we had a very heavy storm about dinner time. All the Midwest is having this frightful weather.

We drove to Detroit in a jeep station wagon with a student from ID and Angelo and I drove half the way and Kasimir the other half. (I remember we took over some of the time because Kas seemed a bit wild, he took a circular off-ramp off the freeway so fast, we had to go right up the grass bank, and it seemed like the car would roll over!) *On Sunday we looked around the downtown a little and saw one or two new buildings then went out to see the General Motors that Geoff wrote the Italian article on. We saw some earlier factories by a very good Detroit man - Kahn. (This was the person that Uncle Wally had worked with, doing steel calculations.) We went from Detroit to Toledo in Ohio, to drop Angelo there, as he has had an offer to take over a factory, so we went to look it over.*

Kas and Geoff and I came back and got here about 1.30 last night, we felt very tired as we had seen such a lot in two days and done over 700 miles. Today has felt hotter than ever, so this evening Geoff and I took a meal- shrimps, salad and potato salad- down to the lake. We sat until it was quite dark and I was just in a bathing costume so felt nice and cool. We've been sleeping a little better, I got a double window fan from the office, they had four extra ones so lent us one and we get a breeze blowing over us all night. We decided the air-conditioning would make our days in the hot offices worse than ever.

July 1ˢᵗ

Only three weeks now till we leave Chicago! Geoff has had all this week off to work on the competition, Angelo is on holiday now and I had today and tomorrow, Friday off for overtime on the first model, and Monday is the holiday for Fourth of July so we have had a good burst of work. We're hoping to buy the boards tomorrow to start mounting and put the colours etc on afterwards. You should see our apartment, we have a huge drafting table set up and drawings all over. Everyone here seems to be moving somewhere, John and Jano went off last Friday, we felt really miserable to say goodbye as we have had such wonderful evenings together, they are amazing people, and made our time in California and here, so wonderful, with introductions to all their great friends.

We just had two Norwegians pop in to say goodbye to us, they are off to the West Coast and hoping to spend a year working and looking around. On Saturday we are going to a party at the Malcolmsen's. They're the ones from Ireland, and he teaches architecture with Mies at IIT, they are off to Europe for three months so we may even see them in England. I have just started to make another model in the office, not too big a one I hope.

*July 12*th *Monday*

Thank you very much Daddy for your letter I went straight along to see the cars. (The Morris car showroom.) *They are only 3 blocks from us and are open until 9 pm I chose the colour and everything and paid them a hundred and sixty four dollars and he would mail off the order on Friday and the delivery is supposed to be six weeks from then. However he seemed to think we would get the car by the 12th of August. There are quite a few of them about and they look very nice - of course they look small here compared with all these big boats folk drive around. We did very little except work since I last wrote. George Barnes* (a good friend of my parents on business in the states) *came over on July the fourth weekend, he came around on the Friday as soon as he arrived, and we have had several dinners together, only one at home as we are so disorganised with four of us with drawing boards in the living room and stacks of drawings everywhere. We have to lift a pile of drawings off our bed each night so we can get in! On the Saturday George came with us to a party at the Malcolmsens, they were just leaving for Europe. George was very good to have around, and everyone found he was easy to get along with. He was chatting to Maria and Anna in Spanish, it is so like Italian, and seemed to enjoy his evening at the party. On the Sunday afternoon I took a couple of hours off work and George and I went a long walk by the lake and watched people water skiing.*

On Monday we left about 9.30 am Kasimiro, Angelo, Maria, Anna, George, Geoffrey and I to go and see some houses in the country, and have a picnic lunch. We had a very pleasant day and came home about 6.30 and worked all evening. On Wednesday George came to say goodbye and wanted to take us to a show but Geoff and Angelo didn't dare stop work, so

George and I went to see Cinerama, it was my third time but it's so splendid and I did want George to see it. He was very impressed.

We had long letters from John and Jano already, but haven't had much time to write back. A chap from Geoff's office came and helped us all weekend and another one is coming tonight. I have hopes to finish up over next weekend so I can think about doing some sorting, washing, and packing. It's only one week on Friday until we leave Chicago!

In a paper this morning it said the Queen was having another baby in the spring and is planning on having six! The papers here are really so poor, I will be glad to get back to the Guardian. Everyone has gone off early from the office so I'll pack up and go. The trouble is, it's the hottest part of the day to walk home.

July 15th

I have just booked our trip to Boston, we are flying as we are so short of time. We will actually go to New York first on one plane and then transfer to another plane for Boston, and then we will return to New York. It is cheaper than the train, and the train takes 20 hours. Our luggage will all go Railway Express, direct to the boat, the chairs and some clothes we are having crated to save us buying another trunk. We leave Chicago on Monday July the 26th at 8.15 am. We are leaving our offices next Tuesday July the 20th so we get some time to pack and Geoff still has some buildings in Wisconsin he wants to go and see. What a lot there still seems to do - we're working very hard on the competition drawings and over this weekend should get them just about completed. If you wanted to write to us in Cambridge we shall be there until about July the 31st and the address is C/O Thais Carter, 75 Francis Avenue, we are not sure where we will stay in New York we may stay with Henry if he is in town, but if not, find some hotel. Our hot weather still goes on, the last few days have been another heat wave, and a place in Kansas had 121 degrees. Last summer when we were in Kansas City it was 115!

Everyone has been phoning me in the office to see about having dinner with us to say goodbye, so I guess from now on we won't get too much time to stop and think. It certainly will be exciting to see you on the boat. I hope we can show you all over it, as it is the most modern one you know. You remember it doing the three-day crossing on its maiden voyage? I'm really looking forward to the sail and some lazy days on deck!

*July 26*th*-22,000 ft up- flying from Chicago to New York.*

We are just having the most wonderful flight amid brilliant blue skies and beautiful white clouds below us like mountain peaks. We left home at about 8am and then left the airport about 10. Chicago looked so beautiful across the lake as we left, I felt very sad to be leaving, it had been a very good experience and we had met some great people. (John and Jano were <u>the</u> most amazing. They had been so generous with all their friends and had helped us with our great trip to the west, and then when we returned to Chicago had introduced us to so many people there, and offered us a stay in their house until we got settled with a place of our own. They were really the Best of Friends.

We kept in touch with them for years by writing regularly. When I had Sarah my first baby in 1955 they sent us wonderful american baby clothes. In 1965 Geoff was asked to come over again to lecture at MIT, and in the Architecture Dept. in St. Louis, and also in Chicago. We stayed with John and Jano, but we really had all changed in 11 years, and did not have the same interests in common. They did not have any children, and I think were disappointed about their teaching and the Institute of Design. They had continued with all the wild partying, and Jano had had some bad accidents. I remember she cut her hand very badly while she was cooking, and then she fell and broke her leg, and almost immediately fell again in the toilet and broke her arm, so she had 2 limbs in plaster at the same time. I think they both drank quite a lot.

Later we had a very sad letter from Jano, to tell us that John had been working on the top of a high ladder in their new studio, and had fallen off, and was killed. Their friends Lou and Al Lunak who we had got to know well, came over later to England, and we went with them touring in France. Looking back through the details of our stay in Chicago, I realize that it was a wonderful lively town, with lots of very interesting people, that we were lucky enough to meet. Perhaps we were there at its peak, but I am glad we were young enough for such high energy.)

Back to my letter.

We have had such a hectic time the last few days, we left our offices last Tuesday. My office was so good, and everyone said how upset they were that I was going, and on the last day they gave a huge luncheon for us and invited Geoff. There were over 30 of them came and they gave us a book about architecture in the US and a subscription to Arts and Architecture magazine which is something we've been wanting to have very much. Down the middle of the table, a large horseshoe shaped one, was a card with Bon Voyage on and everyone had signed it! Weren't they good and it was all a surprise, they've never done it for any other folk who left. On Wednesday we went by train to Wisconsin to see some Frank Lloyd Wright buildings. Wednesday evening we were busy packing like mad and Thursday too. We had to go down on Thursday and buy another large trunk and we bought one of the hang- wardrobe type cases too, because things are supposed not to get so creased. By Friday I had to wind up the packing and about 8.30am they came to collect the chairs for crating. I dashed down to the bank before lunch and then came home to find the Railway Express man saying he couldn't send the baggage right to the boat, so I rode over with him to their depot, plus all the baggage and managed to send it all. This moving around is certainly expensive it cost me 26 dollars railway express 18 dollars for the chairs, a hundred and thirty we had to pay income tax. (This we should get back at the end of the year though.)

This is turning out to be a very rough flight. We are just going through some very nasty storm clouds and they are knocking us about all over, we must be dropping 40 ft in some pockets and then going up and sideways the next minute. Everyone has little cartons in case they get sick! We are due in New York about 1.45 Chicago time, then we'll try to get an immediate flight up to Boston as Thais is expecting us before tea.

After we had sent off the baggage on Friday I started to help Geoff and Angelo on the competition. They had been working on it all the time. Friday evening John Cauldwell the English architect I worked under asked us there for dinner, and Saturday Lou and Al Lunak, some friends of John and Jano, took us out for a picnic and to see some more friends who run a wonderful zoo. Saturday evening, Geoff and I worked and all day yesterday we worked with Angelo. Geoff had to finish the report of their work and he was up until about 3.30 a.m. last night typing it out, any way the thing is finally finished thank goodness, we just have to wait and see if we have any luck.

This thumping around has got much worse and has made Geoff quite ill, it is very annoying as it was so lovely before. I certainly hope the crossing is calm as we both of us need a nice rest. I'll just finish this from Thaïs's and post it from Cambridge.

Hi! We have been in Cambridge since Monday evening and it's now Thursday, we have been having a wonderful rest. Geoff was really so overtired on the plane and he was really terribly ill. A lot of the people were, but Geoff seemed so tired already that he just couldn't get off the plane in New York, so we got a wheelchair and some brandy and he went and lay on some grass at the airport and slept. I phoned Thais in the meantime and explained we'd be late and maybe wouldn't come until the next morning. Anyway I found a fairly good train leaving at 8pm and arriving at 12.30 so we took that because Thais' house is so lovely and quiet and I felt sure Geoff would be better if we could get here. Thais and her son met us at the station and we came here and went straight to bed and slept until 1.30 the next day, every morning we have slept until 11. I'm sure it was more exhaustion with Geoff than anything, and of course it was very rough. I was just dying for us to land as it seemed such a long time. Some people on the plane thought Geoff had had a heart attack, so I was terribly worried about him.

This house is lovely it is just surrounded by trees and is so restful. We have to go off to New York this weekend as Geoff has a lot he wants to do there, however he seems to have completely recovered so don't worry about him, he's been eating very well again. We are going on a picnic today in the country, so I must close. Thais has six tiny month old Kittens and they are just tumbling all around my feet. They are so cute. (Thais also had a very interesting student who we met, Edward Said, from Palestine, staying in one of her empty rooms, while he studied in Harvard. He was later very famous as an Orientalist, Historian.)

August 3rd Tuesday, 142 E. 33rd St., New York City.
We arrived on Saturday to stay with Henry until this Friday when we get on the boat. We had a lovely restful stay with Thais, she had a little party for us on the Wednesday. On Friday we got the other two trunks off by railway Express, cost me another 14 dollars! Then I went into town to look at the shops and bought a cool cotton dress, Geoff went to see an architect who has just recently returned from working in Paris. He was very busy working on the Chicago Competition, so Geoff was glad to be able to see someone else's scheme - he hadn't anywhere near finished and it had to be in the following day, Saturday.

The weekend was very hot when we arrived here so we went to Central Park and sat down by the river on Sunday. Yesterday was cooler and we had a very nice lunch with Jean Beckwith, she has had a little girl since we saw her and they are now moving out of New York to a very nice house they are building on Long Island, right on the beach.

About 4pm yesterday we went by train to New Canaan to see an architect called Philip Johnson. He runs the Museum of Modern Art in New York and has built some very lavish houses in the new Canaan area - Geoff had written one of his news letters about them, so he asked us out there to have dinner with him. We had a very pleasant evening in his wonderful house looking out onto beautiful trees and they're all floodlit as a part of his house. It is very like a Mies Van der Rohe house and is all glass. He took us to see some of his other houses and to his office to look through his new work, he was very helpful. We came home about 1.30 am. so have slept on quite late this morning. I just went out and got Geoff's trousers pressed while he did the washing up for me, we're now off to see a Japanese house in the Museum of Modern Art.

Tomorrow we go to see Steinberg - you know the wonderful cartoonist. Geoff's Italian editor wrote especially to ask him to do an article on him, so we were able to make an appointment to see him tomorrow. This evening we are going out to dinner with Henry and a friend of his, and all this whirl stops on Friday at 12 when we sail, on the new SS. United States. I was planning to send this letter to you at home, but I guess by the time it arrives you will have left to go down to Southampton so I will send it to Geoff's family.

That was the last of my letters from America.

Our last day in New York we had arranged the interview with Saul Steinberg, it was our most memorable visit to interview anyone. He and his wife were both Rumanians, living in the centre of Manhattan, on the street with the elevated railway. He had studied architecture in Milan, Italy, the town where Edilizia Moderna is based. His drawings are very architectural, so I guess we were not surprised to be asked for an article on him. We first met in his office in the first floor of his house, and after an hour or so he asked us to go in to meet his wife in the living part of the house, she was a very friendly, jolly person. We sat around the dining table drinking excellent European coffee and talking. About 5.30pm. Alexander Schneider, the violinist came in to see them, wearing a crazy baseball cap, not looking at all like a world-famous violinist. After a while they were asking if we enjoyed watching baseball, but we told them we had never seen any, they were rather amazed and said as we were leaving the US the next day, we must certainly go with them to see the big Dodgers game in Brooklyn. Steinberg, Schneider and Geoff and I all went off in Schneider's huge open car, over the Brooklyn Bridge to the game, I don't remember too much about the play, but we were talking with Steinberg about the psychology and the mental stress on the players. He had once toured with one of the top teams for one season, and had been really studying the pressure and the strain on the highest paid players. If they had a bad season or a series of bad games, they would be dropped from the team, with a huge financial loss. It was already a very high finance, pressure game.

After the game was over we went back into Manhattan and went out for dinner, and afterwards went to a theatre to meet Utta Hagen, the actress, who was playing in New York at the time. She was a friend of Steinberg and Schneider. While we sat talking after she finished her performance she asked us if we enjoyed the New York nightclubs, and again we said we had never been to one. After she was changed into her own clothes, we set out for a series of night clubs, we still had Steinberg and Schneider, and now Utta, and Geoff and me. Steinberg was very amusing, he kind of looked like a parson, with glasses and something about his collar made it seem clerical. All the nude girls in the floorshows took a delight in teasing him, but he was absolutely undaunted! Guess it had happened to him a lot. Finally they got us back to Henry's apartment about 4.30 am, the morning we were leaving. Our interview with him had lasted more than 12 hours! We would have five days resting on the SS United States to recover, before arriving in Southampton.

We boarded the ship early, and all our suitcases went down to our cabin, but we stayed on the deck with Henry, and took in the bustle and last exciting views of Manhattan, and the skyline as we sailed out. Finally, after we had lost sight of the skyline we went down to our cabin for the first time, and there on the bed was a letter from the shipping people in Chicago, saying the weight they had charged us for, was not correct, we owed a few dollars more so they had kept the crates in storage in their warehouse in New York! The storage costs were several dollars a day. I was so mad, it meant we had left all our crated things in New York. I had gone with them in Chicago, when they weighed our chairs etc., and they had allowed for the weight of the crates, but after they had crated them, they had ended up slightly heavier than they had estimated. This turned out to be a long saga when we got back home to England.